The
Wenner-Gren
Foundation

For Anthropological Research, Inc.

Anthropology Put to Work

W ENNER- G REN I NTERNATIONAL S YMPOSIUM S ERIES

Series Editor: Leslie C. Aiello, President, Wenner-Gren Foundation for Anthropological Research, New York.

ISSN: 1475-536X

Previous titles in this series:

Anthropology Beyond Culture
Edited by Richard G. Fox & Barbara J. King, 2002

Property in Question: Value Transformation in the Global Economy
Edited by Katherine Verdery & Caroline Humphrey, 2004

Hearing Cultures: Essays on Sound, Listening and Modernity
Edited by Veit Erlmann, 2004

Embedding Ethics
Edited by Lynn Meskell & Peter Pels, 2005

World Anthropologies: Disciplinary Transformations within Systems of Power
Edited by Gustavo Lins Ribeiro and Arturo Escobar, 2006

Sensible Objects: Colonialisms, Museums and Material Culture
Edited by Elizabeth Edwards, Chris Gosden and Ruth B. Phillips, 2006

Roots of Human Sociality: Culture, Cognition and Interaction
Edited by N. J. Enfield and Stephen C. Levinson, 2006

Where the Wild Things Are Now: Domestication Reconsidered
Edited by Rebecca Cassidy and Molly Mullin, 2007

Since its inception in 1941, the Wenner-Gren Foundation has convened more than 125 international symposia on pressing issues in anthropology. These symposia affirm the worth of anthropology and its capacity to address the nature of humankind from a wide variety of perspectives. Each symposium brings together participants from around the world, representing different theoretical disciplines and traditions, for a week-long engagement on a specific issue. The Wenner-Gren International Symposium Series was initiated in 2000 to ensure the publication and distribution of the results of the foundation's International Symposium Program.

Prior to this series, some landmark Wenner-Gren volumes include: *Man's Role in Changing the Face of the Earth* (1956), ed. William L. Thomas; *Man the Hunter* (1968), eds Irv DeVore and Richard B. Lee; *Cloth and Human Experience* (1989), eds Jane Schneider and Annette Weiner; and *Tools, Language and Cognition in Human Evolution* (1993), eds Kathleen Gibson and Tim Ingold. Reports on recent symposia and further information can be found on the foundation's website at www.wennergren.org.

The Wenner-Gren Foundation
For Anthropological Research, Inc.

Anthropology Put to Work

Edited by

LES W. FIELD AND RICHARD G. FOX

Oxford · New York

First published in 2007 by
Berg
Editorial offices:
1st Floor, Angel Court, 81 St Clements Street, Oxford, OX4 1AW, UK
175 Fifth Avenue, New York, NY 10010, USA

Berg is the imprint of Oxford International Publishers Ltd.

Library of Congress Cataloguing-in-Publication Data

Anthropology put to work / edited by Les W. Field and Richard G. Fox.
    p. cm. — (Wenner-Gren international symposium series)
    Includes bibliographical references and index.
    ISBN-13: 978-1-84520-600-0 (cloth)
    ISBN-10: 1-84520-600-2 (cloth)
    ISBN-13: 978-1-84520-601-7 (pbk.)
    ISBN-10: 1-84520-601-0 (pbk.)
    1. Applied anthropology. I. Field, Les W. II. Fox, Richard Gabriel, 1939-

    GN397.5.A653 2007
    301—dc22

                              2007006651

British Library Cataloguing-in-Publication Data

A catalogue record for this book is available from the British Library.

ISBN 978 184520 600 0 (Cloth)
ISBN 978 184520 601 7 (Paper)

Typeset by JS Typesetting, Porthcawl, Mid Glamorgan
Printed in the United Kingdom by Biddles Ltd, King's Lynn

www.bergpublishers.com

In memory of John W. Bennett and his delight in breaking through academic orthodoxy.

Contents

Acknowledgments

The Wenner-Gren International Symposium "Anthropology Put to Work/Anthropology That Works?" was held at the foundation's office in New York City on 19–22 May 2005. The symposium was the 136th supported by the foundation, but it was the first held in Wenner-Gren's new office space on Park Avenue South. For the first time in over thirty years, the foundation was able to host an international symposium "at home." We were very glad our symposium led off in the new space, and it served us well—better than any castle in Austria would have!

We are much in debt to Laurie Obbink, who has directed the international symposium program for many years—and always with verve, savvy, and loyalty to the foundation's goals. Not only the foundation but also anthropology has profited greatly from Laurie's long-standing dedication. Maugha Kenny, the foundation's director of finance, is someone else who aided us—behind the scenes—by making sure the new space had equipment, furnishings, and a general ambience conducive to making our symposium a "go." Victoria Malkin at Wenner-Gren helped us throughout the pre-publication process to make this volume the best we could. Hannah Shakespeare at Berg Press proved to be a capable and considerate acquisitions editor, and Jane Kepp copyedited with the precision and pinpoint accuracy of a sharpshooter. We would also like to acknowledge the important contribution Craig Howe made during the Wenner-Gren symposium.

Fox came up with the idea for this symposium when he was still president of the foundation, which means that the current president, Leslie Aiello, is not to be taxed for any misconceptions or failings it might have had. We sincerely thank Leslie for her goodwill and generosity toward this "inherited" undertaking.

Participants in the Wenner-Gren Symposium

Linda Basch, National Council for Research on Women
Pamela Block, State University of.New York at Stony Brook
Jennifer Burrell, State University of New York at Albany
Mercedes Doretti, Argentine Forensic Anthropology Team (EAAF)
Douglas E. Foley, University of Texas at Austin
Gelya Frank, University of Southern California
Charles R. Hale, University of Texas at Austin
Craig Howe, independent scholar
Joanne Rappaport, Georgetown University
Nandini Sundar, Delhi School of Economics
Sandy Toussaint, University of Western Australia
Andrew Walsh, Wilfred Laurier University and University of
    Western Ontario
Drexel G. Woodson, University of Arizona

Introduction

How Does Anthropology Work Today?

Les W. Field and Richard G. Fox

We had military governments many times [in Argentina] but this one was particularly bloody and thousands of people disappeared. And so, when democracy returned—that was '84—there was the need to recover the remains of the people that had disappeared... The first time I went into a grave, I basically was very concentrated on what I was doing... I was able to work ... and I realized that I felt [good] about doing something concrete..., meeting with the families of victims and feeling that there was some concrete thing that we could contribute ... to try to do something about what happened in the past.

—Mercedes Doretti, on becoming a forensic anthropologist

From its beginnings, cultural anthropology claimed to work. By "work-ing" we mean that anthropologists claimed they had the training and skills to gain knowledge necessary and useful to society. This knowledge could be theoretical or practical or some mix of the two, but it was, early anthropologists insisted, of benefit to society that people know it. The rationale for why such knowledge benefited society might even shift. In anthropology's early days, for example, researching primitive societies was said to matter because their customs reflected previous evolutionary stages. Later, it was because primitive societies showed the range of human cultural possibility. Whether such knowledge claims "work," that is, whether they are accepted and rewarded, is a matter of conventional understanding in the wider society—a projection of education, media, the market, and the other institutions that create judgments of value to society. Whether anthropology works, therefore,

[handwritten margin notes: Factors that contribute to whether anth knowledge "works"]

1

is something anthropologists cannot proclaim or legislate on their own, although they can try to convince society that what they know has high value. Knowledge claims that a society rewards at one time, furthermore, may not be well regarded at another, as phrenology, parapsychology, eugenics, and a heap of other discarded sciences attest.

Our first proposition—the one that motivated us to organize the symposium on which this book is based—grew out of our perspective on these knowledge claims and how they have been and will be put to work. For anthropology to work in the future, we suggest, anthropologists may need to change their orientations, methodologies, and pedagogy— or, better put, they may need to accept the changes now impinging on them. Our proposition about the future depends, however, on a particular view of anthropology's past.

Is anthropology's history a succession of grand theories, competing schools, and great men and women thinkers? No doubt it is in part, but we also need to recognize that anthropology's history has to do with the pursuit of work—jobs, income, financial security, and the legitimacy in society that underlies all the foregoing. One significant measure of whether past anthropology "worked"—and one not necessarily dependent on some abstract measure of anthropology's worth—is whether anthropologists found jobs to do and what those jobs were. For anthropologists to find work, anthropology had to "work"; that is, its knowledge claims had to be accepted as valuable in the wider society. We therefore use the word *work* in two senses: it refers to the jobs anthropologists did or hoped to do, and it also refers to anthropology's legitimacy in society, which made those jobs available.

At the beginning, when little was settled, anthropology claimed to work in multiple ways: to train and advise colonial administrators, to collect information useful for governing internal minorities such as American Indians, to collect artifacts for museums and set up displays of them, and to undertake university research and teaching as one of the liberal arts or sciences. By the 1920s, many of these knowledge claims had proved not to work. Colonial administrators judged anthropology's knowledge of kinship and ritual esoteric, and the American government turned away from ethnographic research and survey. From this time onward, anthropology in the United States came to work mainly as a museum and university subject, although it never entirely gave up claims that it worked—that is, could be applied—in the wider society. In the United Kingdom and France, anthropology's knowledge claims were even more restricted, because museums played a smaller role in those countries, and recognition of anthropology as a legitimate scholarly discipline, at least in terms of university appointments, came later and on a smaller scale.

The Great Depression and, even more, World War II and its aftermath momentarily brought anthropology back into working directly with the state and its practical objectives. Anthropologists joined multidisciplinary projects during the depression and the war, by which social science was put in the service of the burgeoning American welfare state. After the war, anthropologists took part in international development and labor management projects, which had similar managerial objectives (see Bennett 1996: S26).[1]

In the 1950s, academic anthropologists mostly withdrew from this kind of work. The reason, according to John Bennett (1996), was a resurgent interest among them in building grand theory. Shortly thereafter, proponents of the radical critique of anthropology, focused on the need for "relevant" research, distanced themselves further from what had come to be commonly labeled "applied anthropology." In the radical view, applied anthropology was inherently compromised by association with colonial administrations and state managerial policies (see Bennett 1996: S24). The boundary between anthropologists whose work was applied and those whose work was basic or pure—a boundary, we argue, that is increasingly fuzzy nowadays—was strengthened during the 1960s and 1970s. The "crisis of representation" in the 1980s and 1990s further fortified this boundary, as an all-pervading relativism cast doubt on the very knowledge claims that allowed anthropologists to work in public.

Anthropology's history for us therefore consists of when, where, and how it was put to work. Among the many claims anthropologists made, some worked at one time and not another, others never worked or not for long, and in any case, what worked and what did not were hardly at the disposition of the anthropologists. As we began to organize a Wenner-Gren International Symposium on how anthropology was being put to work at the beginning of the twenty-first century and how it might be in the future, this view of anthropology's history provided us with three premises:

1. The jobs senior anthropologists do or have done recently may not be those that young scholars can or will do in future.
2. The current sense of crisis that many academic anthropologists (mostly in the United States) have about their mission misses the fact that important changes in anthropology's work have already occurred. In particular, there has been a steady erosion of the

boundary between applied and basic research in terms of where and with whom anthropologists work and what kind of anthropology they produce.

3. Most importantly, applied and basic research do not represent separate scholarly positions or divergent intellectual stances; they reflect different jobs done by anthropologists. That is, they have frequently reflected the degree to which anthropologists have obtained protected and well-rewarded jobs in academe, where they can undertake what is called "basic research"—and then whatever else these anthropologists or others do gets labeled "applied." As access by anthropologists to such highly privileged academic jobs decreases, the boundary becomes increasingly fuzzy. The fact is that most anthropology has been "engaged" and "public" in intention—and thus, in a general sense, applied—whether or not that intended public saw it as legitimate and authoritative and whether or not the anthropologist's job description called for application.

Some personal experiences can clarify this last point. Fox's work (1985) on the interplay between British colonialism and Sikh identity in northern India was not applied in a narrow sense, but when he was called upon to address militant Sikh congregations in the United States during the Khalistan agitation in the 1980s, it became so. Militant Sikhs scrutinized his research for what it might say about the degree of separation between Hindus and Sikhs, in aid of the movement to carve a separate Sikh state out of India. Fox also found himself, on the basis of his historical research, defending Sikhs against accusations of terrorism after the assassination of Indira Gandhi in 1984. One dean at Duke University even asked him to warrant that a Sikh who had recently moved into the dean's neighborhood would not be making bombs in his basement.

Field, by contrast, began research with California Indians in the employ of one unrecognized tribe, the Muwekma Ohlone of the San Francisco Bay Area. His research agenda, interview and life-history formats and scheduling, and access to archival materials were all arranged and planned with and through the tribe. Only after working on a variety of projects connected with their federal recognition petition for almost a decade and doing similar work with other unrecognized coastal groups did Field begin to explore projects that departed from specific "applications" of anthropological research relevant to the tortured relations between the federal Indian bureaucracy and the unrecognized tribes. But this move also took place, in large part, at the instigation of members of Indian communities.

The best way to see that our future work may not be what we do or claim to do today is to view our past from the vantage of the present. How passionately we disown much of that past and the way anthropology was put to work then! We are dismayed that Franz Boas, American anthropology's founding father in the early twentieth century, robbed Indian graves for skeletons and concocted a false burial to fool a young Inuit into letting science have his father's corpse. We are ashamed that Alfred Kroeber, Boas's early student, betrayed Ishi, his Indian friend (or captive, depending on your view), and sent his brain for scientists at the Smithsonian to study and preserve. And what sort of folly was it that might have led Margaret Mead, a later Boas student, to be hoaxed in the 1920s by Samoan young women who made Samoa out to be just what Mead wanted? Accusations made in the 1970s of anthropology's complicity with colonialism and its fellow-traveling with American imperialism similarly impugned anthropology's history on the job (see Freeman 1983; Hymes 1972; Starn 2004; Thomas 2000).

We anthropologists have often been quick to disown this past, as if we could purify ourselves by vilifying our ancestors. There is no need to worship these ancestors, but there is another lesson we need to take from the past—in respect of our future. These past "failures" should tell us that anthropology worked differently in the past. Boas and Kroeber, for example, believed in a salvage anthropology that could take liberties in the name of science in order to rescue American Indian customs and languages before the native societies disintegrated. If Mead was truly hoaxed, it came about because of a naive faith in ethnographic rapport, long before anthropologists began to work with populations and in a world where the boundary between good guys and bad became fuzzy. All three worked at a time when anthropologists needed to gain legitimacy within universities, and no doubt the then current image of the sober and unbiased scholar, for whom science came first, conditioned what they did and the way they presented themselves.

To be sure, we must uncover past instances of naiveté, complicity, and duplicity in anthropology if we are to improve our understanding and better our knowledge—of ourselves and thereby of the world we study. At the same time, we had better take the lesson that anthropology can be put to work in different ways and that anthropologists have had to respond to the job opportunities available to them at any one time.

In planning our symposium, therefore, we conceived of anthropology's future in a way fundamentally different from that of anthropologists who have recently called for a "public" or "engaged" anthropology re-focused on critical social issues (see Basch et al. 1999; Lamphere 2003; Scheper-Hughes 1995). No doubt these exhortations are well intended, and the anthropologists expressing them are in earnest. For us, however, this image of anthropologists "reaching out" from protected academic positions to a vaguely defined "public" is elitist and out of touch with the working conditions of many anthropologists, especially those junior and untenured. We also have strong doubts that anthropologists can be whatever they want to be; the "just do it" sentiment behind these fervid appeals seems more in line with both nationalist and individualist American ideologies than with the current realities of scholarship in the United States. Furthermore, the exhortations by senior anthropologists for an engaged, public anthropology assume a crisis situation that we think is neither new nor sudden. In our experience, younger anthropologists have had to respond to this "crisis" for at least two decades.

We based our symposium, therefore, on the premise that profound changes have *already* occurred in anthropology, leading to new kinds of work for a large number of anthropologists. We decided to focus our symposium on this work as a way of making it better known and more instructive to young anthropologists. We did not assume that there is an essential anthropology, based in the academy, that needs to become better at managing public relations and "reaching out" or that needs to reassume the authority to name the important social issues of the day. Rather, we presumed that new anthropological work has responded to changing social and cultural demands, and we doubted that anthropology could determine on its own which issues to highlight. For us, the meaning and significance of an "anthropology in public" is neither obvious nor simple, because there is no singular, dominant anthropology that allows us to determine when and how to "engage" with "the public."

We hoped to bring together at the symposium a sample of the many new forms of work in which anthropologists engage, but we know that this volume represents only a handful of examples. In the event, we had fewer participants from outside the United States than we expected, and certain workplaces, such as the corporate world and private philanthropies, needed greater representation. We believe, however, that the contributors do show that anthropologists are put to work in diverse ways today and that anthropology has changed profoundly because of it.

Although this volume cannot cover all the new career scenarios, we think it does identify the degree to which the work of anthropologists has changed. We hope it will aid graduate students and early-career scholars to accept these changes, without feeling that something essential to anthropology has been lost, and to adapt to them, because there really is no other choice for most young anthropologists. Others have documented the current dearth of academic jobs and the increased vulnerability of untenured—in many cases, never-to-be tenured—junior faculty, and we see little point in reiterating these projections here. We want to focus instead on what these changed conditions of work, these new career scenarios, mean for the way anthropology gets done differently and the way, in the process, our basic operating concepts get modified.

The contributors to the volume indicate that the new conditions of anthropological work require significant departures from standard and widely accepted principles of cultural anthropology. In what follows, we discuss the chapters in relation to these significant departures.

From Rapport to Collaboration

The most significant departure concerns the concept of ethnographic rapport and reflexivity in fieldwork. Ethnographic rapport in its canonical version—this is, the image of the anthropologist among the "natives," building up trust and friendship with them in return for information—has come under attack for being disingenuous in several ways. Peter Pels (1999: 107) finds a fundamental "duplexity" in ethnographic fieldwork, in that "the anthropologist poses as someone wanting to be converted to a 'native' audience during fieldwork and as someone who has been converted (but, perhaps, has returned to 'normal' ways) when reporting on this fieldwork ... back home." Pels also reminds us that "rapport" helps the anthropologist overcome native reservations about the anthropologist's ulterior motives, when in fact the academic career underwritten by the fieldwork is precisely an ulterior motive.

Another contradiction is that ethnographic rapport invokes a sameness between anthropologist and "native," at least enough to facilitate communication, whereas ethnographic texts construct difference or "otherness" (see Argyrou 1999). "Rapport" also suggests an equality in the relationship between anthropologists and their subjects, when the norm is for the poor and vulnerable to be our target populations. Finally, the concept of rapport assumes that the anthropologist gets along well with members of the society or population under study, even to the point of wanting to minimize the group's dysfunctions or internal conflicts. Robert Edgerton (1992) called this the "myth of primitive harmony."

Such a "goodthink" concept works poorly in a world in which anthropologists study drug dealers, ethnic militants, religious fundamentalists, and others who, although caught up in circumstances, nevertheless are not underclass heroes or oppressed "good guys." Even when anthropologists do work with people who are the "good guys"— such as members of indigenous peoples and other oppressed ethnic minorities—political and ideological factionalism, religious diversity, sexism, unethical behavior, and the power of individual personalities can no longer be glossed over so that anthropologists can represent a unidimensional "indigenous voice." Although most anthropologists recognize how poorly the concept of rapport fits ethnographic reality today, we often cling to this concept as an essential one to transmit in graduate training and to use in evaluating the worth of field research by young scholars. The chapters in this volume provide an alternative to the concept of rapport, as we discuss shortly.

The concept of "reflexivity" is a recent addition to or elaboration of "ethnographic rapport" that only makes for more difficulty. "Reflexivity," when it focuses on the mutual changes in anthropologists and their interlocutors created by ethnographic interaction, is insightful but hardly novel or revolutionary: it seems obvious that successful field research has always depended upon some such mutuality. When "reflexivity" goes farther and focuses the ethnographic text on the anthropologist's psychological response and self-realization through fieldwork, it is possible that such reflection only exacerbates the inequalities in ethnography by underlining the privilege of exploring and publishing the anthropologist's self-actualization. Ostensibly studying others, the anthropologist, in effect, chronicles himself or herself. The excesses of that route, epitomized by the postmodernism of the 1980s and early 1990s, appear to have passed, yet anthropologists still commonly use the term *reflexivity* in an unexamined way that could connote self-indulgence. As with "rapport," the work to which anthropology is put today supersedes a self-indulgent reflexivity and demands a new ethnographic relationship based on collaboration. Although it is possible, as Luke Lassiter recently wrote (2005), to see much continuity in the ways "rapport," "reflexivity," and now "collaboration" have been used in the history of ethnographic research, we see real differences in the deployment of these concepts and, consequently, real advances in ethnographic methods.

collaboration

This concept of collaboration—as a method of ethnographic research, as an epistemological principle, and as a means of putting knowledge to work—developed into the most significant commonality among the contributors to this volume. Lassiter (2005: 84) defined collaborative ethnography as "the collaboration of researchers and subjects in the production of ethnographic texts, both fieldwork and writing." He underscored that quite different goals and imperatives could emerge within each collaborative project. His own work, which spans research among the Kiowas and among urban African Americans, exemplifies the ways in which different kinds of collaborative fieldwork relationships nourish very different results. Lassiter's work emphasizes that notions of collaboration must not become vague general principles that do not move much beyond "rapport" and "reflexivity."

The contributors to this volume work collaboratively for specific reasons. Some of them embrace collaboration in response to predicaments and opportunities encountered in their research. In many communities, anthropological research methods and goals must be reconciled with criteria and agendas developed by leaders and other intellectuals from those communities. Often our contributors actually work in the employ of the community, thereby reversing the conventional power relations that often typified fieldwork in the past. In some instances they have developed collaborative relationships with academics from other disciplines or have combined anthropological research with goals and orientations derived from other disciplines. Still other contributors endorse collaborative efforts as a solution to their broad critique of anthropological theory and practice.

Joanne Rappaport's work in Colombia, for example, has demanded political and social collaboration with indigenous intellectuals and social movements, without which ethnography would have proved impossible. That collaboration, in turn, transformed her theory and methods, leading to what she calls "co-theorizing." Rappaport found that her collaborative work complexly resonated with the history of politically committed social science done by Colombian scholars.

In a parallel fashion, Mercedes Doretti's Argentine Forensic Anthropology Team (EEAF) developed because the politics of human rights, married to the methods of forensic anthropology, produced new methods and forms of knowledge that required ever-evolving negotiations between anthropological, political, and local practices and goals. The resulting collaboration comprised a complex ensemble of expertise, ethics, and desires produced as all the interested parties—anthropologists, governments, nongovernmental organizations (NGOs), and families of victims—came together. Doretti's use of the term *negotiation* evokes the manner in which anthropological work, as in Rappaport's research, becomes so embedded in complex relationships that the anthropologist can no longer impose her research priorities. For both Rappaport and Doretti, collaborative relationships shaping the research they did obviated any consideration of the people with whom they worked as "informants." Those relationships underscore the degree to which both the anthropologist and the people with whom she worked became "interlocutors."

Gelya Frank also recounts the transformation brought about in her anthropology through collaboration, in this case with residents of the Tule River Indian Reservation in central California. This collaboration developed because the Yokuts bands at Tule River had been working up their own projects and historical agenda. Frank turned to another discipline, occupational therapy, to further her own and the community's goals. By bringing occupational therapy and anthropology into the collaboration, Frank found her ability to make space for changes in the conception of her research steeply augmented, and she advanced the efforts of the Tule River community in relatively rapid order.

Pam Block's chapter, too, is concerned with the teaming of occupational therapy with anthropology, but she offers a very different story, focused on the making of a new career—her own—and the new disciplinary and professional collaborations she forged. In her case, collaborations took place within the context of a university deeply enmeshed in corporate America, one in which "for-profit" calculations took precedence over canonical notions of basic research. Block shows the new personal and disciplinary collaborations this sort of university required, and hers is a cautionary tale indeed. Apart from the inevitable problems anyone would encounter in forging a new kind of cross-disciplinary career, she details how difficult it is to describe her work to both anthropologists and occupational therapists. The collaborations that Rappaport and Doretti must achieve "in the field" have their counterpart in the career collaboration that Block must create at home in the university.

Charles Hale and Drexel Woodson each discuss collaboration in more general ways and within the context of anthropology's history and future. Hale wishes to erase the distinction between basic and applied research in favor of what he labels "activist anthropology," which is both collaborative and politically engaged. He recognizes that collaborative approaches, operationalized as activist anthropology rather than as cultural critique, have not been broadly accepted in American scholarship, despite their ethical virtues and their production of results valued by the communities involved. He warns us that activist anthropology will never survive in the new corporate American university unless it highlights its superiority in producing theory and analysis, and his chapter showcases the methodological and epistemological advantages of collaborative and activist research over canonical pure research in anthropology. Although Hale recognizes the contradictions that activist research can generate, both within the anthropologist's epistemology and methods and between the anthropologist and the communities in which she or he works, he argues that activist anthropology is still characterized by ethical superiority and better payoffs for the anthropologist's collaborators relative to those achieved through an instrumental applied anthropology.

Woodson offers the work experience of an anthropologist firmly committed personally to maintaining a distinction between pure and applied research. His commitment grows out of the multidisciplinary development work he has been doing for over two decades in Haiti. He uses theory and epistemology elaborated in basic anthropological research to assemble field methods he and the larger research team deploy in the applied, "policy-relevant" work they do in Haiti. Their goal is to develop "social indicators" of Haitian domestic economy and development that NGOs will regard as valid and reliable. These indicators, which are qualitative and quantitative benchmarks of social, political, and economic conditions in Haiti, depend upon fine-tuned collaborations between Woodson and Haitian interlocutors, as well as between Woodson and team members from other disciplines. A different and perhaps more trying collaboration takes place with international NGOs, who have the ultimate say about the worth of these social indicators in terms of eliciting funds for Haitian development.

These multiple collaborations, Woodson relates, require a process of "bracketing, compressing, and simplifying" information and then "probing and unpacking" it—a process that is profoundly reflexive as an outcome of the work itself, rather than a self-absorbed reflexivity. Woodson says his work is energized by the interplay between pure and basic research, which we take to mean that his ethnography follows basic research methods, whereas his data are directed toward applied purposes. His collaborative work with NGOs has substantially transformed the ethnographic data he collects and presents and, in turn, the methods by which he collects them.

This transformation signifies to us that the distinction between pure and applied research is no longer salient, as Rappaport argues in the case of Colombian anthropology, just as the work-based reflexivity

Woodson highlights disavows the self-interested variety that has been associated with basic research in the past two decades. Linda Basch explores another angle on these topics. Like Frank and Block, she has found a disciplinary home outside anthropology, as director of a network of women's research and policy NGOs. Abjuring the pure-applied dualism as well, Basch instead names a creative and explicitly reflexive tension between the instrumentalism that characterizes her daily work life and the descriptive empiricism of anthropological inquiry. Without doubt, Basch values her training and her professional identity as an anthropologist for what they contribute to the goals and agendas of the projects she works on with feminist NGOs. But she also considers the insights she has gained concerning the internal dynamics of interdisciplinary and academic-nonacademic collaborations in the making of those projects an essential part of her role as an anthropologist in this work. She suggests that anthropologists have a strong, multisided role to play when they work with other kinds of professionals, and that their attention to work process as well as final product is one of their specific contributions.

A New Reflexivity

The reclamation of reflexivity is further detailed in the chapters by Sandy Toussaint, Nandini Sundar, and Andrew Walsh. Toussaint describes her work career in Australia as a different kind of collaboration from the one Doretti detailed: it is based on doing both teaching and research and on moving between the lives and locations of her interlocutors and the university. Like Hale, Toussaint is concerned with the effects of corporate control on the university, and like Woodson, she has worked with scholars from other disciplines. But in her chapter there is no closure on these disjunctures; she relates the potential of such collaborations, including the potential for failure. One non-anthropologist scholar with whom she collaborated did not follow even the basic contours of collaboration with Aboriginal communities. Competition over productivity in the university has led to competition for scarce resources such that some otherwise valuable research projects are never funded. In any individual case of collaboration, bridging the vast differences between the quotidian harshness of marginalized Aboriginal people and the privileged world of the university may not succeed.

Toussaint makes it clear that such failed collaborations have multiple losers, not only colleagues from other disciplines but also, and most sadly, the Aboriginal communities, whose land claims and other struggles for social justice do not necessarily end well. The anthropologist can come to be perceived by the people themselves as having let them down, no matter how hard she worked to help them. In turn, she feels dreadful for their plight, in a reflexivity that comes "on the job" rather than in the mind. Toussaint's chapter balances the more positive presentations of collaboration by Rappaport, Frank, and Hale, but she remains fully committed to such collaborations because they are anthropology's work today.

In Sundar's chapter, collaboration also characterizes anthropologists' relations and negotiations with public interlocutors and with scholars from other disciplines with whom she has worked on development projects among tribal communities in India. Calling attention to dist-inctive conditions shaping the development of anthropology and other social sciences in India, Sundar, like Toussaint, recognizes the difficulties and, in the Indian context, the dangers of collaboration. The history of anthropology in India, as it developed among indigenous scholars in a colonized society, gives her a special viewpoint on the nature of anthropological collaboration. She is uncertain that a single anthropology exists that can be cross-fertilized by other disciplines, uncertain about what constitutes the anthropological canon when what is written in so many Indian languages is considered ineligible for inclusion, and humbly uncertain about applying anthropological knowledge in the face of the frequently dire economic and political problems facing communities where she has worked.

She also honors the hard work of the early Indian anthropologists in legitimating anthropology as a basic research discipline in India and themselves as worthy researchers in the face of colonial prejudice against indigenous scholars. These hard-won past victories for Indian anthropology and for Indian universities mean, especially given the sectarian violence that now afflicts India, that the risks of a collab-orative and activist anthropology are much higher. Hale, too, affirms the tensions between the scholarship he advocates and the indigenous movements with which he works. But Sundar, from her South Asian vantage, is far less sanguine about the outcomes of collaborative enterprises for anthropology's interlocutors and about the security of the anthropological discipline within the boundaries of the university where it is housed.

With Walsh's chapter, the kind of reflexivity characterizing Toussaint's and Sundar's contributions reaches a higher pitch. His analysis introduces an alchemical allegory, offering the idea that anthropologists spin golden publications out of fieldwork straw, at least in part to explain both to Walsh himself and his Malagasy interlocutors exactly what he is doing in Madagascar and how he makes a living doing it. By emphasizing anthropology not only as work but as a job, Walsh explores the obsession with product in academic work, recalling Hale's suggestion that the hyperproductivity required by corporate universities just might be turned to the advantage of collaborative activist anthropologists. If Basch implied an emphasis on process as much as on product, Walsh explicitly argues for a new valuation regime in anthropology, one that allows for failure to produce—publications, for example—and that turns our reflexive attention to the processes of doing fieldwork, teaching, and writing and to what is gained from them by all interlocutors. After all, Walsh points out, alchemists learned to work with elements in ways that future generations of scientists have taken tremendous advantage of, notwithstanding their failure to produce gold. No doubt Walsh's radical view ultimately envisages whole new meanings not only for anthropology, collaborative or otherwise, but for all kinds of work.

From Fieldwork Epiphany to Fieldwork Realism

In this volume we contest another part of the anthropological canon, the hoary notion that successful fieldwork can be measured by whether the anthropologist comes back a "different person," altered forever and immeasurably by the ethnographic encounter. Ethnography as "vision quest" is one of the oldest and most destructive parts of the anthropological canon. It displaces training in analytic methodology and field methods with an unmeasurable psychological change—why do we need field methods when the true test of good ethnography is whether the anthropologist has a personally transformative experience in the field? It also supports, unfortunately, anthropologists' claims that they are different from ordinary scholars—political scientists and sociologists, after all, don't have epiphanies during fieldwork. This claim to being chosen not only often gets anthropology dismissed but also interferes with the collaborations across disciplines on which we now depend for work. Worse, it puts a burden on fledgling anthropologists, who must authenticate their professional standing by narrating ethnographic epiphanies and who often wonder how much transformation is enough to qualify.

The stereotype of anthropological fieldwork as comprising personal epiphanies has vanished from the chapters in this volume. Significant life changes might have occurred during each contributor's fieldwork, but for these writers such changes appear to be neither implicit and off-stage nor, in a Malinowskian sense, erotically charged (as was presumably the case for many anthropologists during most of the twentieth century). Nor are these life changes explicit, overbearing, and the focus of interest, as they have been in the recent postmodernist turn. The profoundly relational nature of fieldwork, in terms of the intertwining of anthropologists' and their interlocutors' lives and minds, is perhaps best expressed by Rappaport's term, *co-theorizing*. This term neither sidelines the active involvement of the anthropologist and her profound investment in the ethnographic experience nor fetishizes that experience to the detriment of the other interlocutors and *their* profound investments in the process. Walsh's emphasis on process over product in the job of doing anthropology also helps to undermine the mystique of fieldwork without detracting from its importance. Other contributors' skepticism and caution about collaborative ethnography, elaborated particularly by Sundar and Toussaint, provide another vantage from which to more realistically value the process of ethnography. In an extraordinary instance of this kind of realism, Doretti has managed to engage in ethnographic work that surely has profoundly changed her, without relying on the trope of the ethnographic epiphany.

Block, Frank, and, by implication, Basch remind us that anthropologists can undergo profound personal changes outside of fieldwork, even though these locales are not part of the canon in anthropology. Block and Frank both describe the profound alterations that their self-concepts and career scenarios underwent as they adopted knowledge from other disciplines and found work in non-anthropology university departments. We can perceive a similar substantial self-awareness arising in Sundar as she recovers the battles for anthropology and indigenous scholarship fought by her predecessors in India and balances them against the claims on her generation of researchers for activism.

From Holism to Situational Comparison

Another part of the anthropological canon disputed in this volume is the notion of holism—that is, the idea that the anthropologist studies everything in a society or, in a more recent form, that the anthropologist develops an overarching view of a society from small-scale research. Toussaint explicitly attacks the icon of holism from two perspectives, presenting the work world of the anthropologist as composed of fragments that cannot be seamlessly reassembled and the world of the Aboriginal communities in which she works as characterized by incongruence, disruption, and suffering that is irreconcilable with a holistic worldview. From another angle, Woodson presents indicators as co-theorized tools of evaluation that do not pretend to reflect the entirety of Haitian rural life. The mirage of holism is clearly tangential to the work Woodson does, both methodologically and in terms of its expected outcomes.

Rappaport, Frank, and Hale work locally and specifically, their anthropological purview defined by the goals and agendas of the people they work with and study. Basch's work is in a sense divorced from locality, because it brings people together from many divergent locations. Finally, in a location where anthropologists historically have deployed the mirage of holism in an almost de rigeur fashion—the Indian reservation—Frank put anthropology to work for a community that had no such expectation. This is another outcome of the kinds of collaborative work pursued by the volume's contributors—some of anthropology's burdens can be lifted because the frameworks for doing anthropology are not determined by anthropological legacies.

Although not holistic, these chapters do allow for broad comparative perspectives in ways that differ from the comparisons of whole societies that have characterized much of anthropology's history—until recently, when the problems with such holistic comparisons led to the demise of most comparative anthropology (see Fox and Gingrich 2002). The old notion of holistic comparison disdained ripping parts or aspects of a society out of the entire social complex, in dismissal of the trait comparisons found in early evolutionist anthropology. That kind of anthropology being long dead, it is time anthropologists returned to a comparative perspective, based on social practices and beliefs, where context is acknowledged but not taken to the point of invalidating comparison.

Rappaport, Hale, Frank, Toussaint, and Doretti all give us instances of collaboration with local people in which the variables that make each instance somewhat different—indigenous politics, national history, imperialist relations, and local beliefs—afford or, better, promote insightful comparisons of the anthropological collaboration and indigenous activism possible in different circumstances. In the chapters by Block, Frank, Woodson, Toussaint, Doretti, and Basch, we can take a comparative perspective on how anthropology—and individual anthropologists—can adapt to the new corporate university and globalized world of NGOs or not-for-profits and still retain a strong identity as professional anthropologists. The contributors here and in their other writings allow for comparisons on many specific topics: indigenous social movements and community projects (Rappaport, Frank, Sundar,

Toussaint), the use of anthropological fieldwork techniques in occupational therapy (Block, Frank), the alleviation of poverty and other kinds of social suffering (Woodson, Sundar, Doretti, Toussaint), and the difficulty of reconciling university life with fieldwork (Walsh, Toussaint, Hale). They do not represent the work at their field sites or in their research projects as providing insights into whole cultural systems, as, for example, in Clifford Geertz's attempt to take the Balinese cockfight as exemplary of the society or his belief that he could learn about all of Indonesia by studying social life in one small town. The conditions our contributors encounter in their fieldwork make these holistic claims unfeasible, implausible, and indeed impossible.

This rich and alternative diversity offers readers perspectives that are grounded in what is going on in the discipline right now, rather than in recommendations for anticipated changes. This is not unintentional and is part of this volume's orientation toward the teaching and training of graduate students.

Putting Anthropology to Work: A Pedagogy

The importance of teaching and training new anthropologists never left central stage as we wrote this introduction, not to mention as we planned and organized this symposium. Many of our contributors came out of graduate programs in anthropology that either partly or in some cases completely neglected to teach fieldwork methodology or to instruct graduate students at all about how one becomes a professional anthropologist or prepares to find work in our field. As recently as the 1990s, discussions of fieldwork and methods in graduate classes were characteristically gossipy in tone, treating the release of Malinowski's diaries, for example, as a titillating exposé rather than as an opportunity to understand the relationships—collaborative and quite possibly combative—by which Malinowski obtained ethnographic information. Doubtless, many programs still neglect these essential aspects of training new anthropologists or relegate them to the margins of more highly valued theoretical discussions. Yet graduate students increasingly demand exactly such classes, as well as advisement that focuses on preparing for collaborative field methods, writing for anthropological journals, assembling professional credentials, and preparing to apply for and work in non-academic jobs. We envision this volume as directed toward graduate students' demands for information about these issues, not in a didactic or directive way in which we opine what should be done, but by way of real examples.

It may be useful for students to consider the multiple kinds of careers described in this volume, as well as the ways in which different kinds of collaborative methods and epistemologies developed under distinct circumstances. In that light, the book could be put to productive use in classes focusing specifically on fieldwork methods, as well as in first-year graduate theory classes. A more profound significance for the volume could be to support the resurrection of another kind of collaborative fieldwork—that between students and mentors. By the 1980s, graduate students were already being told that the days in which they could expect to work with their professors at the latter's research sites were long over. As Lassiter and his students showed in *The Other Side of Middletown: Exploring Muncie's African-American Community* (2004), students not only are asking to learn collaborative research methods but frequently are interested in creating such projects with their professors. Reviving this kind of collaboration in ethnographic research could have profound consequences for the way anthropology's interlocutors understand our research methods and the way individuals, both students and interlocutors, become trained in the doing of ethnography.

The most important way this book could be taught is as part of a wholesale shift in the orientation of graduate training toward the kinds of circumstances in which most anthropologists now work. This would mean including the work of non-academic anthropologists in the lists of required reading on which graduate students are tested and understanding that work as part of a greater, more inclusive canon. In short, the training of graduate students must increasingly match the jobs and work those students will end up doing, and it is toward that goal that this book is designed to contribute.

Note

1. The Western Electric Hawthorne project is the best-known instance of anthropology's involvement in industrial labor management before World War II. See Mayo 1933, Warner and Low 1947, and Chapple 1943 and 1946 for contemporary statements about this research; see Landsberger 1958 and Schwartzman 1992 for retrospective critiques. Instances of multidisciplinary projects that incorporated anthropology are the cross-cultural studies of basic personality sponsored by Abram Kardiner in the 1930s and 1940s (Kardiner

1945; Kardiner and Linton 1939) and, somewhat later, the study of premodern and modern economies headed by Karl Polanyi (Polanyi 1944; Polanyi, Arensburg, and Pearson 1957). The major example of the use of anthropological research during the Second World War is Ruth Benedict's study of Japanese culture "at a distance," *The Chrysanthemum and the Sword* (1946), but anthropologists participated in more direct ways that, in retrospect, often seem unfortunate (see Mead 1979; Starn 1986). After World War II, anthropologists rushed to join the other social sciences in the study of development and the "new nations" (see Kluckhohn 1949; Linton 1945; Steward 1950, 1956) at the outset of the atomic era and the Cold War.

Anthropological Collaborations in Colombia

Joanne Rappaport

Colombian ethnographers have for decades engaged in a committed anthropology marked by political and social collaboration, blurring the lines that separate what their North American colleagues call applied anthropology, advocacy, and pure research (Jimeno 1999; Rappaport 1990). In the past few decades, the communities that Colombian anthropologists traditionally studied have begun to do their own research, forcing a shift in the terms of dialogue between external scholars and communities, as well as in the expectations that communities have of researchers. In this chapter I examine the way an engaged Colombian ethnography emerged over time and tease out of its history a sense of what collaboration has meant to Colombian researchers.

I focus on social scientists whose work with popular movements has revolved around the construction of a research agenda, as opposed to those whose relationships with social movements have been confined to advocacy. I look especially at the development of participatory action research in the late 1960s and the 1970s by Orlando Fals Borda and La Rosca de Investigación y Acción Social (Circle of Social Research and Action) in collaboration with Colombian indigenous and peasant organizations, and at the work of the anthropologist Luis Guillermo Vasco in the 1980s with the history committee of the indigenous community of Guambía. Vasco's approach, unlike La Rosca's, privileged the field as a site of co-theorizing between academics and grassroots researchers. In considering how these scholars saw the research process transformed by collaboration, I home in on the locus of theorizing, the nature of agenda building, and the creation of horizontal relationships between researchers and community.

The kind of collaborative research conducted by Colombian academics contrasts with many examples of collaborative ethnography in North America. Contemporary North American anthropologists have written extensively about the significance of collaborative writing (Hinson 2000; Lassiter 2005; Lawless 1993; Ridington and Hastings 1997), but such writing does not purport to transgress the boundaries between applied and "pure" research. Rather, its fundamental goal is the production of a new kind of ethnography geared largely to a scholarly readership—that is, a new kind of pure research.

In contrast, Colombian anthropologists' attempts at collaborative research break down these boundaries in crucial ways. Their commitment to collaboration is tempered by an equally significant engagement with activism. Thus their research is simultaneously pure and applied, though perhaps such distinctions do not cut to the core of what this research is about. Unlike the collaborations of most applied researchers, these scholars' collaborations with popular organizations are essentially political, geared toward promoting social justice from the grassroots, which makes their research more activist than applied. At the same time, their commitment to community-based research agendas results in work that is not pure in an academic sense, because it is not driven by academic theory (Strand et al. 2003: chap. 4)—although, as I demonstrate, they also produce innovative scholarly publications. Finally, what most significantly distinguishes these Colombian activist-scholars from their North American colleagues is their focus on field practice as a space in which social analysis and political action can be generated, as opposed to an emphasis on writing as a vehicle for scholarly collaboration.[1]

This Colombian collaborative heritage bears implications for research conducted by foreigners in Latin America, as well as for the work of nationals. Indeed, it provides us with an alternative intellectual lineage that we can engage in building a new anthropological agenda for the twenty-first century. In the second half of the chapter, I bring this lineage to bear on my own collaborative relationship over the past decade with the Regional Indigenous Council of Cauca (CRIC), a major Colombian indigenous organization.

Initially, CRIC members sought me out after having read my published and unpublished work on the colonial history of the Nasa ethnic group (Rappaport 1998). I was first asked to coordinate history workshops in local communities with the objective of facilitating the collective study of colonial reservation titles whose contents had passed into the oral domain and had become a kind of mythic charter for communities and for CRIC. Later, I was invited to participate as a team member in a study of the history of CRIC's Bilingual Intercultural Education Program (PEBI). In the process, I discovered that collaborative research does not revolve exclusively around the production of a written text by a research team. Instead, it requires extended exchange with a broader range of activists, transcending the project itself. At the same time, it constitutes a key space for generating a new kind of anthropological theorizing that spans the divides between pure and applied research, between the academy and those undertaking research within popular organizations.

My approach to ethnography is heavily indebted to these Colombian researchers. Although it has resulted in scholarly writing, I have attempted to follow the Colombian example by shifting my emphasis from writing to analytical dialogue in the field. This has led to products that are of utility to the organizations with which I have worked and has contributed even more to the development of a distinct grassroots research methodology. In this sense, my notion of what ethnography is and the ways in which it can be harnessed in an activist context has been permanently altered. The link between theory and ethnographic interpretation has moved, for me, away from being forged through solitary academic pursuit and toward fostering an appreciation of the way collaborative research can promote co-theorization with the communities we study. Reflexivity has come to be redefined, in my experience, as a process of contemplating the epistemology of our theoretical dialogue. This has reshaped my methods, my interpretive strategies, and the contents of my research, redefining ethnography for me in significant ways.

The Militant Research of La Rosca

In 1972, a book titled *Causa popular, ciencia popular* (Popular cause, popular science) appeared in Colombia, published by La Rosca de Investigación y Acción Social, a network of Colombian social scientists and journalists advocating militant research alongside popular movements (Bonilla et al. 1972). La Rosca members proposed abandoning the university—or at least rejecting the traditional research methodologies of the academy—to employ their scholarly skills in the service of popular sectors by inserting themselves as researcher-activists into local and regional struggles. They argued in favor of establishing research priorities in conjunction with local militants, studying the history of the militants' organizations, and then returning the results of their research to them (Bonilla et al. 1972: 44–46).

Participatory action research

Participatory action research, as this approach came to be called, presupposed "that the researcher himself is an object of investigation: his ideology, knowledge, and practice are judged in light of popular experience. The exploitation that occurs when people are studied as 'research objects' (a veritable sacking of their cultural values and of the treasure-house of their experience) is abandoned, leading to a respect for them, their contributions, their critiques, their intelligence" (Bonilla et al. 1972: 46, my translation). Final authority would rest with the popular sectors and not the researchers (1972: 47). La Rosca proposed, in essence, that popular sectors "expropriate" scientific knowledge, techniques, and methodologies (1972: 48).[2]

La Rosca's task did not conclude once its research was completed. Its members advocated a methodology that they called "critical recuperation," which turned research results toward activist ends:

Critical recuperation

> Critical recuperation is achieved when, on the basis of historical information and an adequate understanding of current conditions, militant researchers arrive in communities to critically study and learn about the traditional cultural base, paying special attention to those elements or institutions that have been useful in the past to confront the enemies of the exploited classes. Once those elements are determined, they are reactivated with the aim of using them in a similar manner in current class struggles. (Bonilla et al. 1972: 51–52)

Local peasant practices of labor exchange and institutions such as the *resguardo* (or reservation, an institution that ensures collective land rights for native peoples) and the *cabildo* (the *resguardo* council, which operates as a semi-autonomous entity) were the sorts of practices La Rosca hoped to study and subsequently reintroduce into communities (1972: 52).

The best-known of La Rosca's efforts is the publication of a treatise by Manuel Quintín Lame (1971 [1939]), a Nasa leader who forged a land-claims movement in the Colombian southwest during the first half of the twentieth century (Castillo-Cárdenas 1987; Rappaport 1998). The posthumous appearance of Lame's writings reactivated his memory among the Nasa of Cauca and the Pijao of the neighboring department of Tolima, helping to spur the Regional Indigenous Council of Cauca (CRIC), founded in 1971, to include in its organizational objectives Lame's demands for reclaiming land within the *resguardo* structure and for strengthening *cabildos* (Avirama and Márquez 1995). La Rosca members produced historical pamphlets reviving the memory of eighteenth-century hereditary chiefs who created *resguardos* in the region (Bonilla 1977), and they introduced a series of picture maps through which local history could be collectively recaptured (Bonilla 1982).[3] The products of La Rosca's research, although not academic, would not have appeared if not for the intervention of these activist-scholars. The continued significance of these publications in indigenous organizations—where they are still studied and used by people at the grassroots—points to the possibilities of a collaborative model that transcends academic writing.

La Rosca also produced some academic documents, such as Orlando Fals Borda's *Historia doble de la costa* (Double history of the coast), a four-volume experiment in narrating the history of the agrarian struggles of people living along Colombia's Atlantic coast (Fals Borda 1980–86). *Historia doble* is organized in two channels, one narrative and the other theoretical and methodological. Fals intended the narrative channel to be consulted by leaders of agrarian organizations and the theoretical channel to be read by politically committed intellectuals and academics. A series of comics, pamphlets, and audiovisual materials was to be produced for the rank and file of the social movements in the region (Bergquist 1990: 160).

The ethnographer Luis Guillermo Vasco made an insightful critique of La Rosca's methods with the hindsight that came from his collaborative experience in the indigenous community of Guambía in the 1980s. He argued that the politically committed scholars of the 1970s made the positivist error of separating field practice from the theoretically informed interpretation of data—the error, precisely, of the organization of Fals Borda's history of the Atlantic coast (Vasco Uribe 2002: 454–57). As a result, he said, La Rosca's attempt to "return" its research to the communities in which it had worked was not entirely successful; La Rosca members did not recognize the position of power they occupied as scholars or that they, like other researchers, had constituted the groups they studied as objects of analysis (2002: 457–58). Ultimately, many aspects of La Rosca's project were academic in their intent and unassimilable (at the time) by the social movements with which they were concerned (Bergquist 1990; cf. Fox 2005).[4] In short, La Rosca's political commitment did not preclude its adherence to traditional ethnographic procedures or its insistence on employing theory originating in the academy.

Theorizing and Co-theorizing

The African American sociologist W. E. B. DuBois argued in *The Souls of Black Folk* (1989 [1903]: 2–3) that racial minorities in the United States keenly perceived that they at once stood within the North American social system and were marginalized by it. This produced what he called a "double consciousness," a dual identity that carried the potential of granting a privileged perspective on social life, which he termed "second-sight." Following DuBois's lead, African American scholars have taken up the challenge of producing theory, something that as early as 1970 Delmos Jones (1970: 251) argued would be crucial in creating a "native anthropology." The scholars I have in mind, particularly the anthropologist John Langston Gwaltney (1981, 1993) and the feminist Patricia Hill Collins (1991), proposed that such a body of theory could arise only out of collective reflections with common folk who, drawing on their life experiences, could theorize in collaboration with academics.

La Rosca's project involved workshops of the sort used by Gwaltney and Collins, but La Rosca's community meetings were directed primarily toward establishing research priorities and collecting information, not toward generating theory out of local cultural forms. Indeed, workshops are a prime vehicle for social research in Colombia (Riaño-Alcalá 2006), constituting a practice that permits information gathering, collaborative strategizing, and political action simultaneously. This format contrasts with the tendency among North American ethnographers to privilege one-on-one interviews, which control the interview situation to a greater degree than is possible in the communal setting of a workshop.

Workshops, however, are a necessary but not sufficient tool for promoting theorizing among ethnic minorities and other popular groups. The generation of theory from below became possible in Colombia only in the 1990s, after a layer of indigenous activists was trained in structural linguistics at Colombian universities and began to experiment with the use of linguistic forms as conceptual guides in cultural research.[5] It was necessary for them to learn what theory was and why it was needed before they could subvert the theory learned in the academy.

One of the explicit areas of activity of the members of CRIC's Bilingual Intercultural Education Program (PEBI) is theoretical production. The theorists in CRIC's ranks are indigenous linguists and students of cosmovision—a kind of a politicized take on cosmology—because it is from indigenous languages and shamanic knowledge that these activists derive their theoretical building blocks. By theory, they mean the conceptual vehicles that guide the analysis and interpretation of cultural forms and the construction of strategies for revitalizing cultural practices and reintroducing them into social life. Although such conceptual frameworks may originate in indigenous cultures, they are also, as I illustrate later, appropriated from the theoretical traditions of the dominant culture and recast according to native priorities.

Theory may be employed to guide the production of narrative, as I describe shortly for the Guambiano History Committee (which is affiliated not with CRIC but with the Indigenous Authorities of Colombia [AICO], another indigenous organization) and for the history of PEBI. But theorizing also takes place when activists use language and cosmovision to coin new definitions of citizenship that are incorporated into their political strategies, a process reflected in the translation of the 1991 Colombian constitution into indigenous languages (Ramos and Cabildo Indígena de Mosoco 1993; Rappaport 2005) . The generation of theory is therefore both an intellectual exercise and an activist objective. Theorizing is a means of imbuing political organizing with cultural significance, a process necessarily punctuated by moments of research and reflection. The ultimate objective, however, is political, not intellectual. In other words, this is a kind of "situated theorizing" (Haraway 1991) in which not only does intellectual practice emerge out of the theorists' ethnic positioning but, more importantly, political activity is guided by their research.

In instances in which external scholars collaborate with members of indigenous organizations on research projects, we might also speak of "co-theorizing," or the merging of differently situated theories. As I describe in the following section, co-theorizing involves the forging of connections between indigenous-created concepts and the theories and methodologies that politically committed academics draw on from their own traditions. Indigenous theoretical frameworks are privileged in this process, but they are expanded through the contributions of external theory and method, so that the conceptual frameworks of both the indigenous researcher and the professional anthropologist are transformed.

Theorizing in Guambía

The Guambiana linguist Bárbara Muelas Hurtado has argued that the rolling and unrolling of geographic and social space governs the relationships that Guambiano families establish with their surroundings: "When one or more people who live in a house are invited to leave for other sites, they are invited with the expression *pichip mentøkun,* which literally means 'let us unroll.' The opposite situation, when they are invited to return home, is *kitrøp mentøkun,* which means 'let us roll up' or 'let us collect ourselves'" (Muelas Hurtado 1995: 32).[6] Similarly, this action of rolling and unrolling defines Guambianos' relationship with time:

> As the years unfold, in lived time, in the voyage of life and through the world, the ancestors have marked a path, they have opened a trail on which those who come behind, their descendants of today, must advance to make history. The past goes in front, and the future comes behind. It is as though our ancestors had returned to look for their descendants or as though those who have already left (died) had returned to "judge" what their descendants have accomplished in their absence. It is as though a turn were made in the vast circular space, a new meeting with the ancestor, [of] past and future, an illusion, a hope, in Guambiano thought.
>
> The space before us and lived time (conserved in tradition) orient human life. They go ahead [of us] in life, and [continue] after life. The space that is left behind and time not yet lived are a space and a time that must still unroll. (Muelas Hurtado 1995: 35–36).

Muelas's linguistic anthropology would form the basis for the creation of a Guambiano conceptual space in which time is conceived as a spiral and history is narrated in a nonlinear, spiral fashion (Vasco Uribe, Dagua Hurtado, and Aranda 1993; see also Rappaport 2005: chap. 5).

It was in a collaborative project organized by the Guambiano History Committee, in which Bogotá anthropologists Luis Guillermo Vasco and Marta Urdaneta participated, that Guambiano theorizing came to fruition. The history project was conceived after the Guambianos reclaimed a large expanse of land in 1980 that had earlier been usurped from them, which they ultimately incorporated into their *resguardo* territory. The research was aimed at establishing the primordial claim of the Guambianos to that territory. Although title to the land is vested in the *cabildo* and is in no danger of being revoked, local non-indigenous historians had for decades argued, without any evidence, that the Guambianos originated in Peru and were relative newcomers to Guambía. The *cabildo* hoped to deploy historical research to debunk these theories and establish the Guambianos' centuries-old attachment to their territory. Rigor was thus at a premium. Vasco and Urdaneta were inserted into research teams composed of elders knowledgeable in oral history and young Guambianos eager to learn to do research. The external scholars concentrated, respectively, on oral history and archaeology, topics of study dictated by the indigenous authorities.[7]

The methods espoused by these interethnic teams were collaborative in both the collection of materials and their analysis. Urdaneta, for example, worked with her Guambiano colleagues to develop classifications in Guambiano of historical time and topographic space, which were then employed as guides for establishing an archaeological chronology and, ultimately, for generating an interpretation of Guambiano prehistory that explained the nature of Guambiano territoriality (Tróchez Tunubalá, Camayo, and Urdaneta Franco 1992; Urdaneta Franco 1988). Vasco and his Guambiano co-researchers developed theorizations of the shape of time modeled on Guambiano material culture, which provided a theoretical foundation for a narrative of land loss, forms of capitulation and resistance, and territorial claims in Guambía (Vasco Uribe 2002: 466–73).

Unlike standard anthropological research or even La Rosca's approach, the work in Guambía subordinated the professional ethnographer's methods and epistemology to those of the indigenous collectivity (Vasco Uribe 2002: 449). This subordination is one of the hallmarks of what I call "co-theorizing." The oral history project encompassed large groups of people who reflected in public assemblies on the historical narratives of elders. Vasco wrote that he was initially confused by the procedures used at these meetings, where breakout groups seemed to mull interminably over discussion points without reaching firm conclusions, a process that was repeated in plenary sessions. Ultimately, he concluded that what appeared to be aimless discussion was, in fact, purposeful:

> The work in breakout groups organized by indigenous people in their meetings was, in reality, a research meeting, in which knowledge of a problem was intensified through discussion, in which they confronted the knowledge of every participant with that of the rest in order to finally arrive at group knowledge... My idea that there were no conclusions at the meetings was wrong; there were conclusions, but they did not take the same form as those with which I was familiar, nor were they written. Later, it became clear to me that after the breakout groups and the multiple discussions that ensued in them, in the mind of every participant lay certain conclusions: a broader knowledge of the problem than there had been before the meeting, now that it was no longer personal knowledge but knowledge held by the entire group. (Vasco Uribe 2002: 461)

Vasco had to learn to "roll and unroll" at these assemblies, because this was what the Guambiano researchers saw themselves as doing. This meant also walking the territory with the elders (Vasco Uribe 2002: 303), using toponymy as a guide to learning the past (2002: 295–96), and conceiving of history and territory as unrolling from a central topographic point (2002: 293). The result was a historical narrative based in the topography of Guambía and organized as a spiral that continually sighted and resighted on primordial events. The spiral format, a topographic manifestation of Bárbara Muelas's notion of "rolling and unrolling," provided the theoretical framework through which this history was organized.

It would be too simplistic to suppose that Urdaneta's and Vasco's only contributions to the project were technical. True, the Guambianos mined the two scholars for their scientific knowledge and methods, as La Rosca had proposed two decades earlier.[8] But the anthropologists also functioned as interlocutors, co-investigators, and co-theorizers. Vasco emphasized that the texts they wrote were dialogic: "Our objective was to build dual texts, at once oral and written, at once indigenous and Spanish, where the various authorities each had their place and fulfilled their roles within the needs of the moment" (Vasco Uribe 2002: 318). Although for the most part the distinctive voices of the outsiders are muted in the seamless pamphlets published by the *cabildo,* in at least one piece—which appeared in an academic anthology—the language of the anthropologist was interjected into the historical narrative (Vasco Uribe, Dagua Hurtado, and Aranda 1993), laying bare the moments at which Vasco's contributions became critical. This text has abrupt transitions between oral narrative and ethnographic explanation, the latter drawing out the implications of what is expressed in the narration. This ethnographic voice appears to be Vasco's and provides important clues to the way co-theorization took place: the ethnographer's eye helped to alert Guambiano theorists to the implications of the conceptual frameworks they had derived from linguistics, thus deepening their interpretations.

It would be a grave error to focus exclusively on the exceptional texts that the collaborative teams produced. Most publications of the Guambiano History Committee are less elegantly written and theorized than the article just cited (see also Dagua Hurtado, Aranda, and Vasco 1998). The vast majority are less layered, less explicitly theoretical, and composed in more accessible language. They were self-published by the *cabildo* for use in schools, where the major concepts are recast in the Guambiano language, returning them to the oral domain. Moreover, the most important contributions of the project were never written at all. As Vasco (2002: 462; see also Riaño-Alcalá 2006) contended, the team's major objectives were achieved through the development of a collective ethnographic research methodology, not through the creation of ethnographic texts. In the long run, the purpose of this methodology was to infuse Guambiano social life, especially in the political and educational spheres, with a self-conscious notion of culture in the hope of revitalizing native lifeways.

In this sense, Vasco's (and the Guambianos') understanding of ethnography as practice contrasts with the North American emphasis on ethnography as text, the latter approach suited to the academic objectives of our craft but not to the collaborative enterprise. But I can take this comparison even further. Vasco did not reduce practice to the collection of research data (as La Rosca did) but focused instead on generating theory and applying it to the analysis of materials collected during the research. He also focused on how this knowledge was brought to bear in resolving the social problems the community faced. That is, ethnography became an exercise in political action.

Research in the Intercultural Milieu of the Indigenous Organization

The experiences of Vasco and Urdaneta in Guambía suggest that what is at stake in collaboration is the bridging of epistemological and methodological differences in the service of a political agenda. The collaborative research process had to admit the possibility of theorizing from a Guambiano cultural standpoint if it was to be successful. Indeed, this is what makes the project so inspiring. But the bridging of cultural differences is not exclusive to the Guambiano-academic divide. Equally significant is the bridging of differences between the culture of the academy and that of indigenous organizations that serve as umbrella groups for native peoples of various ethnicities who do not necessarily share epistemologies. As anthropologists, we have been trained to study the kind of epistemological difference that Vasco and Urdaneta encountered in Guambía, but we are less attuned to the far subtler cultural order of the multiethnic indigenous organization, whose contours appear self-evident because its organizing strategies hold so much in common with those of other social movements.

In order to get at this organizational culture—which is crucial if we are to comprehend collaborative research within the indigenous movement—we must examine the social dynamics of research within such organizations. This task implies a comprehension of the interculturality of indigenous politics, including the articulation of non-native supporters of indigenous organizations—in CRIC, they are called *colaboradores*—and their role in the research process.[9] *Colaboradores'* positioning as "researchers within" suggests that it is not only indigenous culture that is at stake in the collaborative research enterprise but also the intercultural milieu of the organization, in which political methodologies are adapted to research ends and research is transformed into political strategy. The presence of *colaboradores* in the research process problematizes what co-theorization might mean, because although they are not indigenous, they are central actors in the emergence of indigenous theory and form an integral part of the indigenous movement, forcing us to reconsider where activist theorizing originates.[10] I use my experience in CRIC as a guide to exploring these issues.

When CRIC militants speak of research, they do not refer to the long-term, argument-driven collection and analysis of information in which academics engage, the kind of work that ultimately crystallizes on the printed page. Instead, they refer to communal spaces of reflection, intuitive processes, organization-building activities, and the production of tools for political action. Although the results of academic research may resonate in many ways with this plan of action, and scholarly researchers may be enthusiastically engaged as interlocutors, the methods and objectives of the two groups are quite distinct.

Vasco's reflection on his difficulty in interpreting the results of Guambiano assemblies points to the essentially communal nature of indigenous research in Cauca. The workshops in which research priorities are determined are generally quite large, sometimes involving up to a hundred people, and include participants with varied experience in the organization who belong to diverse generations of activists and exhibit an uneven command of indigenous languages. After plenary sessions in which the leadership presents background information and proposals, assemblies generally divide into breakout groups to consider discussion questions provided by the coordinators.

When too many breakout group members are young or inexperienced, or when the leader adheres too closely to the discussion questions, the result is a disjointed series of one-sentence responses elicited from the discussants one by one and then reported back to the plenary by schooled participants or by *colaboradores* in what could be interpreted as a translation into movement discourse. When there is some consistency in the membership of the breakout groups, however—for instance, when members share common organizational experience and are not afraid to speak out, something I have seen happen when participants are mostly bilingual teachers or catechists—lively debate and stimulating conclusions are presented to the plenary, leading to a spirited reinterpretation of the smaller groups' findings. At its best, the workshop strategy results in a powerful blueprint for research and action that is harnessed in the political activities fomented by the workshop, as well as in a host of materials ranging from curricula to pamphlets informed by collective discussion.

Collaborative research, then, not only involves working in a team with activists but also permitting the communal environment of the workshop to guide the research. Activist-researchers frequently possess (or are open to learning) the skills needed to frame research questions and to gather and interpret information. But workshop participants are not researchers in any standard sense. Notwithstanding this fact, in organizations such as CRIC it is in large assemblies that research guidelines are frequently set and the results of research evaluated. Therefore, as academics involved in collaborative relationships with indigenous organizations, we cannot lose sight of the interpretive space that workshops afford, nor can we ignore the suggestions made by their participants. Collaboration thus begins to take on broader proportions.

Guidelines for a History of PEBI

In order to work through this issue, I reflect on a project in which I participated, charged with preparing a history of CRIC's Bilingual Intercultural Education Program (PEBI). Although I was influenced by the work of La Rosca and the Guambiano History Committee—I was attuned to the necessity of collectively establishing a research agenda and to the significance of co-theorizing—CRIC's methods and concerns played an important role in shifting my notion of the purpose and nature of ethnographic research.

When I embarked on the project, I naively assumed that our re-search would be conducted within the confines of the research team, supplemented by workshops at which communal interviews would be conducted and the results of our research evaluated. I discovered, however, that a series of workshops held in 2000 and 2001—before and immediately after I joined the project—had already compiled the research guidelines. In total, approximately one hundred people attended at least one of these meetings. The majority were indigenous bilingual teachers or PEBI activists, but leaders in the communities where the workshops were held also attended, since most such meetings are hosted by localities.

The goal of the earlier workshops had been to define the project and devise a research plan, including the generation of research questions. Initially, the group decided it would conduct a systematic survey of the activities and accomplishments of the program's various components, which included curriculum development and primary research in cosmovision and linguistics. Such a detailed critical inspection is called a *sistematización,* a genre that is widespread in popular education and alternative development planning in Latin America. A *sistematización* is a combination of descriptions of the organization's activities and the results of collective evaluation of issues facing the group. As I understood it on the basis of previous examples of this genre produced by CRIC (2000), the *sistematización* was a compendium of raw data organized into categories, followed by a brief evaluation of the project; its written results were conveyed in a largely undigested and somewhat schematic format.

When I began work with the project, I questioned the utility of the *sistematización* format because of its unmanageable final product. I was also attentive to the critiques I had heard from many Nasa-speaking activists who preferred embarking on a history project, largely with the aim of learning a new set of research methodologies. In contrast, most of the *colaboradores,* who had administrative experience in a variety of organizations, opted for *sistematización,* which was more familiar to them.

As I soon discovered in the first workshop I attended, the Nasa speakers intended to wrest control of the project from the *colaboradores,* underlining the fault lines within the organization that would impinge on our research. Ultimately, the history format won out, thanks to the critical mass of Nasa speakers at the workshop. But even though the group opted for a historical approach, the research questions that were to guide our work were essentially guidelines for a *sistematización.*[11] There were fifty-one questions, the vast majority of them presentist in orientation, in large part evaluating key PEBI policies that had made education a fulcrum for community organizing and had fostered the development of a self-conscious notion of indigenous culture. Few of the questions were retrospective.[12]

Reconciling History with *Sistematización*

The research team, made up of a Nasa linguist (Abelardo Ramos), a *colaboradora* (Graciela Bolaños), and me, was obliged to build a bridge between the *sistematización*-oriented questionnaire given to us by the workshop participants and the history we hoped to narrate. Three concepts emerged from the guiding questions to become pivots of the historical narrative we eventually published (Bolaños et al. 2004). First, we focused on the development of the school as a community organizing tool rather an institution devoted exclusively to education. This is what CRIC calls the concept of community control. Second, we looked at the way cross-cultural dialogue and the appropriation of ideas across cultures—which we called interculturalism—provided a philosophy for building a pluralist movement.[13] Finally, we studied the way cosmovision—a concept that articulates the need for a balanced universe with a return to indigenous ritual forms, which developed out of seminars held among shamans in the 1990s—furnished a new pivot for identity construction at a moment when the movement replaced its class-based objectives with a politics of peoplehood. In other words, our conceptual framework originated in none of the individual cultures of indigenous groups in CRIC but in the culture of PEBI as an organization.

Unlike the guiding questions, we did not situate PEBI policies in the present but used the guidelines as a lens for interpreting the past. That is, while recognizing that interculturalism and cosmovision were approaches that had gained currency in the past decade (community control was a guiding concept from the beginning of PEBI), we believed they could still serve as powerful hinges for making sense of the way early activists harnessed external ideas and struggled to revitalize cultural forms. By organizing our history around these notions, we were able to situate historical narration in the present, making it more meaningful for contemporary indigenous readers and providing a three-channeled reading of the history of PEBI.

The participants in the workshops that produced our research strategy attended just a few of the interviews we conducted with key regional and local historical actors. They were not active in the writing phase; Ramos, Bolaños, and I did the writing as a team, negotiating the narrative line by line.[14] Although the history we wrote was of an education program, the two CRIC team members, following the directives of the workshops, insisted that it be more political than pedagogical in scope. This taught me an important lesson about CRIC's research priorities and the nature of CRIC's educational programs. In the early stages, I had envisioned a spiral history, given that Nasa activists, like the Guambiano historians and Vasco, had embraced this motif as central to their cosmovision (Anonymous 2000). Nevertheless, Bolaños and

Ramos felt that the use of a spiral organizing model would reduce our narrative to a Nasa-centric history, ignoring the interculturality of the program and the participation of activists from other ethnic groups in the project. Their strong intercultural stance is what led us to adopt a conceptual focus based on organizational culture as opposed to one of the various indigenous cultures represented in CRIC.

Socialización

Although the authors of the research guidelines did not help to write the history, their insights were again at a premium when the book was completed and we began what in CRIC is called *socialización,* or the collective grassroots evaluation of a project. Thus, in a sense, the book was but a pretext for two important arenas of organizing that took place immediately before and after its publication. At a 2004 meeting to plan the *socialización* workshops directed at bilingual teachers and community leaders, which began in 2005, PEBI activists probed the relationship between the conceptual structure of the book and CRIC's political objectives. They were largely concerned with the tension between PEBI as an education program and PEBI as a political organization.[15]

On one hand, our interlocutors proposed to delve into what they saw as a dialectical relationship between pedagogy and politics. They sought to comprehend how their creation of intercultural pedagogical methodologies constituted a political act. They wanted to reflect on what tools PEBI history offered to stimulate the evaluation of the teaching methodologies and didactic materials they had generated over the course of more than twenty years. On the other hand, they were keen to interpret ways in which the three conceptual axes of the study could be reconciled with CRIC's general political program, which promotes the defense of the communal land base, the deepening of political autonomy, and the promotion of indigenous culture. In particular, they questioned how they were to understand autonomy in light of the strategy of appropriation of external ideas that characterizes interculturalism and how this might impinge on indigenous culture. In summary, what PEBI activists hoped to do with our book was to turn it into an organizing tool whereby local teachers and community leaders reflected on the program's objectives at yet more workshops. The book was by no means a conclusive study but a small step in a communal organizing process.

The Role of the Anthropologist in Collaborative Research

Like Urdaneta's and Vasco's roles in the Guambía history project, my role in the PEBI project was grounded in the methodological contributions I could make to the team: sharing my skills as an interviewer and assisting in writing a coherent and persuasive narrative. But these were not the only contributions I made, nor did the PEBI collective conceive of my collaboration in such narrow terms. To conclude this chapter, I offer my reflections on what else I contributed to the enterprise and how it transformed my notion of ethnographic practice.

Earlier I cited a La Rosca text asserting that collaborative research transforms "the researcher himself [into] ... an object of investigation: his ideology, knowledge, and practice are judged in light of popular experience" (Bonilla et al. 1972: 46). In other words, collaboration implies a kind of "being-looked-at-ness," which the film critic Rey Chow (1995: 180) argued is at the heart of the autoethnographic endeavor. For Chow, autoethnographers are simultaneously the subject and the object of their research; the fact that they have been examined ethnographically by others informs the way they look at themselves. I have reflected in other publications on how "being-looked-at-ness" is central to the ethnography produced by Nasa intellectuals (Rappaport 2005: chap. 3). What I examine here is how it is also a fundamental element of collaboration, forcing the external ethnographer to look at herself, just as indigenous participants do—a brand of reflexivity that transcends the inward-looking and individualistic thrust of North American cultural critique, which Charles Hale (2006a and this volume) has contrasted with activist anthropology.

I went into the PEBI history project accepting that although historical narration is situated in the present, we would need to harness current experience to a retrospective interpretation of the past. Ramos and Bolaños did not entirely understand or subscribe to this premise, because it meant evaluating the past as something different from the present—as somehow, from their point of view, politically imperfect. For instance, as we evaluated narratives of PEBI's early attempts to lodge the educational project in indigenous lifeways, we confronted the fact that the incipient understandings of culture as a constellation of customs that characterized PEBI in the early 1980s clashed with current notions of an integrated cosmovision that permeates all aspects of everyday life and political practice. The latter implied that the earlier efforts had not been entirely successful, something Ramos and Bolaños were reluctant to accept.

At the same time, because we were charged with harnessing the research guidelines supplied to us by the workshops, we had to employ current concerns with cosmovision, community-based education, and interculturalism to interpret the past. Now wearing the hat of the historian, I was initially uncomfortable doing so. My self-appointed task was to lay bare the way I thought past and present could be reconciled, forcing Ramos and Bolaños (and me) to evaluate the research strategies I was accustomed to using and to try to place them in dialogue with the ideas articulated by CRIC. In this sense, I was being looked at by them and, subsequently in the *socialización* planning, by the PEBI collective.[16]

The "being-looked-at-ness" of my collaboration with CRIC resided not only in the way its members looked at me but also in how I looked at myself as a researcher—the extent to which I needed to transform my future research practice to conform with their methodologies. In a sense, then, "being-looked-at-ness" on the part of the external collaborator is a kind of reflexivity. Unlike the reflexive turn in anthropology, however, which focuses on the ethnographer herself, the kind of reflexivity I came to practice homes in on the process of co-theorizing that I first learned of through the work of Vasco and the Guambiano History Committee. Co-theorizing turned my reflexive sensibilities not toward myself but toward the dynamics of the group of which I was a member. This reflexive posture not only involved confronting the difficulties I had in subordinating my more solitary interpretive strategies to the collective approaches of CRIC; it also meant learning to adopt my colleagues' theorizations in my own research, so that interculturalism moved in both directions.

Such a transformation did not take place exclusively in the scenario of writing PEBI's history. It also happened when I sat down at my computer and composed my own essays, which would be read by both CRIC activists and my academic peers. In this sense, collaboration resulted in a dialogue in which CRIC was not the object of my research or my assistance but another interlocutor, thus expanding the intellectual networks through which my work traveled and from which I derived intellectual sustenance. Such an approach diverges from the premises of applied anthropology, which is a one-way process emanating from the anthropologist and directed toward a client population. To achieve my collaborative goal, I could not entirely subordinate my methods to those of CRIC but had to confront the two in my research and writing practice, using what I learned from Ramos and Bolaños to both question and expand on the academic premises upon which I worked.

Only then could we engage in a true collaboration involving mutual respect and dialogue.

The three concepts that framed our project all came out of the intercultural milieu of the indigenous organization. Accepting this framework was for me a significant step, because it forced me to discard the essentialist baggage I brought to the project—not just my notion of what constituted "indigenous" or "Nasa" but also my notion of what an indigenous organization was all about and who belonged to it. I came to see that it would be impossible to study indigenous organizing without taking account of the place of the indigenous movement in the larger Colombian political universe and of the border-crossings of its diverse members. This led me to recast my understandings of identity formation, informed by the anthropology of the north to focus exclusively on ethnic subjects. I came to understand that the fluidity of ethnicity in Colombia goes beyond such concerns, taking on a distinctly political tinge that is deeply constructivist, not essentialist. Even when CRIC activists speak of something like Nasa culture, they are pointing to political strategies, not existing states of being. I do not think I would have come to understand this point if not for the collaborative experiences I have enjoyed over the past decade.

Collaboration is thus a transformative experience. It not only affects the organizations with which external scholars work, making possible a deeper commitment to politically inspired research, but also leads those scholars to rethink their own craft, to roam beyond the academy in search of theory and method, to embrace a new layer of interlocutors, and to rethink the ways in which they reflect on themselves and others. In short, collaboration cannot be seen as a paternalist application of anthropological skills in a practical context; it must be seen as an innovative vehicle for revitalizing anthropology in the twenty-first century.

Acknowledgments

The research on which this article is based was conducted between 1996 and 2003 in various locations in the department of Cauca, Colombia. It was funded in 1996–97 by Colciencias, the Colombian national science foundation, under a grant awarded to the Instituto Colombiano de Antropología; in 1998 and 1999 by summer academic grants from the Graduate School of Georgetown University; and from 1999 to 2002 by an International Collaborative Grant from the Wenner-Gren Foundation for Anthropological Research, which provided funds for the creation of a collaborative team of indigenous, national, and international researchers. I thank the members of our team, which included Myriam Amparo Espinosa, David Gow, Susana Piñacué Achicué, Adonías Perdomo Dizú, and Tulio Rojas Curieux. I have written about my experiences in that team in other venues (Rappaport 2005). Each member collaborated with an indigenous organization or community. I worked with the Bilingual Intercultural Education Program (PEBI) of the Regional Indigenous Council of Cauca (CRIC). I thank Graciela Bolaños, Abelardo Ramos, and Inocencio Ramos, as well as the entire PEBI team, for their hospitality and dialogue. Denise Brennan, Les Field, Richard Fox, and the other participants in the Wenner-Gren symposium provided me with helpful commentary on an earlier draft of this chapter.

Notes

1. I distinguish in this chapter between a North American insistence on the primacy of ethnography as a genre of writing and a Colombian focus on ethnography as field practice. This distinction does not preclude the significant point made by Gelya Frank (this volume) that both pure and applied forms of anthropological research in the United States are seen largely as exercises in writing. My argument regarding the nature of Colombian participatory action research also coincides with the discussion of activist anthropology advanced by Charles Hale (this volume).

2. The participatory action research of La Rosca is not to be confused with the participatory approach currently in vogue in rural development (Chambers 1997; see also Cooke and Kothari 2001). Although the latter advocates grassroots participation in development projects, it does not involve the sort of collaborations with radical organizations that were central to La Rosca's objectives, nor do its aims revolve around bolstering the capacity for militancy of the grassroots, as La Rosca advocated. In addition, building on the influence of Marxism in the Colombian social science of the 1960s and the wide participation of students and scholars in leftist parties and movements, La Rosca sought to imbue its research with a class (and later an ethnic) consciousness that is generally missing from the panorama of rural development practitioners.

3. Víctor Daniel Bonilla, a member of La Rosca, was active in CRIC at its founding. I was initiated into the Colombian indigenous movement (and introduced to its intense factionalism) in the late 1970s by Víctor Daniel, who

also encouraged me to begin to analyze the archival materials I had collected by juxtaposing them with the histories prepared by La Rosca. Gonzalo Castillo, also of La Rosca, was made aware of Lame's book by the indigenous community of Ortega, Tolima, where the manuscript was carefully stored and consulted by native authorities (Castillo-Cárdenas 1987). Lame's treatise has since been reissued (Lame 2004 [1939]); the new publication includes an indigenous take on Lame's biography, rendered in comic-book form (Nene and Chocué 2004: 103–10).

4. In a sense, Bergquist's critique is unfair. Although La Rosca's pamphlets, books, and picture maps were inaccessible to many indigenous activists in the 1970s, they have become accessible today, when there is a significant layer of schooled native militants who are not only readers but also identify themselves as researchers. In March 2006, at a meeting of the CRIC leadership to discuss strategies for writing an organizational history, participants continually brought up these materials.

5. An MA program in ethnolinguistics was developed at the Bogotá-based Universidad de los Andes in the 1980s, with the participation of international scholars as instructors, through a combination of French and Colombian funding. Indigenous activists were provided with scholarships and studied alongside non-native, tuition-paying students. The program spawned other MA programs in provincial universities, including the Universidad del Cauca, and attracted indigenous linguists trained in more traditional linguistics programs.

6. The ø is used in the Guambiano alphabet for vowels originating at the center of the tongue, like the French *u*.

7. The history committee also collected extensive archival materials from a number of Colombian and Ecuadorian repositories. However, its members did not have the skills to read and assimilate these documents, and the hundreds of pages of copies they amassed went unconsulted.

8. The Guambiano History Committee explicitly recognized the relationship between research skills and power, as it stated in one of its narratives: "When the Spaniards came, they arrived doing research. They grabbed those who lived in Cajibío, whom they called Novirao, and they taught them Spanish. They asked them about everything. They called those who knew the most and they asked them, so as to learn all there was to know about the Guambianos. When they had found out everything, they began to dominate them, to exact tribute, to organize things and people in their own way. They sent the hereditary chiefs to collect everything they wanted, to take it to Popayán [the colonial capital]" (Vasco Uribe, Dagua Hurtado, and Aranda 1993: 9).

9. *Colaboradores* are for the most part former leftists who sought out the indigenous movement as a prime site for constructing a new proposal for

nationhood in Colombia. Like the members of La Rosca, they hoped to pro-mote the class struggle in the countryside, although today's movement has come to espouse a discourse of ethnic peoplehood that *colaboradores* have also embraced. However, unlike La Rosca members, *colaboradores'* primary identity is that of activists and not researchers.

10. The quandary over where to place *colaboradores*—whether they belong "inside" or "outside" the movement—hints at the essentialist lens through which we have become accustomed to viewing indigenous organizations.

11. CRIC is a multilingual environment in which members of various indigenous ethnic groups and *colaboradores* communicate largely in Spanish. Only half of the Nasa are fluent in the Nasa language. Many of the most radical proposals for cultural revitalization come from the Nasa speakers within the PEBI collective, who are frequently at odds with Nasa activists who are monolingual in Spanish and with the *colaboradores* (see Rappaport 2005).

12. The fifty-one questions are analyzed in Rappaport 2005: chap. 5.

13. Interculturalism is a pedagogical movement that advocates the appro-priation of external theories and methods into an indigenous cultural matrix in order to stimulate research and, ultimately, foster political pluralism (López 1996). An antidote to multiculturalism, it is meant to empower subaltern groups, as opposed to simply tolerating their presence.

14. One of the obvious skills that external researchers bring to the table is the ability to write up results in a coherent and persuasive fashion, something that the activists—whose writing skills were confined to curricula and political documents—could not do. Vasco and Urdaneta also functioned as scribes for their research teams.

15. *Socialización* activities have been ongoing, mainly in the teacher train-ing programs coordinated by PEBI. However, in August 2005 I attended a work-shop organized to begin to conceptualize a broader history of CRIC, at which we engaged in a *socialización* of the PEBI book. Participants included not only PEBI activists and bilingual teachers but also the founders of CRIC—men and women in their sixties and seventies—who had been charged with writing a history of the organization. Given the objectives of the workshop, the contents of the book were not discussed in any detail; instead, participants used the PEBI history to project their goal of writing a history of CRIC. They reflected on how the moments in PEBI's history recorded in the book shed light on ways to think about the history of other localities. They were concerned, in particular, with methodological issues and with the possibilities of training elders to participate in historical research. Moreover, they emphasized the significance of interpreting history through vehicles other than published books, including visual images and video. Finally, they spent a great deal of time elaborating on the purpose of a CRIC history: to ignite the organizing

flame under an increasingly apathetic youth—a very different objective from that of the PEBI history, which was to stimulate further research among bilingual teachers.

16. Ramos and I are currently working on a dialogic article about our experiences on the team, to be published by *Historia Crítica* in Bogotá. In it, Ramos narrates his own confrontations with the team and lays out what he learned in the process.

Gray Spaces and Endless Negotiations

Forensic Anthropology and Human Rights

Mercedes Doretti and *Jennifer Burrell*

In the past two decades, human rights commissions, international tribunals, and local judiciaries investigating past human rights abuses have increasingly turned to forensic archaeologists, biological anthropologists, and, to a lesser extent, social anthropologists to provide crucial evidence in their proceedings and to oversee the recovery of victims' remains. As demand for these areas of expertise in human rights cases grows, largely in response to the insistence of human rights nongovernmental organizations (NGOs), the disciplines of forensic archaeology and anthropology have become increasingly well known and even popularized. Indiana Jones movies and television shows such as *CSI* and *Bones* now dominate the popular imagination about work in this field, attributing to the forensic anthropologist an allure infused by classic anthropological exoticism, high technology, and humanitarian interest. As a result, the market for popular and academic forensic books continues to increase.[1] Forensic anthropology programs proliferate, their phones ringing off the hook with calls from prospective students. And forensic anthropologists increasingly find themselves navigating between a variety of political pressures, funding imperatives, and human rights concerns.

This state of affairs, however, is recent. Applying traditional archaeological and biological anthropological techniques to the field of forensics and to human rights cases remains problematic and fraught with obstacles in many countries of the world. In addition, this kind of forensic work was initially embraced and fostered by human rights organizations and not by academic departments and universities. For these reasons, forensic anthropology applied in the service of human rights offers a unique perspective for examining what we call the "gray spaces," that is, the way this anthropological work often falls in between or outside of traditional anthropological subject matters and academic concerns. It also takes place at the interstices of local political agendas, NGOs' wishes, national programs, and the work of international organizations. These gray spaces add another dimension to the role of forensic anthropologists: finding a middle ground on which to carry out investigations, a search that includes negotiations of roles, positions, politics, and funding requirements.

Besides these considerations, forensic anthropology applied to human rights cases raises different kinds of questions in relation to how anthropologists might engage social and political worlds and what kinds of "products" might emerge from this engagement. The goals of our work, and the methods, techniques, and engagements used to achieve them, are often quite different from the concerns of anthropologists based in academic institutions. We often speak to different audiences, and distinct kinds of inquiries inform what we say and how we present our findings. As a consequence, the kinds of "results" that emerge from our investigations are categorically different. This constellation of actions and considerations is also colored by the particular Latin American contexts of our work.

In order to illustrate how these issues and concerns come together in the work of our group, the Argentine Forensic Anthropology Team (Equipo Argentino de Antropología Forense, or EAAF), and in forensic anthropology and human rights in general, we describe the Latin American political experience and the national contexts in which forensic anthropology applied to human rights cases incubated and grew. We show how and why national teams were formed to carry on investigations once the mandates of commissions of inquiry had expired. We follow this with an explanation of the structure of an EAAF forensic investigation in order to illustrate the ways in which anthropological, political, and local knowledge and considerations come into play and are negotiated. These examples clarify the interstitiality of forensic anthropology applied to human rights investigations and show how anthropological engagement in this arena is the result of a carefully constructed and orchestrated and often delicate balance between professional expertise, ethical dimensions, and political contexts.

The Latin American Experience

Societies emerging from periods of political violence characterized by gross violations of human rights and humanitarian law face the difficult task of confronting their pasts while working to prevent reoccurrences of such abuses. During the 1970s and 1980s, the countries of Latin America were shaken by periods of intense violence and repression. Severe and extensive human rights violations were committed, primarily by states under the control of military governments. (Peru and Colombia are exceptions to this generalization.)

At the start of the 1980s and into the 1990s, these countries began to move toward reinstating democratic governments. With the establishment of democracy came the immediate need to investigate the human rights violations of the recent past. The extremely limited role of judiciary bodies, and often the complicity of forensic experts within those bodies, was questioned and in some cases redefined. It became clear that improvements in the administration of justice were crucial to reinforcing the new democracies. During the last two decades, trials of perpetrators have been held at the national and international levels. Although these investigations led to the conviction of guilty parties in some countries, in others amnesty proclamations allowed those responsible to avoid conviction, even when investigations were and still are being carried out.

Since the 1980s Latin American archaeologists and anthropologists have been called on to assist in the recovery and analysis of evidence related to large-scale human rights violations in their countries. In some countries, violations continue to occur. Responses to this challenge have been the formation of forensic anthropology teams in Argentina (1984), Chile (1989), Guatemala (1992), Peru (1999), and, most recently, Colombia (2004). The Argentine Forensic Anthropology Team (EAAF), of which Doretti was co-founder, was established in 1984 as a nongovernmental, nonprofit, scientific organization that applies forensic sciences—mainly forensic anthropology and archaeology— to the investigation of human rights violations in Argentina and worldwide.

In most cases, the initial request for the involvement of forensic anthropologists and archaeologists comes from human rights NGOs and associations of families of victims, not from the judiciary, the medical examiners' offices, or the government. This is consistent with the fact that in many countries, the majority of abuses were or are committed by the state, and new democracies have limited political power or will to investigate them. Even when the responsibility for human rights abuses is spread more evenly among the parties in a conflict, in most cases none wants a full investigation of the crimes of which they have been accused.

Because of these kinds of considerations, anthropologists and archaeologists applying forensic anthropology to human rights cases find themselves outside the precinct of academic institutions and independent research, working in the NGO world and serving as consultants and expert witnesses for governments, special commissions of inquiry, and judiciary institutions. Often, law enforcement agencies themselves are accused of the crimes under investigation. Although our investigations take place specifically at the request of NGOs, grassroots initiatives, and international commissions, these agencies often carry their own institutional histories and levels of credibility in terms of what they mean and represent to local populations. When we work at their behest, we, too, are associated with these local meanings.

Nevertheless, these organizations are frequently less problematic locally than are national governments, particularly in transitional states. Our connection with them, we have found, frequently helps families and sometimes communities to situate the work we do within a larger humanitarian context. In other words, for many people we become the face of larger projects of democratization and transition, even though our connection with these projects may be indirect or may be through organizations that represent different aspects of this relationship.

The work performed by forensic anthropologists is technical and scientific but often has strong political consequences. This often implies constraints and seemingly endless negotiations within the political framework in which we have to work. Unlike in academic research, in this context we anthropologists do not dictate the rules of engagement— although neither do we passively accept them, especially when they prevent us from being able to fully investigate a crime. In other words, we recognize that dialogue and collaboration with the state sector are often necessary in order to accomplish the goals of providing evidence, restoring bodies of victims to loved ones, and upholding the right to an investigation. At the same time, when negotiations compromise the integrity of an inquiry, we cut them off, an action we have taken when no other ethical recourse was available. For example, in the case of the El Mozote massacre in El Salvador, amnesty laws passed in 1993 led to a cessation of the investigation. We resumed work on it in 1999 when new political contexts permitted us to do so.

On the other hand, the community of forensic anthropology and archaeology is currently well established in Latin America and has amassed a substantial history of investigatory experience with the UN and international tribunals in the Balkans, Africa, and Asia. In February 2003, the Latin American Forensic Anthropology Association (ALAF) was created, in part to provide a forum in which to utilize the experiences of forensic practitioners throughout the region for standardizing methodologies, implementing ethical and professional criteria, and developing mechanisms to ensure the safety of forensic practitioners and their families. Additional goals include advocating for the use of forensic evidence in judicial proceedings, defending the scientific and technical integrity of the practice, and providing a mechanism for accreditation. Among the new challenges is the need to move beyond immediate cases to produce scientific research based on our experience. This in turn will improve the tools available for the investigation of human rights cases.

The formation of ALAF, in short, provides a space for engagement in academic and other kinds of debates that previously have been unavailable to us because our resources have been directed primarily toward immediate human rights crises and inquiries around the world. It also constitutes, as Cardoso de Oliveira (2000) noted for Brazil, an important mechanism for moving from the "periphery"—because of our applied emphasis and our base in Latin America—to new centers of legal and anthropological practice and disciplinary debates.

The Argentine Case and the Formation of EAAF

In the summer of 1984, democracy returned to Argentina after eight long years of dictatorship. As many as nine thousand people were "disappeared" by the state during that time, and no serious investigation had been allowed. It was generally known (although not officially acknowledged until years later) that many had been thrown from airplanes into the Argentine Sea, and therefore their remains would probably be irretrievable. But many others were buried in anonymous graves in the "John Doe" areas of cemeteries all over the country. At the first opportunity, judges, relatives of disappeared people, forensic doctors, police, media personnel, and the curious gathered at cemeteries, frantically searching for remains of the missing. The press photographed bulldozers digging up several individual graves at once, skulls and other bones flying from their shovels.

Untrained cemetery personnel tried their best to recover skeletal remains but left behind small bones, including teeth, and other evidence such as bullets. The bones were broken, lost, or mixed up. Skulls were piled in one place and postcranial bones in another, destroying the relationship between the skull and the rest of the skeleton. Television screens showed doctors holding skulls with gunshot wounds. Though in all likelihood these were the remains of disappeared people, no one knew to whom among the victims they might belong, to what episodes they were linked, or who specifically was responsible for their deaths. Furthermore, no one knew what to do with the remains once they had been recovered. The evidence necessary for identification and for legal cases against those responsible for the crimes was being destroyed.

There was no precedent in Argentina for dealing with massive exhumations. The forensic physicians in charge of recovery, whose familiarity was with cadavers, had little experience with exhumations or analysis of skeletal remains. In addition, some doctors had themselves been complicit in the crimes of the previous regime, by either omission or commission. In Argentina, as in most of the rest of Latin America and other regions as well, forensic experts are part of the police, the judiciary system, or both, or are otherwise affiliated with the government. Therefore, during undemocratic periods, their independence is severely limited.

After several massive exhumations, the need for a scientific alternative to these procedures became obvious. The National Commission on the Disappearance of People (CONADEP), created in 1984 by newly elected President Alfonsín, and the Grandmothers of Plaza de Mayo, a human rights organization, asked the Human Rights and Science program at the American Association for the Advancement of Science (AAAS) for assistance. The AAAS sent a delegation of forensic scientists to Argentina, including Clyde Snow, one of the world's foremost experts in forensic anthropology. Snow called for a halt to all unscientific exhumations and asked archaeologists and anthropologists to get involved.

Only a few advanced students of archaeology and social anthropology answered his call, a phenomenon we discuss later. Under Snow's direction, and using techniques from traditional archaeology and forensic anthropology, this small group participated in exhumations in which data were properly collected, documented, and analyzed. The collected evidence served to convict several high-ranking military officials and to identify disappeared people and restore their remains to their families.

Clyde Snow returned to Argentina many times over the next five years. The volunteers he trained formed the Argentine Forensic Anthropology Team, EAAF. After 1986, EAAF expanded its activities beyond Argentina and has since worked in more than thirty countries in Latin America, Africa, Asia, and Europe.

A significant percentage of this international work has been to assist in forming national teams in Guatemala, Chile, and Colombia, among other countries. In the United States, Physicians for Human Rights and the Science and Human Rights program at the AAAS partially supported these efforts and conducted training and forensic work themselves. Important international forensic efforts were set up by special UN tribunals to investigate war crimes committed during the Balkan wars and the Rwandan genocide. The newly established International Criminal Court also has a forensic component. Snow has been at the center of most of these efforts, providing training and advice as well as working on cases.

EAAF applies forensic sciences to the investigation of human rights violations to assist the families of victims, train local teams, and provide evidence to courts. In the long term, EAAF aims to contribute to the historical reconstruction of the recent past, which is often distorted or hidden by parties or government institutions that are themselves implicated in the crimes under investigation. EAAF members frequently act as expert witnesses and consultants for local and international human rights organizations, national judiciaries, international tribunals, and special commissions of inquiry such as truth commissions.

Defining Engagement: An Interdisciplinary Approach

Whether focused on a human rights investigation or a "normal" criminal case, forensic work is definitively an interdisciplinary effort. Forensic anthropologists and archaeologists, forensic pathologists, biological anthropologists, radiologists, ballistics experts, crime scene investigators, and geneticists—to name the main disciplines that can be involved—pool their expertise to maximize the information obtained from the evidence. In addition to this aspect of the work, forensic workers in human rights cases are sensitive to the fact that what they do is often part of the process of restoring dignity, trust, and respect for people who have suffered severe abuses. In many cases this trust may initially be difficult to establish and requires extensive work with families of victims and with community leaders who support local investigation initiatives.

Within the context of a human rights case, the work of the forensic team often involves three steps: the preliminary investigation, the archaeological work, and the laboratory analysis. The preliminary stage of an investigation is what distinguishes forensic human rights cases from others, and for this reason we discuss it in greater detail. Typically, it includes the examination of state, judicial, police, and military files, cemetery and registration office records, and other kinds of documentation related to the case under examination. Often this historical information has not been collected before, or the data collected by others is insufficient or neglects questions related to forensic issues.

EAAF members spend considerable time interviewing witnesses and survivors and collecting information about the case as well as antemortem or physical information about the victims for identification purposes. Human rights organizations and sometimes local judiciaries (if they have not been involved in the conflict) play a crucial role in finding eyewitnesses and putting a case together. Because these cases frequently arise at moments of transition from civil conflicts, wars, or state terrorism, nongovernmental organizations often fill the gaps created by complicit judiciaries, police forces, and other investigators. Often at great risk to their members, they form a bridge between an investigative body and witnesses, survivors, and relatives of victims. Even in democratic transitional moments, witnesses and relatives of victims frequently feel more comfortable releasing information to a local NGO or giving testimony before a court of law or national or international commission of inquiry with the support or mediation of an NGO. Truth commission investigators usually rely on the work of NGOs as a starting point for their investigations. EAAF members also conduct assessment trips to the area to be examined or excavated and evaluate the available information about it. Forensic anthropology, archaeology, and social anthropology are all helpful in this preliminary investigation.

In order to collaborate and build relationships with local communities, EAAF champions direct contact between the forensic team, local NGOs, and the presumed relatives of victims before the forensic work begins. This allows local people to understand the procedures that will be performed and to ask questions, and it gives EAAF the opportunity to consider local people's expectations, doubts, worries, and objections. In most cases involving political disappearances, the relatives of victims have been badly treated by officials, who often deny the very fact of the disappearance of their loved ones. It is important, we think, to reestablish a link of trust and respect.

The crucial importance of restoring the remains of loved ones and burying them according to local practices transcends culture and religion. The desire for justice and acknowledgment of past abuses is also a strong demand in many countries. EAAF's experience with different national cultures, religions, and political situations has shown that exhumations and reburial ceremonies related to human rights violations have a strong healing effect on families of victims and on communities. In some situations, however, exhumations are not supported, or they need to be done taking religious issues into account. Therefore, as part of the preliminary stage of an investigation, we also verify that the families of the victims want the work to be done. Their cultural and religious practices regarding death and burial should be respected as the investigation proceeds. In El Salvador, for example, families of victims who are Seventh-Day Adventists often do not want exhumations performed. In Argentina, a minority group of relatives of victims does not want to recover the remains of their loved ones unless the military publicly takes responsibility for their deaths; they see exhumations as a type of blackmail to silence them or a compromise they are unwilling to accept.

In Indonesia, a largely Muslim country, families of victims expressed concern about autopsies or examination of skeletal remains, because according to their religion the body should not be cut or disturbed after death. However, they added that if the truth about what had happened or even justice could be achieved by these procedures, they would accept the need for exhumations. Muslim religious leaders in Aceh explained to us that religious concern could be overcome if a clear purpose was achieved by doing forensic work, and they would be willing to explain this in a public campaign in conjunction with other religious leaders and Muslims in general. If these kinds of issues are not taken into account before doing the forensic work, it may fail, producing more pain and suffering to those whom we are trying to help.

There are often nonconflictive ways to respect victims' families' decisions in the extreme case of their total opposition to exhumation. EAAF does not intervene in cases where families do not support exhumations. For example, we completed a final mission to El Mozote, El Salvador, leaving certain mass graves untouched due to the wishes of family members. From a legal standpoint, this can be done without compromising an investigation because, first, most tribunals and commissions order forensic work for a very limited number of select cases, and second, to prove legally that a massacre occurred, not all bodies need to be discovered and examined. From historical and documentation standpoints, we can often still provide an estimate of the total number of victims by other means.

A new accompaniment to forensic investigation that is emerging is psychosocial support for families experiencing the exhumation of the remains of their loved ones. Having remains returned provides closure for many families; it offers the irrefutable proof that their loved one is really dead. But mourning under such circumstances is a complicated and unusual process at the individual, family, community, and national levels. Community and individual counseling has been developed by local NGOs in Guatemala and Zimbabwe and serves as a model for other countries undergoing similar processes. Our experience has shown that local or regional NGOs already familiar with the culture, language, religion, and individual situations of victims offer extremely valuable benefits to families involved. They have a firsthand understanding of the political climate and may also be more effective in the reparations stage of the resolution of a conflict.

EAAF devotes considerable energy to training national forensic teams. We see this as essential for continuing recovery and identification beyond the mandates of commissions of inquiry or tribunals. The period during which such adjudicatory bodies operate tends to be short, especially relative to the time necessary to exhume and identify victims of a conflict. More than twenty-five years after the peak of the repression in Argentina, EAAF is still searching for the disappeared. Similar investigations in Chile, Peru, Guatemala, and many other countries will continue for years. National forensic teams are essential to ensuring that the rights of families are met.

Gray Zones and Negotiations

As the foregoing explanation of a forensic investigation of a human rights case demonstrates, anthropologists working in this field bring to bear a wide variety of skills, training, technical expertise, and experiences. We combine elements from historical ethnology, social and cultural anthropology, political anthropology, activism, advocacy, and the more obvious technical practices of archaeology, biological anthropology, and forensic medicine. At the same time, the nature of the work places us outside of academe and often outside of judicial and legal structures.

Although we are interested in academic debates, the purpose of our work is to ensure that the basic right to truth and to a fair investigation is upheld. Although we ultimately try to provide positive identifications and to restore remains to the families of victims, we are also subject to national political contexts and constraints. Sometimes we have to wait years to obtain legal permits. Sometimes investigations are so circumscribed that we can, for example, restore remains to families or make positive identifications but not name causes of death. Sometimes we are permitted to collect ballistic evidence but not to analyze it.

Why are forensic anthropologists working in human rights situated between so many disciplines and subdisciplines, academic trajectories, and political requirements that traditional anthropologists and archaeologists are not subject to? First, the framework in which human rights work is conducted is not always friendly to the independent expert. Independent forensic experts are often called not only because a country lacks specialists but also because institutions that should have conducted investigations did not do their job or are suspects in the same crimes. And yet for legal reasons, forensic teams working on human rights cases may have to work with representatives of those very institutions. It can be uncomfortable to work outside of academic institutions or in situations where tension with official institutions exists. In these cases, we must weigh our role as engaged anthropologists and activists against the human rights goals and principles for which we work: upholding the right to truth and to an investigation, and identifying and restoring the remains of human rights victims to their families.

In many ways, a forensic investigation is a more restrictive framework than an academic one. The work is conducted within the framework of a judicial system or special body with a mandate that basically establishes what will be done and the questions or points of expertise that must be addressed. We have a limited amount of time, normally a few weeks, to do our work, and we have to maintain a chain of custody for the evidence as well as confidentiality of findings and discussions. We are nominated as expert witnesses, and as such we may be cross-examined by other experts or defense lawyers, which implies that we must refrain from speculation when interpreting the evidence. Often it is difficult to make the judicial community understand the limits of certainty in our discipline.[2] Standard deviations in methods for establishing age at death on the basis of skeletal remains, for example, may often be a problem. Information about cause and manner of death is not always clear or absolute when one works only with skeletal remains.

Working on forensic and human rights cases often comes with complicated emotional baggage. Unless there is some legal constraint, we believe families have the right to observe exhumations, and so they are often present at our field sites. This point sometimes awakens resistance in the academic and forensic communities, whose members are more accustomed to working in isolation. Also, as part of our work we often share extremely intense, private moments with people we hardly know, and then we rarely see each other again. A clear current of affection often exists between anthropologists and relatives of victims—a strong and peculiar bond.[3] But we know extremely little about each other. From both sides, the memory that binds us may be too painful for us to stay in contact.

Human rights organizations are often seen as ideologically motivated by definition. Many anthropologists and archaeologists are more comfortable working for the United Nations than for the legal system of a given country at the request of a human rights organization. For example, many assume that working for the UN is more neutral than working for Amnesty International. In our experience it is often the reverse. Despite the image of neutrality the UN attempts to put forth, as an intergovernmental body that is the closest thing to a state institution in this globalized world, the UN is also one of the most political institutions around. In any case, we are acutely aware that because of the politics of funding and access, our work may, in particular contexts at particular times, be understood by association to be inspired in ways that we do not necessarily intend.

Resistance from parties involved with criminal investigations in human rights cases is frequent, and it may take months or years of negotiation to finally be able to investigate these types of crimes. The parties involved, or weak transitional governments following dictatorships or civil wars, often use any possible tool to delay investigations. On more than a few occasions, when final permission was granted for a forensic investigation, we met with resistance from officials and the judiciary who tried to limit our role to the "humanitarian identification of remains." In practical terms, this may mean collecting no evidence at the crime scene that relates to understanding what happened there or that can provide information about cause and manner of death and possible perpetrators. For example, from time to time we have been forbidden to collect ballistic evidence, which aids in re-creating what happened. Our response to these kinds of situations has been that as expert forensic witnesses, we cannot discard the collection of relevant evidence during a criminal investigation unless we have a written order from the prosecutor or judge in charge not to collect it. Not surprisingly, this kind of instruction rarely appears in writing, and so most of the time we have been able to proceed.

Thus, discomfort and tension emanating from a number of areas are constant realities for archaeologists or anthropologists involved in this kind of work. Argentina is a good case for illustrating the kinds of obstructions and tensions that arise. One notable observation regarding the earliest forensic work in human rights cases in Argentina, in the early 1980s, was the lack of involvement of academic archaeologists and anthropologists in this new field at a time when their expertise was sorely needed to rebuild the nation. Why this was so sheds light on the complications and complexities of postwar societies.

First, the brutality of the dictatorship left many scientists frightened to become involved in any activity with political connotations. Because military coups had been cyclical in Argentina, many people believed that sooner or later the military would return to power and punish those who had helped gather evidence against it. Second, under the military government a positivist, apolitical, and rather naive conception of science was promoted, and the social involvement of scientists was strongly discouraged. This isolated social scientists from contemporary society and from other kinds of communities, such as those of the indigenous, mestizo, and dispossessed people of the countryside. Archaeology and bio-anthropology were confined to the ancient dead, devoid of any connection to living people.

Third, some archaeologists and anthropologists preferred to devote their efforts to reconstructing institutions devastated during the war, such as universities and the National Research Council. Fourth, for some, because this kind of forensic work was inherently political, it was not scientific enough and did not promote serious scientific research. Yet another group of archaeologists and biological anthropologists recognized the urgent need for a scientific forensic archaeology in Argentina and valued the pioneering work being done, but for personal or professional reasons could not become involved themselves. Finally, the social science community was affected by the repression, and some social scientists disappeared or were imprisoned. Part of the academic community went into exile during the dictatorship and never returned or had yet to return when this work commenced.

As a result, when Clyde Snow began his search for professionals to begin the scientific investigation of a recently discovered mass grave, only a few advanced students of archaeology and social anthropology were in a position to answer his call. Importantly, this group of young volunteers was independent of scholarly institutions, a fact that, on the one hand, gave them great autonomy. On the other hand, that same autonomy and lack of connection delayed the entry of forensic anthropology into the academy, an association that undoubtedly would have helped to consolidate and develop the specialty.

In sum, most of the well-established archaeologists and biological anthropologists in Argentina at the time thought the forensic field was too new, too risky, too political, or insufficiently scientific to be included in the practice of the disciplines. However, early forensic work in Argentina and the rest of Latin America provided a new dimension to archaeological praxis and opened the door to the involvement of archaeologists in human rights issues. Though archaeology is now more widely used in human rights investigations worldwide, some of the same disagreements over the relationship between science, academe, and human rights work are alive in many countries.

Aspects of these tensions are reflected in the historical trajectory of academic debates over what is commonly referred to as the "reburial issue." Many governments and scholars now recognize the rights of indigenous people with regard to archaeological sites and, more significantly, to the human remains of their ancestors. Despite some initial friction, forensic archaeologists and more academically oriented archaeologists are finding common ground and recognizing common goals. Both subdisciplines, they are coming to recognize, are in the business of exhuming historical remains that are eventually returned to families or extended kinship groups. In pursuing this goal, and in standardizing rigorous scientific methodologies and ethical codes and procedures, the techniques and practices of both are enriched and improved, whether one is excavating a ten-thousand-year-old tomb or a mass grave from the 1970s. Moreover, these kinds of debates point to how anthropologists should be aware of the political implications of their research, whether they work in forensic archaeology in Argentina or in the classic archaeology of ancient Greece, where the issues are often less direct and visible (Doretti and Politis 2003).

Forensic findings in a human rights investigation may also have political consequences, because the crimes under investigation were politically motivated. The parties involved often tend to politicize them to justify their actions and to prevent investigation and prosecution. Without being disingenuous about what is at stake, we can say that anthropologists and archaeologists involved in human rights investigations are, in a way, returning to the principle of investigating a crime, regardless of motive, only with years of delay. In this sense, they are part of the depoliticization of such crimes and part of the effort to return to the rule of law.

Shaping Engagement

Anthropologists, particularly cultural anthropologists, have historically worked with "informants," the subjects of their studies, and often produce "results" for other anthropologists. In this sense, too, forensic anthropology utilized for human rights investigations is categorically different. The results of our investigations—reports, executive summaries, book chapters, press conferences, and popularly accessible formats such as comic books—are specifically targeted to the audiences who request them, usually NGOs, local communities, international tribunals, and peace commissions. This lends a substantially different quality and voice to their presentation. For example, commissions of inquiry require generalized reports with a limited number of case studies that demonstrate a range of abuses. Funding agencies might require executive summaries of successful missions, describing the work they paid for and the kinds of results the work produced in local communities. Often, local NGOs and families request a more popular format for information that is potentially traumatic for them and sometimes difficult to comprehend. In other words, our goal is to present the results of our investigations in the most accessible manner for the various audiences that have requested them. In doing so, we seek to lend whatever transparency we can to processes that have been obscured and hidden. We deliberately avoid narrative strategies that hide or complicate the meaning and results of investigations.

We recognize that these "results" are weighted differently in academe, but we measure our productivity in other ways: by collecting evidence and translating it into final products to be used in different kinds of forums or by the families of victims to understand the experiences of their family members and themselves within larger contexts. Because of the enormous undertaking of these steps, coupled with negotiation of the gray spaces and ambiguous zones, we have not, for the most part, engaged in theory building, although we hope to address theoretical projects through the creation of ALAF.

Finally, the identity of our "informants" and the nature of our work with them are categorically different from what is found in other kinds of anthropological investigations. We work with both the living and the dead and hope that both will provide clues to and details of a bigger picture. The living have a right to know what happened, and they provide us with the kinds of details that help us make sense of and interpret the histories marked on the remains of their loved ones. But how and where the truth is delivered matters. As the Argentine human rights activist Juan Méndez has argued, "knowledge that is officially sanctioned and thereby made 'part of the public cognitive scene' acquires a mysterious quality that is not there when it is merely 'truth.' Official acknowledgement at last begins to heal these wounds" (cited in Hayner 2002). Families and local NGOs, then, rely on us to convey the histories that they have entrusted to us to the forums where their becoming public will set the wheels of justice and reparations into motion.

Conclusion

In Latin America, the origins and practice of forensic anthropology have been drastically different from those of developing countries. Forensic anthropologists in Latin America have pioneered several areas of forensic sciences and human rights investigations. At EAAF, when we initially started our work twenty years ago, we needed to distance ourselves from legal-medical systems and other governmental institutions that had reportedly committed crimes or had lost credibility during lengthy periods of human rights violations. We worked outside these organizations, incorporating new scientific tools for human rights investigations. In order to have a long-term effect, and taking advantage of increased interest in international criminal law and the domestic incorporation of it, we now work toward incorporating international protocols for human rights work into domestic criminal procedures. In a way, then, in the past two decades we have come full circle.

Coming full circle, however, does not mean that the negotiations that give forensic anthropology applied to human rights cases its distinctive form cease or lessen. These negotiations and the gray spaces and interstices between subdisciplines and agendas are intrinsically linked to the growth of the field and the politically charged contexts in which its work takes place. In this sense, the negotiations and gray spaces inherent to our work both define the limits of forensic anthropology as an engaged practice in the field of human rights and push at its boundaries, opening new arenas and new possibilities.

Appendix: EAAF Recommendations

On the basis of our experiences working as forensic anthropologists for truth commissions, special commissions of inquiry, and national and international tribunals, the EAAF has developed a number of recommendations. Some of them are the results of two workshops organized in 2002 and 2003 by the International Committee of the Red Cross in Geneva at which forensic pathologists, anthropologists, archaeologists, lawyers, and human rights activists developed guidelines regarding people missing and disappeared during wars and internal conflicts. Several of these were discussed at length in this chapter, and we provide no further details for them.

The effectiveness of institutional bodies that are established for fixed time periods would be strengthened by the following:

1. Improving the relationship between families of victims and forensic teams.
   1.1. Facilitating the right to truth of families of victims.
   1.2. Seeking approval from families for exhumations and respecting cultural and religious funeral rites.
2. Creating mechanisms to continue the recovery and identification process beyond a commission's or tribunal's mandate.
3. Whenever possible, improving contacts between independent forensic experts and local judiciaries, prosecutors, judges, and lawyers.
   This recommendation includes giving presentations to local judiciaries and lawyers, with basic information about how the forensic sciences, mainly forensic anthropology and archaeology, can contribute to judiciary investigations. This also provides a valuable opportunity to discuss the way evidence is handled in a particular country, to discuss cases done in other parts of the world as well as specific local ones, and to understand the concerns of the legal community.
4. Whenever possible, training and promoting local teams and local forensic experts.
5. Whenever possible, maintaining contact with local human rights organizations.
   At times of massive human rights violations in a country, the judiciary normally loses much of its capacity to impartially investigate crimes committed by the state or by armed parties in a civil conflict. Truth commissions are usually created during transitional moments at the ends of civil conflicts, wars, state terrorism, and so forth. Thus, local nongovernmental organizations (NGOs) often fill part of the gap. At times, at great risk to their members, they form a bridge between the investigative body and the witnesses, survivors, and relatives of victims. Even during democratic transitional moments, witnesses and relatives of victims often feel

more comfortable releasing information to a local NGO or giving testimony before a court of law or a national or international commission of inquiry with the support or mediation of an NGO. Truth commission investigators usually rely on the work of NGOs as a starting point for their investigations, and therefore these connections are essential to our work and to ongoing national investigative processes.

6. Improving access to DNA.

Informing the relatives of a disappeared person that the remains being analyzed do not correspond to their loved one is very difficult. But it is equally difficult to tell them that we are unsure whether or not a particular set of remains matches, and because we have no way to resolve this doubt, the remains must continue to be stored. Traditional forensic anthropology techniques are limited when sufficient antemortem evidence cannot be obtained. This was often the situation until the early 1990s, when it became possible to recover DNA from skeletal remains. At this point, genetic testing quickly became a tool in human rights investigations. Access to it, however, is still very expensive.

EAAF has depended on the generous pro bono work of laboratories in the United States, Canada, and the United Kingdom, but they can accommodate only a limited number of cases every year. As a partial remedy to this problem in Argentina, EAAF has established a genetic blood bank composed of blood samples from relatives of disappeared people who visited our Buenos Aires office from 1998 onward. This bank makes possible genetic analyses necessary for identifications whether or not close relatives are present or alive. This technique will become especially crucial in countries such as Zimbabwe, where HIV is affecting at least 25 percent of the adult population.

7. Protecting possible killing and burial sites.

Whenever possible, it is important to protect possible killing and burial sites if they are not being investigated at the time of discovery. In this way they will be available to families of victims and investigators working in the future.

8. Preserving crucial evidence and forensic reports for possible ongoing and future investigations and prosecutions.

Uncovering evidence of human rights crimes does not necessarily mean that justice is immediately achieved. Many human rights violations are investigated but not prosecuted, mostly because of amnesty laws, limiting the role forensic evidence can play in judicial processes. However, as new mechanisms are developed in the field of international criminal law and as old cases are brought back to trial (in Argentina and Chile, for example), it is important that vital evidence and reports be preserved in order to be used in future trials.

9. Creating witness and informer protection programs.

In each commission or tribunal there is usually a core group of ten to fifteen—perhaps fewer—key witnesses to major incidents. Often these people need protection, including, in some cases, eventual safe emigration to another country. Usually this type of commission has no mechanism for dealing with witness safety. An ad hoc measure may eventually be enacted, depending upon the commission's specific mandate, the way it is interpreted, and the flexibility of the international, national, and regional bodies that may assist in the process. Though setting up a witness protection program is clearly a complicated issue, we think it is extremely important to include some sort of mechanism from the planning phase as a matter of course.

10. Providing counseling or psychological support for persons who testify and for families and friends of victims before, during, and after exhumations.

11. Providing counseling or psychological support for forensic personnel and for staff members who receive testimonies for commissions.

Sometimes the overwhelming weight of the testimonies of witnesses, victims, and their families produces conflicting feelings of exhaustion, guilt, and depression in the researchers who are investigating atrocities for truth commissions. In some instances, international investigative missions have provided psychological support, but this is still the exception. Counseling may prove especially helpful when these commissions extend their work to a year or more, as they often do.

12. Promoting the incorporation of international forensic protocols for human rights investigations into domestic criminal procedures.

Incorporating international forensic protocols for human rights investigations into domestic criminal procedures is essential. Doing so will ensure that scientific tools and mechanisms developed for human rights investigations will have a longer-term effect. Along these lines, the United Nations has produced several documents relating to forensic science and human rights.

Notes

1. Consider, for example, the huge popularity of two bestselling authors, Kathy Reich and Patricia Cornwall, whose main characters are forensic specialists. *Bones,* the Fox Network's recent program, is based on Reich's forensic anthropologist protagonist, Temperance Brennan.

2. This predicament—the fixedness of law versus the flexibility of anthropological understandings—has perhaps most famously been addressed in cultural anthropology by James Clifford (1988) in relation to the Mashpee.

3. This relationship is addressed at greater length in the thirty-eight-minute film *Following Antigone: Forensic Anthropology and Human Rights* (EAAF/Witness 2002).

Collaborating to Meet the Goals of a Native Sovereign Nation

The Tule River Tribal History Project

Gelya Frank

Anthropology's core jurisdiction is the production of knowledge about culture. Its hallmark is the writing of ethnographic texts. Yet in the United States, and perhaps elsewhere, anthropology has been profoundly affected by other disciplines and forced to retrench (Peacock 1999; Turner 1993). For one example, practice professions dealing with human populations, such as education, nursing, law, medicine, and occupational therapy, have imported ethnographic approaches, recast as "qualitative methods," and now claim expertise in the area of culture. For another, cultural studies and ethnic studies programs have influenced the way anthropologists think about culture and have made it more possible for them to engage with the political agendas of the constituencies they study. Interdisciplinary and collaborative approaches trouble the jurisdictional model based on exclusive control of a conceptual and methodological domain, as described by sociologists of the professions (e.g., Abbott 1988). In fact, borrowing across disciplinary boundaries is not only usual but central to the revitalization of academic professions.

The nexus between anthropology and occupational therapy provides a case in point. Education in occupational therapy was initially a Progressive Era innovation arising in the settlement movement, which took place outside the university. It was followed by practical training courses sponsored by the United States surgeon general in World War I, restricted to women only. Education for the profession, whose practitioners were female, had its strongest base in the mid-twentieth century in state colleges whose purpose was to provide practical training. Infiltration into private, elite research universities came slowly. The first master's-level program in occupational therapy was instituted in 1947 at the University of Southern California, providing a new platform for the academicizing of this mainly female profession.

The profession drew from anthropology and other mainstream disciplines in the 1980s and 1990s to establish greater academic credibility and autonomy while developing its new, cutting-edge discipline, occupational science. The development of elite scholarly textual practices in occupational therapy was needed to challenge long-standing prejudices in Western culture and the academy that devalued the knowledge and practices associated with manual activity and female-gendered work. Anthropologists now working in occupational therapy, many of whom are also occupational therapy practitioners, are developing concepts and methods that can potentially help to revitalize anthropology by complementing and infusing its textual emphasis with performative approaches—that is, approaches based on doing.

The Tule River Tribal History Project, piloted on the Tule River Indian Reservation near Porterville, California, took such a performative approach. The Tule River Tribe is composed of descendants of formerly independent tribes known collectively as Yokuts.[1] The project employed common tools of anthropological fieldwork such as recording interviews with tribal elders. But its effectiveness was amplified and transformed by drawing on the conceptual background and practices of occupational therapy. Those involved in the project did this by engaging tribal elders in history-making activities such as constructing their own genealogies and family trees using computer programs.

Moreover, the project put collaboration in the foreground in several ways. It created an opportunity for conversation and exchange of practices between anthropology and occupational therapy in a field situation. It also created an intercultural space in which indigenous and non-indigenous collaborators worked together to promote the Tule River Tribe's nation-building goals. Finally, in the service of constituting a tribal legacy, the project's activities were structured to promote cooperation and communication so that different generations and diverse families within the Tule River Tribe could collaborate with one another, an effect that the tribal elders themselves noticed by the end of the pilot project (Frank 2005).

The history project achieved remarkable successes during twelve weeks in the summer of 2004. The promising trajectory of the project was interrupted for a year and a half, however, by unfulfilled commitments and administrative tangles in the intertribal agency that co-funded the pilot using State of California Tribal TANF prevention funds.[2] This impasse was broken when the Tule River Tribal Council voted in February 2006 to establish an official, standing Tribal History Committee to build on the pilot project's achievements and to develop tribal goals and budget recommendations for the next three to five years.

Although the initial twelve-week phase of the project was collaborative in its goals, it in fact had many features of a professional consulting relationship and a service-provider model. The project director (an anthropologist and occupational scientist) and staff (occupational therapy graduate students) were seen by the tribal leadership and membership as supplying expertise to fulfill goals that the tribe had not yet managed to fulfill on its own. The establishment of the Tribal History Committee meant that the Tribal Council took over the direction and implementation of the history project, allowing the academic partners to take a more fully collaborative, supportive, and facilitating role.

The Tule River Tribal Council's decision to initiate the history project grew out a long-standing goal, "to preserve the Tribe's history" (Environmental Concern, Inc. 1972). I became associated with the tribe as a graduate student in anthropology who volunteered in 1972–74 to assist the Tribal Council in meeting this goal.[3] The ideas of "occupation" and "engagement" in the Tule River Tribal History Project emerged from my teaching at the University of Southern California in the Department of Occupational Therapy during the founding of a new discipline known as occupational science. Ideas about "engaging in occupations" to support social transformations, however, reach back to Boasian anthropology and its influence on Pragmatist philosophers and Progressive Era initiatives, including the settlement movement, labor reforms, and the founding of progressive education and occupational therapy. The history project's position at the intersection of anthropology, occupational therapy, and the nation-building goals of a California tribe went beyond anthropology's traditional focus on text and representation. It was part of a movement to incorporate occupational, activist, and performative approaches when working with indigenous peoples and postcolonialist agendas (Field 2005; Glass 2004; Hale, this volume; Hinton 1994, 2002; Rappaport 1994, 1998, 2005, this volume).[4]

Using Occupations to Produce Indigenous Histories

Those involved in the pilot phase of the Tule River Tribal History Project attempted to expand on traditional occupational therapy approaches. Occupational therapists use everyday activities to promote recovery, adaptation, and independence in persons whose function is impaired by chronic illness or disability. Increasingly, the profession is also interested in interventions using activities and routines to prevent lifestyle diseases associated with obesity, such as diabetes and coronary illness. The Tribal History Project proposed the following conceptualization: "Just as occupational therapists traditionally use activities with individuals to support their independence and well-being, the Tule River Tribal History Project uses activities with a tribe to support its collective well-being and sovereignty."

The Tule River Tribal History Project resulted from the widespread satisfaction of tribal members with a twenty-page color news insert commemorating the survival of the tribe that the Tribal Council contracted with me to produce in 2002. It included numerous contributions of articles, photographs, paintings, interviews, captions, and information by and about tribal members (Tule River Tribal Council 2002). This effort represented the first time the tribe had published and disseminated a self-authorized tribal history for mass distribution. The publication was inserted in the Sunday editions of local newspapers and circulated to 37,000 households in Tulare County. Tribal Council chairman Duane M. Garfield Sr. inquired informally, through a staff member, about my availability to write a book to preserve the history of the tribe. In response, I offered to submit a proposal for a project that would provide activities by which tribal members could tell their own history.

The Tribal Council referred the history project proposal to the tribal elders for approval. The tribal elders consisted of 118 tribal members ages 55 and over—less than 10 percent of the population. Perhaps twenty or thirty members attended the regular tribal elders meeting at which the history proposal was presented. Many elders were initially cautious, and some were outspokenly opposed to the proposal. One person voiced fear of the tribe's losing control over its intellectual property, objecting that the elders would be "giving away" their stories to an outsider who would publish and profit from them. Another elder argued that the project came too late to be of any value and asserted, "This should have been done thirty years ago."

The sense that it is "too late" is a common response of Native American tribal members to cultural preservation projects, as Craig Howe (Oglala Sioux) commented on the basis of his experience in developing and presenting tribal histories using museum exhibits and hypermedia:

> In many instances, the public meetings to which the entire community is invited are the first times that community members have gathered

together to discuss tribal history. Aside from the political machinations that often accompany such gatherings, deep-seated issues within the communities are brought to these discussions. Questions concerning authority to speak, personal character, information dissemination, and loss of tribal knowledge are not uncommon. A recurring theme is that knowledge of the "old ways" passed on with the last generation who were educated by the community instead of by formal schools. (Howe 2002: 175)

Nevertheless, a survey of the Tule River tribal elders unequivocally showed their strong desire to preserve their history.[5] Once a public forum was established, the interest and participation of the tribal elders and their families grew steadily in a manner similar to that which Howe described:

> With a deep sense of loss, community members repeatedly say that these projects are too late, that the old men and women who knew the stories have all passed on. Ironically, after having said this, tribal members are identified who do know the stories. And this is one of the benefits of the process that accrues solely to the community: The collective knowledge of the community is recognized. In discussing their tribal histories in public formats, individuals share stories and opinions that other community members are keenly interested in hearing. One outcome of this is that the communities themselves wish to retain copies of all the information gathered during the developmental process, and to make it available to community members. (Howe 2002:175)

A full-time staff of five graduate student fieldwork interns from the University of Southern California Department of Occupational Science and Occupational Therapy quickly and effectively developed methods and protocols for the tribal history-making activities (Kitching et al. 2004). The occupations chosen for the project were described in a brochure distributed to each tribal elder:

Family Trees
Learn to make your family tree. Use our tribal rolls from 1888. We'll help you get started on genealogy software even if you are new to computers.

Digital Photo Archive
Bring your old-time photos for scanning on CD-ROM for the tribal archive. We'll help you index them and make a copy for your family.

Elders Video Interviews
Sign up for a video interview. Tell us about your parents, grandparents, uncles, aunts, sisters, brothers, husbands or wives, children, grandchildren. What were the old people like? What did they do? How did they—and you—survive?

Elders Heritage Roundtable Talks
Reminisce with other Elders about Rodeo Days, *Tripne* Legends, Military Service, School Days, Life On (and Off) the Reservation. Food provided.

Tribal Elders Heritage Website
Choose to have a portion of your family history on the website.

Lively discussions among tribal elders and other adult tribal members took place at the roundtable discussions, which were videotaped, and also at public viewings of photographs from the tribal archive that were digitally projected on a screen. The elders were not necessarily accustomed to having their views sought out. As Luther Garfield, age eighty, one of the oldest and most active participants, commented to one of the occupational therapy interns: "People don't like old people. They run away from them. I guess they think that they don't have anything to say" (Kitching et al. 2004).

Tribal members participated in proposing topics and organizing events, particularly the roundtable discussions. For example, Tribal Council contracts and grants officer Nancy McDarment brought together women in their twenties through their sixties to talk about their experiences on the tribe's women's softball team, the Challengers. Many of them paid tribute to the Challengers' coach, tribal elder Edna Williams, who was present. Another time, elder Ray Flores Sr., a professional guitarist, brought together tribal members to recall the place of music in the everyday life of a previous generation and the improvisational and unique harmonic skills of earlier tribal musicians. A catered lunch was served at the roundtable events to draw tribal members' participation and also to mark the roundtables as collective events through the sharing of food. Tribal elder Maggie Valdez, seventy-eight, another of the oldest and most active participants, insisted on preparing a meal. She provided a full turkey dinner accompanied by the rarely prepared but symbolically important former staple of the Yokuts diet, cooked acorns.

Many elders who participated in the project anxiously inquired about whether the project would continue on a full-time, year-round basis, as had been announced to the Tribal Council by the Tribal TANF administrator. Tribal members of all ages expressed regret that they had not yet taken advantage of the activities that were offered, particularly the chance to make a family tree.

The accomplishments of the project were impressive. Family trees were created by forty tribal members of all ages, many of them working in pairs across generations. For the Digital Photo Archive, about two thousand images dating from the early twentieth century were compiled, contributed by twenty-five different elders and their family members. Video interviews with nine of the oldest tribal members were recorded and transcribed, some with family members acting as interviewers. Nine roundtable talks took place and were videotaped. A tribal history website was launched (www.tuleriver.org). At the conclusion of the twelve-week pilot, tribal elders reported dramatic gains in confidence that the history project could help to preserve tribal history and support nation-building goals (Frank 2005).[6]

From Textual Representation to Performance

Anthropology's area of legitimate practice—its "doing"—is the production of texts through fieldwork (eliciting and recording information) and publication (analyzing, interpreting, and disseminating information). The feminist philosopher Karen Barad (2003) has argued that academic practices in general are overcommitted to representationalism, which treats entities (people, cultures, nonhuman entities, physical phenomena) as if they exist in and of themselves, apart from our interaction with them: "Representationalism is the belief in the ontological distinction between representations and that which they purport to represent; in particular, that which is represented is held to be independent of all practices of representing" (2003: 803). Barad contrasts a move toward *performativity* as a way of knowing through engagement, action, practice, or "doing": "The move toward performative alternatives to representationalism shifts the focus from questions of correspondence between descriptions and reality (e.g., do they mirror nature or culture?) to matters of practices/doings/actions" (2003: 801).

Solidarity with constituencies and commitments to action affect the production and legitimation of knowledge. The anthropologist's classic stance of participant observation—being the "fly on the wall"—reinforces an ontological distinction between representations and entities to be represented. This kind of representationalism had its critics in the American academy as early as the 1930s and 1940s, when Kurt Lewin, the social psychologist and an early proponent of what is now called action research, wrote, "The best way to understand something is to try to change it" (quoted in Greenwood and Levin 1998). A. L. Kroeber's politically disengaged pronouncements of the Muwekma Ohlone as "extinct," for example, continues to adversely affect that tribe's struggle to gain federal recognition (Field 1999, 2003). Les Field's work in support of Ohlone efforts to gain federal recognition is not only representational but also collaborative and performative.[7]

In the United States, applied anthropology is a recognized subfield that includes many people who work outside the academy. The Society for Applied Anthropology (SfAA) was founded in 1941 "to promote the investigation of the principles of human behavior and the application of these principles to contemporary issues and problems."[8] Although the work done by applied anthropologists is often performative, the legitimating tasks of the subfield are basically textual, as in the mainstream of the profession: conducting research to advise governmentally supported agencies, nongovernmental organizations, and private corporations (the anthropologist as expert) and using research to promote the goals of the constituencies studied (the anthropologist as advocate) (Field 2005). A recent movement known as public anthropology focuses on widening the audience for texts produced by anthropologists, but without necessarily changing anthropologists' field practices (www.publicanthropology.org).

Anthropologists' relationships with Native American tribes are becoming more collaborative and also more performative as tribal governments assert their sovereign power to grant or deny permission to scholars seeking to conduct research in Indian country (Champagne and Goldberg 2005; Field 2005). This shift has been gaining momentum since the 1960s and 1970s but has accelerated as gaming industries on some reservations have produced new wealth and political clout for many tribes, following the Supreme Court ruling in *California v. Cabazon Band of Mission Indians* (1987). Tribes are requiring anthropologists to use their knowledge and skills to support the survival of Native American peoples facing poverty and political disenfranchisement, not to focus obsessively on collecting information about traditional cultures (Biolsi and Zimmerman 1997; Deloria 1969; Stocking 2000). Sam Deloria (Standing Rock Sioux), director of the American Indian Law Center, commented on the challenge to adapt and create indigenous institutions:

> If we are going to talk about our cultures and their survival, let's really mean it. Let's put some practical importance into dealing with the

problems that we have with our families and communities and children. For we are creating institutions. Indian tribes are engaged in some of the most delicate and complicated work that is being done in this world right now—trying to adapt social and political institutions to the needs of their own communities, questioning what to change and what to preserve. The only thing that's going to humanize those institutions is us, ourselves, setting down our own standards and insisting on them. (Quoted in Coffey and Tsosie 2001: 209)

Because the mood in Indian country is future oriented, indigenous and non-indigenous intellectuals may be able to find common ground more than ever before—particularly in anti-essentialist theories that offer an alternative to the view that "real" indigenous cultures are past (Clifford 1997; Grossberg, Nelson, and Treichler 1992; Kirshenblatt-Gimblett 1998; Young 2001). Anthropologists must now develop theories and methods of collaboration to engage with indigenous projects while also respecting indigenous cultural sovereignty (Champagne 1998; Coffey and Tsosie 2001; Rappaport, this volume; Smith 1999; Tsosie 2002a, 2002b). Such collaborations may certainly involve the production of texts as documents and reports of activities and events. But the focus and intent of the activities may be primarily performative rather than textual in terms of helping to facilitate tribally driven goals and agendas related to cultural planning and institutional change.

Tribal Histories at Tule River

The Tule River Tribal History Project has been a collaborative effort to promote the production and recording of indigenous histories. It has built on a wide array of history-making practices and the formation of collective memory from prior to the introduction of the history project (Connerton 1989; Halbwachs 1980 [1950]; Nora 1989; also see Basso 1996). Histories are constantly spoken on the Tule River Reservation in the course of everyday conversations, in arguments supporting proposals before the Tribal Council, at formal commemorative events such as the Memorial Day service observed by the Tule River AmVets Post, at the Acorn Feast held recently in autumn, and, of course, at funerals. Written histories produced by tribal members include transcripts of tape-recorded interviews, vocabulary lists gained from tribal elders in Yokuts dialects, and obituaries in local newspapers written by or based on information supplied by family members. Many people own copies of the highly informative application forms that their ancestors filed to gain inclusion on the 1928 California Roll. They also own copies of popular historian Frank Latta's *Handbook of Yokuts Indians* (1949), in which appear accounts by and photographs of ancestors of the present tribe. Many tribal members have extensive photographic collections and maintain scrapbooks. The tribe's collective memories are also "inscribed" in the natural landscape, in the Painted Rocks, in the yearly repainting and repair by the tribal elders of the crosses in the two cemeteries on the reservation, in events such as the occasional Spring Festival at which traditional storytellers and dancers perform, in bodily appearances and behaviors, in rodeos, in graffiti and bullet holes, in sites of car accidents, in swimming holes in the river, in acorn grinding holes used by a great-grandmother on a family's land assignment, in hats and tack hanging in sheds, and in other tools and implements.

A more formal layer of history making has been initiated by the Tule River Tribal Council in asserting its sovereignty through legal battles with federal and state governments. Toward this end, the tribe has engaged both indigenous and non-indigenous consultants to help construct alternative indigenous histories. These are written histories that meticulously cite primary archival and oral materials, placing them critically in relation to existing published histories. They focus on the tribe as a collective entity, an active protagonist protecting its land base and tribal membership. The tribe's recovery of 1,250 acres of prime timberland on the reservation's northeast corner in 1980 serves as an example (Frank and Goldberg n.d.; see also Frank 1980). Collaborating with a team of indigenous lawyers and non-indigenous scholars, the Tribal Council authorized a history based on sources from the National Archives that showed how tribal members came together over many decades to protest the intrusion of non-Indian settlers and timber interests on the reservation and to petition the federal government to provide a remedy. Such formal, alternative, indigenous histories will increasingly be written by tribal members as the education level and professionalization of the tribe's membership continues to rise.

A preference for focusing on family histories that I have observed among tribal members at Tule River appears to go deeper than the sentiment associated generally with a desire to know about one's immediate forebears. It can also be traced to the experience of the California tribes, which underwent the most rapid and devastating colonization in all of North America (Hurtado 1988; Rawls 1984).[9] In the case of the Tule River Indians, the Southern Valley and Foothill Yokuts tribes initially were buffered by their inland location from serious disruption under the Spanish and Mexican regimes. They were also protected from the brunt of the American invasion in California Territory after 1848 by their distance from the gold mines. But the influx of settlers after California statehood in 1850 and the organization of Tulare County in 1852 produced a rupture so severe that it nearly annihilated these tribes (Phillips 1975, 1993, 1997).

Tribal sovereignty was ignored as the federal government redefined the land base beginning in 1853 with the removal of villages under local leaders to the Tejon Reservation at the southern end of the San Joaquin Valley (Phillips 2004). In 1856, some survivors of these tribes were placed on a reservation along the Tule River following a war of extermination that was initiated by settlers (Stewart 1884). The reservation was established on a traditional village site belonging to the Koyeti tribe. Members of the Koyeti, Chunut, Yaudanchi, Wikchumne, Yowlumne, Pankalachi, and other local tribes who moved there to become agriculturalists under government supervision became known collectively as the Tule River Indians. The population of the tribes on this first Tule River reservation peaked in the 1860s at about four hundred persons. In 1873 they were forced by executive order to move to the present reservation in the remote and agriculturally less desirable foothills of the Sierra Nevada. They were told by the government agent to build homes and fence their property, in anticipation that the land would be allotted (that is, deeded) to heads of households. The land assignments were never allotted and technically belong to the tribe, but they are nonetheless treated as inheritable family property.

The reservation population from the late nineteenth through the early twentieth century dropped to about 150 members. The tribe now includes more than 1,500 members, who trace their membership to the original families that settled and lived on the present reservation. Constructing family histories has been pivotal to survival because it is tied to the right to live on the reservation, inherit the use of tribal land, and enroll one's children as tribal members.

Because Tribal Council members are elected from a relatively small population, it is much more likely that a tribal member will serve in tribal government than that a non-indigenous citizen will become a city, county, state, or federal official. When tribal members serve on the Tribal Council, they encounter, often for the first time, the masses of legal and administrative documents that relate to the tribe's survival and functioning as a political entity. Their responsibilities as tribal leaders then engage them performatively in using texts to construct not only family histories but also more formal tribal histories. The Tule River Tribal History Project addresses a need felt by the tribe to create a bridge between the kind of naturalistic history-making activities already engaged in by tribal members and the self-conscious production of histories needed to support the tribe's sovereignty and, in a profound sense, its survival and well-being as a collective entity.

Occupations and Social Transformation

The concept of occupations with which the tribal history project works is fundamentally anthropological and refers to human adaptation. Franz Boas (1960 [1888]) described the "domestic occupations and amusements" of the Central Eskimos when he returned from his first fieldwork, in Baffinland in 1883–84. Cataloguing the array of mundane daily activities carried out by men and women during the winter, Boas emphasized the relationship between survival and the routine organization of activities driven by the seasonal hunt of sea mammals. Boas's catalogue of daily activities in a traditional indigenous lifestyle— preparing food, making clothing, carrying out ritual obligations, and caring for animals—importantly addressed the opportunities these occupations afforded for enjoyable family and community relationships associated with the regular daily cycle of work and rest:

> It is winter and the natives are established in their warm snow houses. At this time of the year it is necessary to make use of the short daylight and twilight for hunting. Long before the day begins to dawn the Eskimo prepares for hunting. He rouses his housemate; his wife supplies the lamp with a new wick and fresh blubber and the dim light which has been kept burning during the night quickly brightens up and warms the hut... The sledge is iced, the harnesses are taken out of the storeroom ... the hunter lashes the spear ... and starts for the hunting ground. Here he waits pleasantly for the blowing seal, sometimes until late in the evening...
>
> Meanwhile the women, who stay at home, are engaged in their domestic occupations, mending boots and making new clothing, or they visit one another, taking some work with them, or pass their time with games or in playing with the children. While sitting at their sewing and at the same time watching their lamps and cooking the meat, they incessantly hum their favorite tunes. (Boas 1960 [1888]: 247)

Later, in the evening, interfamily and intergenerational mingling and conversation took place while people engaged in recreational activities such as carving.

It is clear from Boas's description that sociability and positive emotions were interwoven with daily occupations. Similar accounts of daily and seasonal occupations fill the ethnographies of the California tribes, including the Yokuts ancestors of the Tule River Tribe. Annual ritual activity embraced the solemn Lonewis ceremony in the fall, a week-long gathering of tribes that marked the departure of people who had died during the preceding year, and the more light-hearted Rattlesnake ceremony in spring, with its thrilling shamans' contests (Gayton 1948a, 1948b). Daily life was shaped by occupations of hunting and fishing, gathering grasses and seeds, collecting and preparing acorns—labor that was mostly performed communally and accompanied by conversation. Under the American regime, these routines and habits were adapted to include agriculture activities on the reservation and seasonal wage labor on farms and ranches.

The philosopher John Dewey, founder of the progressive education movement, seized on this basically Boasian anthropological under-standing of the relationship between occupation and the adaptation and evolution of the human species.[10] Writing at the turn of the twentieth century, Dewey saw humans as actively striving to explore and master their world, rather than passively reacting to outside forces. He understood the political implications of empowering children to use their imaginations and to experience their actions as contributing to larger purposes and goals, including the survival and development of the human species, their own ancestral groups, and the American democratic polity. Like his contemporary Maria Montessori in Italy and his predecessor Friedrich Froebel in Germany, Dewey was concerned with promoting learning through exploring, handling, and actively doing things. Like Froebel, Dewey aimed to instill moral and communitarian values (Dewey 1990).[11]

Characterizing the preindustrial lifestyles that were becoming rapidly outmoded for urban youths at the turn of the twentieth century, Dewey wrote about the power of occupations to instill habits of order, industry, and responsibility to produce something in the world: "In all this there was continual training of observation, of ingenuity, of constructive imagination, of logical thought, and of the sense of reality acquired through first-hand contact with actualities... No training of sense-organs in school, introduced for the sake of training, can begin to compete with the alertness and fullness of sense-life that comes through daily intimacy and interest in familiar occupations" (Dewey 1990: 10–11).

Dewey's emphasis on self-discipline and regular habits recalls the rigorous standards often held in traditional Native societies for the acquisition of wisdom and power (see Buckley 2002). Dewey was interested not in enforcing authoritarian control over the "disciplined bodies" described in Foucault's critique of modernity but in fostering individual creativity and its relationship to the survival of the group. Changing conditions in the group's environment called for the capacity to adapt. The Progressive Era, for example, was a period of massive immigration and oppression for the urban working class. Dewey advocated for new educational practices based on experience—on meaningful "doing" (occupation)—as a means to promote democratic participation and empowerment. In this regard, his work was a forerunner to Paulo Freire's pedagogy of the oppressed.

The social ethicist Jane Addams, a colleague of Dewey, applied occupational ideas to meet the needs of impoverished and disenfranchised immigrants in Chicago. Relying on wealthy patrons to support her reformist agenda, Addams was unsympathetic to anarchist and revolutionary approaches to social transformation. Like Dewey, she aimed to promote empowerment through democratic participation in American society. She and her colleagues made the Hull House settlement in Chicago a place where women in the garment trades organized, as well as the site of well baby clinics, child care programs, arts and crafts programs, ethnic clubs, political debates, and antiwar activism. With radical colleagues, the personnel of Hull House launched successful battles to establish child labor laws, public sanitation, and a special court system to deal with juvenile offenders (Addams 1999 [1910]; see also Seigfried 2002).

The first course in occupational therapy was taught at Hull House by social worker Eleanor Clarke Slagle (Loomis 1992). With colleagues in arts and crafts, education, nursing, architecture, and medicine, Slagle founded the National Society for the Promotion of Occupational Therapy in 1917. The profession used occupations such as weaving, chair caning, bookbinding, woodworking, and leather working to rehabilitate people with psychiatric illnesses, physical disabilities, and chronic illnesses such as tuberculosis. The US surgeon general's endorsement of this mission resulted in the training and deployment of occupational therapy "reconstruction aides" during World War I and occupational therapists during World War II, linking the profession's development to national agendas.

Between the wars, Slagle worked closely with Adolph Meyer, then America's foremost psychiatrist, to develop her approach, known as "habit training" (Leys 1990; Lidz 1967; Lief 1948). A close personal associate of John Dewey, Meyer took a Pragmatist view of mental illness, viewing it as a "problem of living" that could be ameliorated by changing the patient's use of time. He described engagement in occupations as the way in which an organism "balances itself in the world of reality and actuality" (Meyer 1921: 5). Slagle and Meyer aimed to offer patients not prescriptions but "opportunities" to engage in occupations to find their own way back to a healthy lifestyle.

Occupational therapists sought to genuinely engage their patients' interest so that they could experience enjoyment in doing meaningful work while convalescing. Cultural meaning and relevance were in the forefront. Tuberculosis patients, for example, were restricted to months and even years in bed. The occupational therapy handicraft program at the Charles Camsell Hospital in Alberta, Canada, established in 1946, provided Inuit and other Native Canadian tuberculosis patients an expressive outlet through traditional arts (Staples and McConnell 1993). Not surprisingly, the Camsell collection of garments, soapstone carvings, and other handicrafts is now housed at an ethnological museum for display and study as part of the region's cultural legacy.

Occupational therapy's Pragmatist impulses have been largely subordinated to the biomedical model in hospital settings (Gritzer and Arluke 1989; see Block, this volume). Consequently, its practices and rationale were increasingly reshaped by scientific reductionism (Kielhofner and Burke 1977) and deference to the conservative political tendencies of the American medical profession (Starr 1984). A movement to restore "occupation" as the core concept of the occupational therapy profession arose in the 1960s with the work of Mary Reilly and her students at the University of Southern California. Reilly's work led to the development in 1989 of a doctoral degree program at USC in a new discipline called occupational science.

Anthropology helped to provide an important new conceptualization of occupational therapy practice in the 1990s (Mattingly 1998; Mattingly and Gillette 1991; Spencer, Krefting, and Mattingly 1993). It also helped to ground the new discipline of occupational science (Zemke and Clark, 1996). Occupational science defines "occupations" as culturally relevant, purposeful activities and routines that give shape, meaning, and value to the experience of individuals and groups (Clark et al. 1991; Yerxa et al. 1990). Significantly, the discipline of occupational science has helped to support occupational therapy's claim to a legitimate jurisdiction in the academy, overcoming prejudice against the kind of knowledge produced by a predominantly female practice (Frank 1992).

Occupational therapy is presently expanding its jurisdiction from the treatment of individuals to interventions with communities (Watson and Swartz 2004). A movement originating in Canada and Australia seeks "occupational justice," defined as equity in access to meaningful occupations for people who are incarcerated or who suffer from other forms of activity deprivation (Townsend and Wilcock 2004). Occupational therapists also now claim a radical political edge by working with populations oppressed by "occupational apartheid" in Europe, Latin America, Asia, and southern Africa (Kronenberg, Algado, and Pollard 2005).

Conclusion

Collaborations between non-indigenous researchers and indigenous peoples in North America call for commitment, trust, dialogue, and alignment in the dynamic area of tribal sovereignty and nation building. The indigenous scholar Craig Howe (2002) argued that an iterative process is needed to develop accountability and trust in collaborations to produce tribal histories:

> It is a very potent experience for community members to revisit many of the important events presented in their tribal histories. In some instances, they are sharing their experience and stories with outsiders for the first time. And their stories are properly their intellectual property. They do not want to invest their time, efforts and emotion if the process is not going to be done right or if the final product is not going to be good in their eyes… Therefore, the process is necessarily iterative, takes place over a period of time, and considerably decenters the traditional authority of the mainstream institution. (Howe 2002: 174–75)

Commitment is easy to invoke representationally as a belief or ideal. But active engagement—what Barad (2003) called "performativity"—is required for the iterative process that makes collaborations truly work. The Tule River Tribal History Project uses history-making occupations to shape new practices among its three constituencies: anthropologists, occupational therapists, and the Tule River Tribe. The history project departs from the familiar anthropological model of recording information from individuals to produce scholarly texts for future reference or advocacy. It aims rather to facilitate and support the engagement of tribal members in creating a collective working legacy to advance cultural preservation, tribal sovereignty, and other nation-building goals.

Acknowledgments

This chapter is based on a paper presented at the conference "Working Anthropology in the Twenty-first Century," organized by Les W. Field and Richard G. Fox and held at the Wenner-Gren Foundation for Anthropological Research, New York City, on 19–22 May 2005. My thanks to the conference organizers and participants for their helpful comments and to Wenner-Gren president Leslie Aiello and conference planner Laurie Obbink. I thank the Tule River Tribal Council and its staff, the Tule River Tribal Elders Program, members of the Tule River Tribe, and the Owens Valley Career Development Center Tribal TANF program. My thanks also to members of the University of Southern California Department of Occupational Science and Occupational Therapy who supported and participated in the Tule River Tribal History Project. Special thanks to Les Field and Joanne Rappaport for their helpful comments through many drafts of this chapter.

Notes

1. According to A. L. Kroeber, about fifty Yokuts-speaking tribes, each with its own territory and political organization, occupied the Great Central Valley of California, or the San Joaquin Valley, from present-day Bakersfield to Stockton. The Yokuts were the largest group in precontact California, occupying about one-ninth of the territory of the state and comprising about one-ninth of the aboriginal population. Kroeber's publications concerning the Southern Valley and Foothill Yokuts tribes were based on interviews with members of the Tule River Reservation (Kroeber ms., 1906, 1907a, 1907b, 1925, 1963). His student Anna Hadwick Gayton did fieldwork there (Gayton 1930a, 1930b, 1946, 1948a, 1948b; Gayton and Newman 1940).

2. The project was co-funded by the Tule River Tribal Council and Owens Valley Tribal TANF. Tribal TANF refers to tribally administered funds under the federal-state welfare program Temporary Assistance to Needy Families. Although TANF funds are typically administered by state and county governments, Tribal TANF programs allow Native sovereign nations to exercise control over the delivery of services in culturally appropriate ways. They also support efforts to promote positive cultural identity under the rubric of prevention. The Tule River Tribal History Project was funded as a prevention program.

3. I became associated with the Tule River Tribe in 1972, when the Tribal Council asked for a volunteer to record oral histories with the tribe's elders. I was completing my undergraduate degree and was about to begin graduate studies in anthropology at the University of California at Los Angeles; I responded affirmatively to the anthropology department chair's solicitation of my interest in the volunteer position. In addition to meeting several of the tribe's elders and recording interviews with them, I showed up daily at the tribal office and, with Chairman Alec Garfield's permission, made copies to familiarize myself with the Tribal Council minutes dating back to the 1930s. Consequently, I became interested in compiling archival documents and initiated a trip at my own expense to the National Archives in Washington, DC. To my surprise, the Tribal Council offered to finance my air travel. I retained copies of numerous documents and was never asked to give them to the tribe, which proved a good thing. On the basis of documents brought home from the National Archives, I was later able to provide testimony for the tribe's legal team to present in a Senate hearing to restore the northeast corner of the reservation (Frank 1980). Also, because a fire subsequently destroyed the tribal building and many irreplaceable documents, as I learned in 2002, I was able to supply the Tribal Council with copies of its minutes from 1936 to 1974.

4. "Postcolonialist thinking" is thinking about how to reconstruct cultural identities in the presence of historical ruptures (Young 2001). It gives "equal weight to outward historical circumstances and to the ways in which those circumstances are experienced by postcolonial subjects" (2001: 58). Post-colonialist thinkers consequently call for interventions that question and revise received histories (Smith 1999).

5. Tribal elders in a pretest concerning the history project ($n = 64$) rated the following items almost at the top of a ten-point scale: the importance of preserving tribal history (9.69), the contribution that knowing tribal history makes to pride in Native identity (9.70), and the importance of tribal history in preparing youths to serve as future Tribal Council members (9.50). The ratings remained at the same level in the post-test ($n = 39$) (Frank 2005).

6. Comparison of pre- and post-test survey results were significant at the .05 level concerning tribal elders' belief in the history project's ability to help preserve tribal history (pre, 5.13, post, 8.46); to help tribal members pool information (pre, 5.70, post, 8.23); to help tribal members identify who was related to whom (pre, 6.92, post, 7.71); and to help others to know more about one's family (pre, 5.05, post, 6.26) (Frank 2005).

7. Field (n.d.) mentions his role in producing an event to partake of the one-time staple food abalone, which older members of the tribe remembered nostalgically. The event helped trigger the production and intergenerational

sharing of new narratives about Muwekma Ohlone history and identity as part of ongoing revitalization efforts by the tribe.

8. SfAA has over two thousand members (http://www.sfaa.net). The American Anthropological Association, the largest anthropology organization, has about ten thousand members (http://www.aaanet.org). In contrast, there are about 37,000 occupational therapists in the United States, with only a small elite engaged as researchers in university settings (http://www.aota.org).

9. Sherburne Cook (1976: 351) calculated conservatively that almost 20 percent of the Native population of California was lost in just the first four years of the American invasion, between 1848 and 1852, plummeting from 71,050 to 60,450. By 1880, the Native population stood at 12,500, or a mere 17 percent of what it was in 1848, when the gold rush started.

10. On the relationships between occupational therapy, Pragmatism, and progressive education, see Breines 1986; Schwartz 1992.

11. According to Alexander Lesser (1981), Boas received an education focused on performativity and communitarian values. His mother, a political radical, founded the first Froebel kindergarten in Minden, Germany.

Doing Cultural Anthropology and Disability Studies in Rehabilitation Training and Research Contexts

Pamela Block

My career so far has been one of using anthropology and disability studies to develop innovative approaches to rehabilitation training and research. Because I have always worked outside of traditional academic anthropology, my experiences may be eye-opening to graduate students who will soon plunge into the unknown world of professional employment. Many of them will find themselves, as I did, working in unusual and unexpected contexts.

Educated as a cultural anthropologist at the doctoral level at Duke University, I received postdoctoral training in two interdisciplinary academic research settings: the Department of Disability and Human Development at the University of Illinois, Chicago, and the Center for Alcohol and Addiction Studies at Brown University. These two experiences grounded me in disability studies, rehabilitation research, and competition for large federal and foundation research grants. Though not a clinician, I am at this writing employed as a clinical associate professor in the Occupational Therapy Program, Division of Rehabilitation Science, School of Health Technology and Management at Stony Brook University, part of the State University of New York (SUNY) system.

Using examples from my graduate, postdoctoral, research, teaching, and scholarly experiences, I discuss both frustrations and rewards I have had in negotiating multiple identities and loyalties. I describe the ways in which disability studies research and activism have influenced my professional practice, how my training in cultural anthropology provided theoretical and methodological support for my disability studies research, and the relevance of my experiences to the so-called boundary between applied and basic research. I also provide some practical "life lessons" meant to guide cultural anthropology graduate students and those who mentor them in navigating the treacherous waters following a successful dissertation defense.

In graduate school, my dissertation chair once referred to an anthropologist of the 1970s whom I admired as being "lost to anthropology" because he had been unable to acquire traditional academic employment and was no longer publishing, or at least not in anthropological contexts. I felt sorry for the man, never imagining that a dozen years later I would find myself placed in the same "expatriate" category. I am still in academe, but I do not teach or mentor anthropology students, nor do I usually publish in anthropology venues. Does this mean I am "lost to anthropology" too?

In his 2004 Malinowski Award Lecture, John W. Bennett said that applied anthropology had been defined in three different ways: as "(1) the study of modern society by anthropologists; (2) small-scale assistance measures to benefit local people involved in the stress of change; [and] (3) interdisciplinary or multidisciplinary socio-cultural research" (Bennett 2005). Bennett preferred the third definition, as do I. Yet all three cause me to wonder why stigma is attached to applied anthropology, for would not many, if not most, anthropologists fall under one or more of these definitions? In his speech Bennett suggested that perceptions of applied versus basic research had shifted to such an extent that many cultural anthropology graduate students were choosing topics that might easily have been considered applied anthropology in the past. It is possible to research social movements as a participant observer and to conduct participatory action research or community-university collaborative research yet not be considered an applied anthropologist. Bennett suggested that the term *applied* could and perhaps should be exchanged for "relevant" or "good" anthropology.

If the difference between "applied" and "basic" or "pure" research can no longer be gauged by research topic or even by methodology, then how do some anthropologists come to be designated "applied" professionals and others not? Perhaps the separation between applied and basic research has more to do with where your office is located and who your boss is than with the type of work you actually produce. If I were to get a traditional tenure-track job in an anthropology department, rather than my current position in the Occupational Therapy Program in the School of Health Technology and Management, would I still be considered an applied anthropologist? Would my research be "purer" coming out of a cultural anthropology program than out of an occupational therapy program? Would it be less pure if I worked in government or industry instead of academe? Does the distinction have less to do with research design than with the ultimate destination of the finished product?

In my case, to add to the confusion, disability studies is commonly mistaken in the anthropological world for a category in medical anthropology, a misunderstanding compounded by my location in a rehabilitation sciences division of a health sciences center. In 2000 I sought in vain to get a disability studies panel approved through the cultural anthropology strand of the American Anthropological Association (AAA) for the organization's annual meeting. It seemed an appropriate venue, given that my research focus is the study of disability rights social movements, the disability community, and wider cultural perceptions of disability. The Society for Disability Studies (SDS) defines the field this way: "Disability Studies encourages perspectives that place disability in social, cultural, and political contexts. Through our work we seek to augment understanding of disability in all cultures and historical periods, to promote greater awareness of the experiences of disabled people, and to contribute to social change" (Society for Disability Studies 2004).

Disability studies is an interdisciplinary field that includes scholars from the humanities, such as history and literature, the social sciences, including anthropology, sociology, education, and psychology, and even some of the rehabilitation sciences, such as occupational, physical, and speech therapy. It grew out of the disability rights movement and is formulated in direct contrast to medical and rehabilitation models of disability, which focus on the physiological aspects of disability, the "fixing" of atypical, "broken" physiology, and the normalizing of physical and cognitive capacity. Within disability studies, disability is seen as part of the continuity of the human condition, as part of an identity reliant as much on socio-environmental factors as on physiological factors. This conceptualization is quite different from that of many doctors and rehabilitation professionals, who tend to approach disability as a biomedical problem in need of a solution (Gill 1998, 2001; Kasnitz and Shuttleworth 2001; Kielhofner 2004, 2005; Linton 1998).

The human and civil rights status of persons with disabilities is poorly addressed at the national and international levels. Disabled people constitute the largest minority on the planet, and the only minority that anyone might join at any time. Estimates suggest that 19.7 percent of the general US population, approximately 52.6 million people, have some level of disability and that approximately 33.0 million people (12.3 percent of the population) have a severe disability (McNeil 2001). Yet in March 2005, Terry Schiavo, a woman proclaimed by the medical profession to be no longer human due to lack of brain function, was starved to death (Johnson 2005a). In addition, a movie winning the 2005 Academy Award for best picture represented suicide as the best course of action for a young woman with a spinal cord injury (Johnson 2005b). Discourses surrounding these two events were indicative of the ways in which disabled people are perceived and valued in the United States. With this in mind, it is sometimes a thin line between disability scholarship and disability activism.

Despite the closer similarity of disability studies to cultural than to medical anthropology, I have learned that if I want my papers and panels accepted in anthropological venues, I must stick with the small group of anthropologists who have formed a disability studies ghetto within the medical anthropology strand of AAA. I see this same group of anthropologists on panels for AAA, the Society for Applied Anthropology (SfAA), and SDS.

Graduate Experience

I received my doctorate in cultural anthropology from Duke University in 1997. During graduate school I took no courses in applied or medical anthropology. I received the message, through the dismissive comments of some of my professors, that applied anthropology was atheoretical and potentially aligned with colonialist, imperialist, or other socially regressive imperatives. A memorable course taught by Richard G. Fox, however, titled "Anthropology as Discipline and Profession," provided the context and grounding for my understanding of the intellectual and methodological roots of my eventual form of anthropology. My practice is based on a solid foundation of the socially and politically relevant rural, urban, and world systems approaches to anthropology and sociology coming from New York and Chicago over the past fifty years (Boas 1962; Mintz 1995; Redfield 1947; Wolf 1997). Fox's course provided a context for understanding the historical power struggles within the academy that resulted in the establishment of anthropology as a discipline and profession. This later enabled me to gain perspective on power struggles going on both within the discipline and between anthropology and other disciplines that have adopted anthropological theories (cultural studies) and methodologies (ethnography and "cultural competence" training) while either criticizing or simply excluding anthropology and anthropologists.

Given the strength of the cultural studies program at Duke in the early 1990s, I was keenly aware of what I perceived to be the marginalized status of cultural anthropology on the Duke campus. I learned to expect at least one derogatory remark about cultural anthropology's collusion with colonialism and imperialism at every event sponsored by Duke's cultural studies program. One of my professors told me that a prominent Duke cultural studies professor referred to cultural anthropology as "science fiction." A rumor circulated among the cultural anthropology graduate students that this person had also told the dean that, given the new cultural studies program, there was no longer any need for a cultural anthropology department on campus. Despite such suggestions, the Duke cultural anthropology program is still going strong. I am not sure the same can be said for the cultural studies program.

One year, the cultural anthropologist Michael Taussig came to campus, hosted jointly by the Duke and University of North Carolina cultural studies programs. At the time, Taussig was in self-imposed exile from anthropology and was based in the performance studies program at New York University. His published exchanges with other cultural anthropologists during the late 1980s and early 1990s revealed deep rifts between him and the profession (Taussig 1989; Mintz and Wolf 1989). While visiting Duke, he was scheduled to give an intimate question-and-answer session for cultural studies graduate students. The cultural anthropology graduate students learned of this session only because one of us was doing an independent study with one of the cultural studies professors. She was invited to the session but was discouraged from telling anyone in the cultural anthropology program about it. Fortunately, she decided to spread the word anyway. A small group of cultural anthropology graduate students arrived late, sat at the periphery of the room, and was silent for most of the session, listening while the cultural studies students asked questions. Finally, at the very end, we began asking anthropology-focused questions. Taussig expressed surprise and pleasure to learn that there were anthropology students present at the session and interested in what he had to say.

I gathered the courage to ask my final question out in the hallway as Taussig was led away to his next meeting. I asked him why his work trajectory (up to that point at least) had moved from documenting real political struggles to writing symbolic representations of struggle (Taussig 1980; 1987). He responded with something vague about separating his scholarly work from his (then campus-centered) activist political practice. It never occurred to me that this question might have something to do with applied versus "pure" scholarship. I only knew that I liked the spirit of Taussig's early research in Latin America. I liked his theoretically complex later work as well but was curious about what had inspired the shift. When I went to Brazil to complete my doctoral fieldwork, I observed that my Brazilian anthropologist colleagues combined applied-activist and scholarly endeavors and did not make distinctions or value judgments about doing applied versus pure research. For example, Sergio Carrara, a social anthropologist and director of the Latin American Center on Sexuality and Human Rights, wrote about the history of public health campaigns against syphilis with a comparative eye toward more recent campaigns against AIDS (Carrara 1996).

Life Lesson 1: Do not be confined by externally applied labels and definitions of what is and is not appropriate anthropology.

Postdoctoral Experience

For most of the time since receiving my doctorate, I have been more concerned with getting and keeping some kind of professional academic job than with how I might be defined and labeled within anthropology. Frankly, I found that a newly minted PhD in anthropology was not particularly helpful in putting food on my table. While writing my dissertation, a comparison of the development of disability services in Brazil and the United States, I lived on as little as $500 per month, hoping my car and computer would survive and writing while living in my mother's summer cabin in the woods. Defending my dissertation and receiving my PhD in the spring of 1997, I turned my attention to the job market.

I had no idea how to navigate in that confusing cattle drive. I had no notion of how the job market worked or how to position myself for employment. I had a vague notion that I would get a postdoctoral fellowship or a job (tenure track or visiting) in an anthropology program. Even then, I had the sense that I would prefer to teach disability studies to students in health and human services, but I had no idea how to proceed in this direction. I mailed out dozens of applications for entry-level tenure track or one-year positions in anthropology programs and received dozens of rejection letters. This was hardly an atypical experience for a new PhD in cultural anthropology, where the job market is so competitive that a single tenure-track job posting might generate two hundred applications. However, there were several ways in which I might have strengthened my chances at getting a job.

Life Lesson 2: Graduate students should prepare themselves for the job market and educate themselves about all alternatives available. Programs should assist them in learning how to prepare a curriculum vitae and cover letter and how to present themselves at job interviews. They should practice their job talks and give conference presentations. Mentors should help students make realistic decisions, on the basis of their individual interests and capabilities, about where to focus their attention in job seeking.

I spent the year after receiving my doctorate working in vocational and residential direct-care services for people with developmental disabilities. I made presentations at a few conferences, but that was the extent of my involvement in academe. I was a finalist in a few interdisciplinary fellowship competitions, but ultimately I was without academic job options, and even my attempts to secure an adjunct teaching position were unsuccessful.

I had worked part-time in disability services throughout my graduate career. Given my focus on disability studies, this was a means to supplement my ethnographic knowledge of the disability service system in the United States. In the many jobs I undertook during graduate school and the year following, I gained valuable understanding as a participant-observer of systemic issues faced by persons with disabilities receiving services from nonprofit and for-profit organizations. I observed what it was like for people with disabilities to exist in these systems. Most importantly for the local disability community, my willingness to engage in direct care meant that my theories and methodologies had substance, because I "walked the talk." I also engaged in activism both as a family member (I have a disabled sister) and by advising a self-advocacy group for adults with developmental disabilities. All very well, but none of this was getting me anywhere in academe.

Fortunately, I found a mentor, a cultural anthropologist who had received his PhD seven years prior to mine. He was about to complete a clinical postdoctoral fellowship program at Brown University. This mentor taught me how to write job letters, identify appropriate post-doctoral opportunities outside of traditional anthropology contexts, and write a convincing proposal that would attract the attention of program directors and researchers with postdoctoral positions to fill. I learned that outside of traditional postdoctoral training programs, a multitude of independent researchers exists who see postdoctoral research associates as a cheap and easy way to bypass complex university employment procedures. Being a member of the "invisible academic underclass" was better than unemployment.

Life Lesson 3: Postdoctoral research positions are not difficult to find if the job seeker casts a wide net and is willing to move to where the work is. Postdoctoral employment is an excellent way to get a foot in the door of academe.

Eventually I accepted a position as a postdoctoral research associate at the University of Illinois at Chicago, in the Department of Disability and Human Development. I devoted four days a week to the job of project director for a research project to increase Americans with Disabilities Act implementation in African American and Latino communities. The principal investigators were community psychologists combining Chicago school theory and Latin American applied political research (Balcazar and Keys 1998; Balcazar, Keys, and Suarez-Balcazar 2001; Keys 1987). I felt right at home ideologically and was privileged to be a part of this vital hub of disability studies. With assistance from mentors and coauthors, I developed my theoretical arguments and began to publish my dissertation research (Block 2000; Block, Balcazar, and Keys 2001). Unfortunately, the job was so overwhelming, especially considering my decision to commute every week between Rhode Island and Chicago, that I had little time or energy to pursue my own research and scholarly interests during the one day per week officially designated for this purpose.

Life Lesson 4: Look for programs and mentors who facilitate independent professional development. When working as someone else's employee, personal research interests are subordinated to those of the employer. If the employer is not committed to the postdoctoral associate's professional development, then the associate will eventually need to choose between finding another job with greater opportunities for professional development and giving up his or her personal scholarly aspirations. This is particularly challenging for anthropologists, because postdoctoral employers are usually from other disciplines and may lack an understanding of career development needs specific to anthropology.

After a year in Chicago, I moved back to Rhode Island, where I was accepted into a formal postdoctoral training program at the Center for Alcohol and Addiction Studies (CAAS) at Brown University. Up until that point I had had little interest in addiction research, but the CAAS faculty encouraged me to develop an independent research program in the area of addiction and disability. The other postdoctoral fellows were primarily clinical psychologists, but this program had accepted several anthropologists in the past, and my cohort happened to include not only me, a cultural anthropologist, but also two others, a medical and a physical anthropologist. This meant I had both peer support and a certain level of institutional tolerance for anthropological approaches to scholarship.

I began engaging in ethnographic research with local disability rights organizations and eventually focused on an organization that provided secondary rehabilitation to persons with recent spinal cord injuries (Block et al. 2001). While developing this area of research expertise, I received systematic training in grant writing. CAAS was essentially a complex grant-getting machine. The entire institute was structured to enable investigators to focus on research and grant writing. Mundane concerns were handled by a team of dedicated and helpful support staff, all willing to assist nerve-wracked postdoctoral fellows trying to write their first grant proposals. One person helped me complete the complex paperwork involved in a federal grant submission, another helped me put together the budget for a multiyear, $450,000 grant proposal. I could never have proceeded without this support; the whole process was simply too intimidating.

Yet I was determined to persevere. Funding was my ticket to research autonomy and increased financial security. After getting a small, internally funded research award to cover the costs, I engaged in primarily ethnographic pilot research. One of the stipulations of the award was that I incorporate quantitative components, because federal funding agencies seldom fund purely qualitative research. I grumbled but complied. Midway through the pilot research I received the good news that my federal grant proposal, written in collaboration with local disability rights organizations, had been funded after just a single submission. This was unusually good luck. In most cases, new and even experienced grant writers must revise and resubmit at least once or twice. Suddenly, I was no longer a postdoctoral fellow. I was a research assistant professor, and half my salary was covered by a three-year grant from the federal Department of Education, National Institute on Disability and Rehabilitation Research, to study health promotion and capacity building for people with recent spinal cord injuries and organizations that support them (Block and Rimmer 2000; Block, Skeels, and Keys 2006; Block et al. 2005).

Joining the Faculty

At the time I worked at Brown University, the CAAS had virtually no tenured ("hard" money) faculty. All faculty supported themselves with research ("soft") money, occasionally supplemented by funding connected with administrative duties (both "soft" and "hard"). It was very stressful to depend on grant income to sustain one's academic career. Postdoctoral fellows who failed to get funding, including my two anthropology colleagues, were forced to leave CAAS. They found clinical, faculty, or new postdoctoral positions, went to work as program directors for other, more successful independent researchers, or left academe to work for nonprofit organizations or in industry. A similar fate awaited faculty whose funding had dried up and who had no further grants in sight. I began to set my sights on more secure employment. After teaching anthropology and disability studies at the University of Rhode Island and at Brown as an adjunct, I found that I enjoyed working with older, nontraditional students and premedical and allied health students. I felt more useful positioning myself to influence future service providers and health care professionals than future anthropologists.

One of my mentors at Chicago suggested that I apply for a position in an occupational therapy (OT) program. The American Occupational Therapy Association defines OT as "skilled treatment that helps individuals achieve independence in all facets of their lives. It gives people the 'skills for the job of living' necessary for independent and satisfying lives" (AOTA 2004). Though not congruent, occupational therapy objectives are not necessarily inconsistent with those of disability studies. Additionally, few occupational therapists have doctorates, yet OT programs are being pressured by their national association, and eventually will be required, to hire only doctoral-level faculty.

Over the course of a year, I applied for positions at two universities, was a finalist at the first, and in 2002 was hired at the second—as a clinical associate professor in the Occupational Therapy Program at Stony Brook's School of Health Technology and Management (SHTM). Although I was not hired on a tenure track, it is possible for clinical faculty to seek tenure review and be granted tenure. Thus, I hope to have access to tenure review without the strain of a tenure clock over my head. I have renewable three-year contracts, and my salary is covered by "hard" money from the state. Many people on the clinical track have taught in SHTM for decades. For the first time in my professional life I have job security, or the closest thing to it, without tenure.

Life Lesson 5: When traditional employment avenues seem closed, be a pioneer. Look across disciplines to find frontier areas where jobs are available. Eight years ago, as I competed with hundreds of other applicants for tenure-track anthropology jobs, I was never told that there were academic fields eager to hire PhDs in my area of expertise. I suspect that occupational therapy is not the only field undergoing this sort of transition.

The Occupational Therapy Program at Stony Brook transitioned to a master's level program in the summer of 2001. Though not a methodologist by experience or inclination, my initial focus at Stony Brook was to help design a research sequence for the program's advanced master's-level students. I taught research design and grant writing. When teaching students research design, I creatively managed to incorporate lectures on qualitative research and ethnography from the perspective of cultural anthropology, along with the history of eugenics and Boas's role in fighting eugenics ideologies (Boas 1912, 1916). I mentored faculty and graduate students in the research, human subjects approvals, and grant-writing processes. Fortunately, these tasks were not all-encompassing. I also taught courses on disability studies to advanced OT students, medical students, and undergraduates.

A New World

As a nonclinical academician on a clinical faculty line, I am aware, on many levels, of my "outsider" status in SHTM and the Health Sciences Center. Stony Brook University is divided in half by a heavily trafficked road. On one side of the road sit the traditional academic disciplines in the School of Arts and Sciences, Engineering, and Business. On the other side sit the hospital and the Health Science Center, including the Schools of Medicine, Social Welfare, Nursing, and Health, Technology, and Management. The condition of the roads and parking is such that, despite the short distance between the two sides of the university, many students travel by bus from one side to the other.

One difference between the two sides is aesthetic. West Campus is a typical state university campus with buildings spread across a large wooded area. In contrast, the East Campus Health Sciences Center is attached to a modernist, high-rise medical complex. There are also clear-cut economic and sociocultural differences in the way faculty members from each side experience their employment at the university. My husband is an assistant professor with a typical ten-month, tenure-track appointment in the Department of Political Science. He is not required to be on campus during much of December and January or June through August. In contrast, like the vast majority of other faculty in the Health Sciences Center, I have a twelve-month renewal contract on the clinical track. I am expected to remain on campus for much of the summer unless I am using vacation days.

My husband's department is similar to the environment I experienced in graduate school, with relaxed dress codes and attendance policies. A twelve-month faculty appointment in the Health Sciences Center means filling out time sheets and the expectation of an eight-hour workday. Those not present in the office during a workday are expected to use sick or vacation time to cover the lapse, though in reality a certain amount of flexibility allows for atypical workdays and working from home. In contrast to the relative informality of my graduate school and postdoctoral experiences, I find myself working alongside colleagues in lab coats or formal business attire.

I am expected to fill out annual "behavior monitor forms" for my OT student advisees. These forms, mandated by the American Occupational Therapy Association, are meant to provide students with guidance and preparation for the workplace. Also completed by students' fieldwork supervisors, the forms record students' attendance, dress, and behavior as appropriate to a professional context. If students score poorly on the forms, they will not graduate from the program. Coming from the bohemian context of a nontraditional undergraduate program followed by an anthropology graduate program, I found the idea of holding students to collectively determined but still essentially subjective standards of dress and conduct odd. When I described to my OT colleagues a scholarly context in which a male classmate might wear a skirt and a female classmate might wear a dog collar and leash, they found this equally odd.

I work with allies within SHTM to establish what we call "a culture of research" in what was, until recently, a primarily clinical teaching school. I am encouraged in this endeavor by the school's administration. For both economic and professional reasons, administrative powers from the upper echelons of the Health Sciences Center and clinical professional organizations have mandated that faculty with master's degrees must get their doctorates, and those with doctorates must publish in peer-reviewed journals and seek external funding. Until recently, faculty in SHTM consisted almost entirely of clinicians with master's or bachelor's degrees. The central focus for faculty was teaching, administration, and community service.

Upper-level university officials have practical reasons for wanting a shift to a research focus. With federal research funding come not only "direct" costs, covering the expenses of research and faculty salaries, but also "indirect" costs, an amount that might be more than 50 percent of the direct costs, to cover the university's "operational" research expenses. Universities have come to rely on both indirect and direct research monies to subsidize other scholarly and administrative endeavors and for sheer fiscal survival. According to figures posted on the Stony Brook University Research Foundation website, research revenue for this SUNY campus increased from less than $10 million in 1973 to roughly $34 million in 1983, $85 million in 1993, more than

$141 million in 2003, and over 162.5 million in 2005 (Stony Brook University 2006). The website states: "Total funds managed at Stony Brook last year exceeded $159 million, reflecting activity in some 1,200 projects involving hundreds of investigators and providing jobs for 1,800 individuals."

Not all SHTM faculty members are happy with the increasing pressure to do research, and some have left rather than adapt to the changes. Yet I myself feel empowered, supported, and appreciated in this environment. My dean, division chair, and program chair have all encouraged my efforts to incorporate disability studies into undergraduate and graduate courses. They have also supported my efforts to establish a research program and to publish and present at conferences. Important for me is an acceptance of my child care needs. I have been not just allowed but encouraged to bring my young children to work occasionally. It is not unusual, especially during summers and school holidays, to see children of all ages in the offices and hallways of the school. While my husband's department welcomes an occasional peek at our children, it offers nothing like the level of acceptance or visibility of children that exists in many SHTM programs.

At the same time, I remain aware of my need to keep up with my peers on more traditional academic tracks, as well as those working in more competitive research contexts. In an effort to cross this divide, I initiated and facilitated an interdisciplinary disability studies faculty discussion group from both sides of campus. I developed curriculum for, recruited adjunct faculty for, and taught within a five-course, fourteen-credit disability studies concentration as a part of the SHTM's Bachelor of Science in Health Sciences major (Block 2004). I forged connections with the Center for Latin American and Caribbean Studies with the goal of pursuing international research and exchange opportunities for students and faculty in the area of disability studies. In the fall of 2004 we brought a Brazilian disability studies scholar to campus.

Since joining the faculty at Stony Brook, I have not only engaged in disability studies research and taught disability studies to undergraduates, graduate students, and medical students but have also mentored a small group of adjunct disability studies faculty. Perhaps it is merely the freedom from worrying about where my next paycheck will come from, but I find the balance of these activities quite satisfying. During my first three years at Stony Brook I completed more than a dozen publications, including peer-reviewed articles, book chapters, encyclopedia entries, and a book review, and I edited a special issue of the journal *Sexuality and Disability.*

Research Activities

When I moved to Stony Brook in the fall of 2002, I decided to leave the administration of my grant at Brown. I felt that a community-based project should stay in the local community where the research was being undertaken. I also felt my time would be better spent completing the actual research and developing new projects than by my getting tangled in administrative transfers and bureaucratic nonsense. When I left Brown, my title on the project changed nominally from principal investigator to co-principal investigator, but I retained control over the research project, and the grant continued to cover one-third of my new Stony Brook salary.

During my first two years at Stony Brook, I spent some time developing relationships with local disability rights and service organizations and learning about the local disability community. Eventually, I received funding for two new grants. I was principal investigator (PI) for a one-year pilot investigation to study barriers to recreational and physical activities for adults with multiple sclerosis. I was co-investigator (Co-I), charged with providing the "qualitative component," for a five-year, twenty-site study of the way organizational factors influence drug abuse treatment outcomes. In addition, I was co-principal investigator (Co-PI) for an unfunded pilot research project to study the influence of peer support on quality of life for children and teens with multiple sclerosis. Thus, including my research based at Brown, by the fall of 2005 I had a total of four research projects of varying sizes and at different stages.

These research endeavors involved developing new, community-based collaborations and working with neurology, rehabilitation, and addiction professionals and disability rights organizations. Sometimes my contribution was methodological—for example, directing the "qualitative component" of the data collection and analysis for a larger, primarily quantitative study. Sometimes I developed community-based research with a qualitative focus and then found a quantitative research partner who created a "quantitative component" for my study. When I was not one of the key investigators, negotiation skills were needed to keep the "quality" in qualitative. For my own studies, I relied on my clinical research partners to translate my methodology into language that grant reviewers would find palatable. I have found that some federal and foundation grant reviewers and members of human subjects research institutional review boards (IRBs) are uncomfortable with "messy" qualitative and community-based research. One IRB member wanted to deny approval for human subjects research to one of my projects because anything with an *n* (number of participants) of less than sixty did not, in his eyes, constitute research.

Life Lesson 6: Whenever possible, try to personally attend IRB meetings at which your project is being reviewed.

Having clinical research partners is a benefit but also a learning and negotiating process for all involved. In a draft of a recent National Institutes of Health grant submission, the neuropsychologist PI referred to children with multiple sclerosis as "patients." He explained that although he had been trained to use the word "participants," he had adopted the biomedical terminology used in the clinical context in which he worked. I pointed out to him that the proposal was about improving quality of life through community, that the focus of the grant was nonclinical, and that, moreover, I was not a clinician. With his approval, I changed every "patient" in that proposal to "participant." In the next draft, however, our mentor, the neurologist co-investigator, blithely changed everything back to "patient" again. I immediately called the PI on his cell phone and started a dialogue about the importance of not referring to people with disabilities as "patients," as if they had no other significant identity. It is just this type of medical-model thinking that disability studies scholars seek to critique and change. So patients again became participants and remained so throughout the rest of the submission process.

A program officer for a foundation to which I recently applied for a large research grant discouraged me from using a community-based research design for this stage of my research. He contended that multiple sclerosis support groups were so different from one another that it would be impossible to measure the efficacy of the intervention model in such non-uniform, community-based contexts. I tried to explain that intervention models developed and implemented in the community were far more likely to be disseminated, adopted, and successfully applied than interventions run in artificially uniform research settings (which, of course, are not truly uniform anyway), but he was unconvinced. I decided that for this submission I would focus on the research innovation of incorporating socio-environmental factors. I suspected this was about as far as grant reviewers for this foundation, which primarily funded medical, psychological, and pharmaceutical research, would be willing to travel, at least for the time being. A future grant submission, perhaps to a funding agency more open to community-based research, would focus on implementing the research design in community-based settings.

Life Lesson 7: Strategies to get qualitative research funded by federal and other agencies that favor quantitative and clinical studies include (1) developing a "qualitative component" to a more traditional quantitative research design, (2) collaborating with a quantitative researcher who can serve as translator or mediator for skeptical grant reviewers, and (3) recognizing the limitations in vision, scope, and financial resources of different funding sources and learning how to structure and time proposal submissions accordingly.

Conclusion

Disability studies research and activism influence my professional practice on several levels. In addition to typical scholarly activities—research and publishing in my chosen area of expertise—I view my position, teaching in the health science context, as an opportunity to educate future health care professionals and disability service providers about disability studies approaches. In the context of curriculum development, research activities, and other scholarly interactions, I seek to educate practicing clinicians and my faculty colleagues.

It is sometimes challenging, however, to remain true to my theoretical and methodological roots. When working almost exclusively with non-anthropologists, it is easy to get diverted onto other tracks, especially when it is so much more difficult to develop large research studies and acquire significant funding when insisting on using qualitative and community-based research designs. I do not always get what I want, at least not as quickly as I would like. Yet I think this is another level at which education is needed. Biomedically minded funding agencies are slowly becoming more open to "nontraditional" methodologies such as qualitative, participatory action, and community-based research designs.

As for the relevance of my experiences to the so-called boundary between applied and basic research, I have to agree with Bennett (2005) that this boundary seems to shift conveniently whenever we need it to do so. Throughout my years of graduate school I was explicit about my intention to combine activism with scholarship. I studied social movements and eventually settled upon the disability rights movement and the study of cultural perceptions of disability as my primary focus. If it had been easier to get a traditional tenure-track position in a department of anthropology, my subsequent scholarship would undoubtedly have been different, but not necessarily better or more relevant than the work I do now. Despite the struggle to remain afloat in academe without much in the way of support from my own profession,

I have been pushed to test boundaries and overcome barriers that I might never have attempted if I had remained safe within anthropology's cloister.

For me, it comes down to deciding on the intended audiences for my scholarship. In a room full of anthropologists, even if few are familiar with disability studies, I feel as if I am preaching to the choir. Certainly, I would like to see disability research valued as a project integral to anthropology, in the same way gender, ethnicity, and sexuality are recognized as areas of study inherently linked to the discipline. Yet if my goal is to practice my anthropology to influence the way people with disabilities are perceived and treated nationally and internationally, then it makes sense to position myself within a health sciences and health policy context such as the School of Health, Technology, and Management. In addition, I like the feeling of being on the academic frontier, on the border between health care services and scholarship. Does this mean I am lost to anthropology? Perhaps I am a prodigal daughter and, like Taussig, will someday return to the fold. Only time (and tenure) will tell.

Acknowledgments

Valuable comments on earlier drafts of this chapter were provided by several colleagues, including Nina Slota, Lisa Benz-Scott, Elizabeth Vanner, William MacAllister, Christopher Keys, and Fern Lebo.

In Praise of "Reckless Minds"

Making a Case for Activist Anthropology

Charles R. Hale

In January 1971 a group of eleven intellectuals—mainly Latin Americans, and none indigenous—met in Barbados to discuss the relationship between anthropology and a topic that had just begun to emerge in national political debates, "indigenous liberation." The declaration that resulted from that meeting, which would later become famous, included the following exhortation regarding "the responsibility of anthropology": "The anthropology now required in Latin America is not that which relates to Indians as objects of study, but rather that which perceives the colonial situation and commits itself to the struggle for liberation. In this context we see anthropology providing the colonized people with the data and interpretations about both themselves and their colonizers useful for their own fight for freedom" (Declaration of Barbados 1971).

This simple but potent statement raises a series of slightly uncomfortable questions for the discipline some thirty years later.[1] Especially after the thorough-going critiques of the 1970s and 1980s, why does support for this type of politically engaged anthropology remain so anemic in the United States? Are there forces intrinsic to the discipline that systematically derail transformation along these lines, even amid near-unanimous expressions of solidarity with the "subaltern"? Or should the explanation focus on the overheated, faintly paternalistic imagery of "Indian liberation" that the Barbados anthropologists deployed? Under what conditions might a new anthropological practice, transformed in the spirit of the Barbados declaration, become institutionalized and legitimated in US graduate training programs, in mainstream agendas for research funding, and in dominant understandings of our discipline?

My answers to these questions comprise four arguments. First, I contend that conditions have never before been so propitious for the institutionalized practice of collaborative and politically engaged scholarship, a method I refer to as activist anthropology. The demand is robust, both from students at the start of their careers and from their future research subjects; critiques from within the discipline have opened ample supportive space; there are strong currents of funding that favor activist research; and broader forces of cultural-political change in the United States, reactionary as they may be, have generated unintended opportunities for activist anthropology. Second, I examine an improbable obstacle to progress along these lines: the rise of cultural critique, a set of theoretical and methodological commitments in anthropology that are generally (and correctly) associated with the conceptual ground-clearing that strengthens the rationale for activist research. Third, I contend that arguments in support of activist research have often been misplaced, resting on ethical imperatives ("We should do this because it is an ethically high-minded way to practice anthropology") and on the usefulness of the resulting knowledge ("The research outcomes have produced this desired practical or political effect"). Although both rationales are important, I have come to believe that in our dialogues within the academy, our primary and most convincing arguments for activist anthropology are its basic methodological and epistemological advantages. I illustrate this point with brief reference to the activist research project in which I am engaged at the time of writing, which is focused on black and indigenous land rights in Central America.[2] In a final section of the essay I explore the possible epistemological advantages of activist anthropology, the most ambitious and, I believe, most compelling argument for doing this kind of research.

My principal conclusion is that the relationship between would-be activist anthropologists and indigenous movements is profoundly contradictory and tension-ridden. It is likely to remain that way. This does not mean that the relationship is fruitless—much to the contrary. It does mean that the rewards accrue in the midst of these tensions. A relatively unexplored explanation for the halting progress toward the institutionalization of activist anthropology in the United States is that we have sought and imagined a relationship of neat convergence between anthropologists and our allies. When contradictions have arisen, they have been cause for disillusionment, frustration, and even abandonment of the effort. Alternatively, I contend that activist anthropology yields better research outcomes precisely *because* its practitioners are obliged to live and engage these contradictions to a greater extent than are those who practice conventional research methods. Far from being deterrents, the tensions need to be understood as key sources of methodological sophistication and analytical insight. The challenge, in sum, is to portray activist anthropology with a greater measure of self-reflection and acknowledged limits than the Barbados anthropologists were able to muster, while at the same time affirming their political vision, energy, and commitment.

Activist Anthropology: A Brief Account

My intention in this section is not to create a definition or to set limits but rather to frame the discussion that follows.[3] In the phrase "activist anthropology," *activist* is an adjective. To me, the word conveys an intention to modify anthropology, to transform the conventional practice in methodological terms. The phrase does not imply that the activist anthropologist becomes an activist—to the contrary, there remains a clear distinction between the two, which is the source of constant productive tension. By the same token, because *activist* is an adjective, the phrase should not be taken to delimit the subject of research—that is, it should not raise the common misconception that activist anthropology is focused exclusively on activists, social movements, people in political struggle. The transformed method must be broad and flexible enough to encompass research on the World Bank or the Mexican state, as well as social movements that contest such powerful institutions. Activist anthropology draws extensively on the cumulative conventional wisdom of our discipline but reorients research practice around a different answer to the basic question, "knowledge for whom?"

Specifically, the practice of activist anthropology involves a basic decision to align oneself with an organized group in a struggle for rights, redress, and empowerment and a commitment to produce knowledge in collaboration and dialogue with the members of that group. In some cases, this alignment is relatively straightforward and unambiguous—for example, one might conduct research in conjunction with an indigenous organization in support of its claims for rights to land and resources. In other cases, the alignment is less direct, more general. For example, I just completed a study of middle-class ladinos, the dominant culture group in Guatemala, focusing on their identity and responses to the ascendancy of the Maya indigenous rights movement (Hale

2006b). The study was conceived through dialogue with Maya activist-intellectuals—indeed, they suggested the topic—but for obvious reasons I maintained a certain distance from them in the everyday conditions of fieldwork. The specific conditions under which the alignment takes place will vary widely. But in all cases, this alignment constitutes a modest attempt to answer the "knowledge for whom?" question in ways that honor and affirm our broader ethical-political commitments in the world.

At the same time, these commitments generate further methodological transformations in each phase of the research process. Establishing an alignment in this way is never as simple an act as it sounds. An organized group in struggle—be it a community, an organization, a movement, or a people—never has the transparency that the phrase "organized group" implies. There are always factions, power disputes, and internal hierarchies, both long-term (e.g., along gender lines) and conjunctural (e.g., between one subgroup that favors militant tactics and another that is more moderate). These require analysis, understanding, and reasoned assessment as part of the very process of alignment.

Once this has been achieved, the researcher has a collective interlocutor (his or her "allies") and a context for dialogue and collaboration, from start to finish. This dialogue yields a refinement of the research topic, a process that is especially challenging to conventional notions of the way research agendas emerge. The point is not to completely disregard the voice of the "scientific community," the cumulative wisdom of university-based theory and methods, but rather to bring that wisdom to the table in dialogue with the particular needs and interests of one's allies, subjecting the two to mutual scrutiny. There is no realistic expectation that this dialogue will yield a perfect fit. The allies will have needs and interests that the research cannot meet, and the researcher—given her training and the particulars of her social position—will have objectives that the allies will not recognize as their own. Instead of a perfect fit, the desired outcome is substantial overlap and the absence of outright conflict. Specifically, they will have worked together to conceive a topic that both view as important, or a research agenda that encompasses this topic while granting a certain autonomous space to the research process.

Transformations of the subsequent phases of research follow the same basic pattern. Activist research methods create conditions for the enthusiastic participation of the allies in data collection, given that they have already acknowledged the value of the research topic and, ideally, see the research as being carried out by and for them. In many cases this participation can open onto a greater emphasis on training in research methods and shared responsibility for data collection, which helps move the research process away from the mysterious realm of expert knowledge and toward more collective and democratic principles. The same goes for data processing and preliminary analyses of results. It is not only an ethical responsibility to make this phase participatory; it also becomes a methodological mandate. People who have played key roles in formulating the topic and collecting the data typically have an enormous amount to contribute in thinking through what has been learned.

Finally, activist research opens a series of broadened mandates and creative possibilities for the design and dissemination of the finished products. It entails an assumed responsibility to make at least some of these products widely accessible and useful to the allies, which means adopting formats other than the standard academic monograph. The very process of addressing this need, in turn, may well influence thinking about the design of the product destined for the academic audience. The point here is not to suppress one design in favor of another but to recognize their distinct purposes, to encourage both (or many), and to encourage mutual influence between them.

Activist Anthropology Comes Home

Since the early 1970s, the political sensibilities of the discipline have moved steadily toward an alignment with the principles that the Barbados anthropologists championed. Such alignments can of course be traced back further, to the antiracism of Boas and Benedict and to antecedent alignments with feminist struggles, with poor, marginalized, and working people, and with people of color. Still, it is certainly safe to characterize North American anthropology, before the cultural and political upheaval of the 1960s, as a bastion of intellectual elitism in which alignment with subaltern peoples was conditioned by a more or less explicit assertion of distance and, at best, paternalist concern. With regard to the study of indigenous Latin America, for example, anthropologists typically combined a distant lament for the destruction of indigenous cultures with a nod to the inevitability of mestizo ascendancy, which often led to ambivalent support for various forms of "salvage" anthropology.

Without going into a detailed analysis of the well-known forces of change, I can note the remarkable contrast some thirty years later. At least judging from the graduate school applications I read every year, it is almost inconceivable that one would choose to study anthropology today without an explicit, if diffuse, sense of solidarity with subaltern peoples and a critique of the dominant forces with which these peoples contend. Such solidarity, in turn, is an essential precursor to the alignment that activist research entails.

Not only have these particular political sensibilities gained prominence, but theoretical developments have reinforced and provided sophisticated rationales for these alignments. The theoretical move, often associated with the postmodern turn but in fact more general and widely affirmed, is to re-present research as an intersubjective process, a complex relationship among differently positioned actors. Whether taken in the direction of critique of ethnographic authority, of feminist standpoint theory, of critical race theory, of radical deconstruction of signification, or even of a moderate extension of Weberian interpretive analysis, this basic move produces a need for precisely the kind of scrutiny that activist anthropology provides.[4]

Although explicit political alignment with research subjects is not the only way to respond to this challenge, it figures prominently among the alternatives. Feminist scholars such as Donna Haraway (1988) and later the "post-positivist realists" such as Paula Moya (Moya and Hames-Garcia 2000) have argued that such alignment can yield special analytical insights and even greater objectivity (of a certain sort), but this step is not necessary for the basic point to apply. Through a general convergence of these diverse currents, it has become standard, indeed almost required, for anthropologists to engage in sustained reflection on this problem: how to ethically justify, analytically represent, and logistically manage the stark inequalities between researcher and subject. Especially when the subjects are alive (as opposed to historical), generally subordinated, and organized to contest subordination, at least a gesture toward activist anthropology's basic principle of alignment inevitably follows.

A third factor favoring some form of activist anthropology involves institutional, career, and life cycles. I admit that my thinking on this point is impressionistic, based largely on my own experiences rather than on broader investigation. But it seems to me that two related processes are at play. First, scholars of my generation (dissertations completed between the late 1980s and the mid-1990s), who were trained in the wake of the successive calls to transform anthropology, are now reaching mid-career and beginning to wield modest influence in decisions regarding training, funding, and program development. At the University of Texas, where, as I write, we are about to hold our third annual "Activist Scholarship" conference, the core group of organizers and supporters includes a number of faculty members at this career stage, with small budgets to draw on and an ability to place a certain institutional authority behind the effort.[5] The same goes, on a smaller scale, for the "activist anthropology" track at the University of Texas. Amid considerable diversity in positions on the specifics—its definition, practice, implications for the discipline, and so forth—it receives general support and little voiced opposition (at least on conceptual or political grounds). I know of strong clusters of faculty with interests along these lines in other major universities, such as Cornell University and the Universities of North Carolina, New Mexico, California at Berkeley, and Toronto.[6]

The second process is demand from students, surely in response, at least in part, to the dire and increasingly polarized political conditions of the United States at early twenty-first century. With little publicity beyond a website, no special funding, and a still incipient administrative structure, the activist anthropology track at the University of Texas receives a constant flow of inquiries, some thirty applications a year, and strong interest in the program from students. My sense, formed through fielding inquiries and reviewing applications, is that the track's central message has great resonance: you do not have to choose between your ethical-political commitments and rigorous, high-level anthropological training; the two can complement each other. In short, a strong demand exists that "we" (a community in the early stages of imagining) are increasingly in a position to meet.

The fourth and final factor opening up space for activist anthropology is counterintuitive and risky but for that reason all the more important to analyze. Especially in pubic universities, we face a rising tide of what Marilyn Strathern (2000) called "audit cultures," a political and ideological transformation associated with neoliberal capitalism. The pressures associated with audit cultures are in many ways decidedly pernicious: the call for practical results at every turn, the application of cost-benefit analysis to determine the allocation of scarce resources, the implementation of stringent measures of accountability—all of which smuggle in highly politicized, market-oriented values disguised in the technocratic language of efficiency, accountability, and hard choices amid scarce resources. As the essays in the Strathern volume make clear, this transformation involves an outward extension into higher education of the same basic principles that have been honed in the private sector and in institutions such as the International Monetary Fund and the World Bank, the bastions of neoliberal capitalism. Yet as we are learning about neoliberalism in general, audit cultures are not seamless; they have openings and contradictions that may be used in unexpected ways.[7]

Two brief examples of these openings, within the general rise of audit cultures in the university, will have to suffice. First, nearly every university in the country has a "service learning" program of some type, often conceived in keeping with neoliberal precepts: recognition without resources, involvement with a depoliticized civil society that takes up the slack left by a downsized state, and no direct challenge to the order of things. Yet rhetorically speaking, service learning has striking similarities to activist research. It opens possibilities for, and has no easy means to exclude, the alternative definition that activist research puts forth.

A second example is audit culture's demand for practical results. The standard response to this demand from progressive academics is to expose its concealed premises of neoliberal governance and to oppose it frontally. Activist anthropology suggests a different tack: diversify the standard understanding of results, asking simply that social justice– oriented evaluative criteria be affirmed alongside market-oriented ones. This approach is far from risk free and could be viewed as compromised. But especially given the broader correlation of forces in today's world, there is much to be said for a carefully conceived struggle from within—a Gramscian emphasis on position rather than maneuver, on negotiation rather than frontal attack.

Internally Generated Difficulties

Let me concede from the outset that in general terms, the most daunting barriers to the advancement of activist anthropology continue to be the gatekeepers within our profession and in the upper echelons of university administrations. It remains fairly easy to discredit a given scholar's research, especially in interdisciplinary university committees, with the observation by a well-placed committee member that the person has become "politicized" and therefore lacks "objectivity." Similarly, as a recent exchange in *Anthropology Newsletter* makes clear, the basic activist anthropology principle of formulating the research topic in dialogue with the research subjects can be derided by gatekeepers of an important funding source as dumbed-down "social work" rather than rigorous science.[8] My sense, however, is that these objections are fairly easily neutralized by the assertion, invoking one of a number of well-established theoretical currents mentioned earlier, that research can be both socially positioned or aligned and unassailably rigorous. The objections tend to carry the day when scholarly rigor (in the "post-positivist" or "situated" sense of the phrase) cannot be adequately defended or when the political forces lined up against the scholar in question are too strong to be counteracted.

The largely unexplored explanation for the anemic institutional advancement of activist anthropology that I posit here is the rise of cultural critique. One reason this explanation has remained unexplored is that in many ways, proponents of cultural critique and of activist research are closely aligned. My ultimate intention is to strengthen this alliance and to affirm the possibilities for creatively combining the two. But this is best accomplished, I am now convinced, by first emphasizing our differences, which at the end of the day are mainly methodological.

Cultural critics pose no objection to the option for alignment with an organized group in struggle. They do not object to the ethical-political principles involved in this choice, nor do they question the goal of generating knowledge useful to that struggle. All this is affirmed. Rather, the objection to activist anthropology is more basic. Cultural critique clears ground for thinking about the world in more expansive and potentially emancipatory ways, the argument goes, whereas activist anthropology, constrained by specific political alignments, undermines complexity and truncates theoretical innovation. The relative absence of contradiction in our portrayal of activist anthropology, ironically, becomes evidence that political fervor has gotten the best of analytical sophistication.[9]

For the purposes of this essay, my portrayal of cultural critique will have to remain general and unelaborated.[10] From the time when the phrase was coined in the mid-1980s, it has come to serve as a gradually expanding big tent, encompassing a wide range of theoretical affinities and textual practices. There are variants of cultural critique aligned with materialist and political economic analysis and others focused specifically on discourse, texts, and forms of expressive culture. The variation is equally great in the writing and expository strategies that cultural critique has spawned, from highly experimental moves to decenter the researcher's authority and give space for subjects' voices to more conventional efforts to combine self-reflectivity with an emphasis on the ethnographic. In places where cultural critique has arisen and developed in close interaction with cultural studies, the boundaries have become even looser and more porous, encompassing the early, politicized interventions of the Birmingham school, initiatives to support and legitimate alternative knowledges, and efforts to decolonize the academy by creating bridges between community- and university-based intellectuals. Indeed, in this most capacious reading, the distinction I have drawn between activist research and cultural critique fades almost completely.

I defend the distinction nonetheless, on the grounds that the center of gravity of cultural critique still makes for an important contrast. That center has four key features. The first is a strong ethical-political orientation toward alignment with subordinate groups and an inclination to produce knowledge that embodies this alignment. Second, a signature analytical contribution of cultural critique is to deconstruct the institutions, knowledge systems, cultural premises, and so forth, that uphold these relations of inequality and dominance. The third is an acute awareness of the power relations built into the research process and a commitment to confronting these inequities explicitly, rather than ignoring or suppressing them. The fourth feature is the contention that we can best confront these inequities through transformations in the text, rather than in research methods: writing reflexively, employing alternative techniques for representing subjects, and, ultimately, producing knowledge that critically probes the cultural precepts of all facets of the process under study.

This fourth feature points to the crux of the divergence. Cultural critics raise questions, contest premature closures, open new interpretive terrain, and plumb contradictions. These interventions at the level of knowledge categories and theoretical frames become cultural critics' principal political contributions; they steer clear of further involvement with research subjects that might transform the way knowledge is produced. They argue, implicitly at least, that direct political alignment yields preordained story lines that support one's allies at the expense of critical engagement.

Framed in this way, the contrast between cultural critique and activist anthropology brings the role of contradiction in the research process to the fore. When activist anthropologists write contradictory elements out of their accounts, in either methodological or ethnographic terms, they inadvertently substantiate the idea that cultural critique generates political analysis of greater complexity, sensitivity, and insight. A persuasive counterpoint can be found in the handful of portrayals of activist research, especially in the genre of reflections on past experiences, that do emphasize tensions and contradictions.[11]

Still, I have been struck by how common it is to find portrayals of activist research in line with the work of Orlando Fals Borda, Miles

Horton, and Paolo Freire, who have advanced path-breaking critiques of elite-oriented knowledge production systems and inspired ample followings but have ultimately conveyed a neat correspondence between researcher and subject, once the hegemonic blinders have been cast aside.[12] Methodological treatises such as that by Davydd Greenwood and Morten Levin (1998) avoid this "felicitous convergence" fallacy, introduce great methodological complexity, and generally deserve greater attention than they have received in anthropology. Both genres, however, tend to lack an appreciation for irony, unintended consequences, and ethnographic disruption of politically structured narratives, precisely the elements on which cultural critique tends to thrive. Using as an example the work in which I am involved in black and indigenous land rights, I briefly explore an approach to activist research that highlights these contradictions.

Mapping Black and Indigenous Land Claims: Contradictions at Every Turn

Since 1998 I have been involved in a series of activist research projects designed to document and analyze claims to land and resources advanced by indigenous and Afro-Latin communities of Central America's Caribbean coastal region. The first two of these projects, although carried out largely in keeping with the principles of activist research outlined here, came with the burden of funding from the World Bank. Elsewhere I have written about the specific contradictions and tensions that arise in such attempts to wage "struggle from within."[13]

By contrast, the participatory mapping project in which I am engaged at the time of writing has been supported by the Ford Foundation (Mexico Office) under conditions that have allowed me and Edmund T. Gordon, the co-principal investigator for the project, a relatively free hand in design and implementation. The funds were received by the Central American and Caribbean Research Council (CCARC), a nongovernmental organization founded by Gordon and me that is devoted to activist research, and are administered by a steering committee consisting of four activist intellectuals from Central America and four US-based scholars.[14] The steering committee selected four sites for the project's implementation, and we are dispensing funds for research in support of indigenous or black community struggles for land rights in each site. During the summer and fall of 2005, Gordon and I directed the research for one of these sites, which involved a territorial claim advanced by fifteen Garífuna communities and the Organización

Fraternal de Negros de Honduras, or OFRANEH, the organization that represents them. The study, carried out by a collaborative team of US-based and Garífuna researchers, had an interdisciplinary scope, including computer-based cartography, ethnography, and legal history.[15]

Although this project had all the makings of an ideal activist research project, it also had its share of problems. The advantages are easy to enumerate. A strong grassroots organization requested and participated actively in the research conception and implementation, giving the project a stamp of legitimacy from the start. Community leaders had their own deep investments in the research, seeing it as having the potential to contribute directly to their high-stakes struggle for control over their resources. Participation in the research activities by well-known Garífuna intellectuals helped create bridges of fluid communication (including use of the native language) and confidence between the research team and the subjects. Finally, because they conceived of the research process as part of their broader effort to advance and secure a territorial claim, community leaders played an attentive role in validating the research results. These four features—organized endorsement, community participation, local collaboration, and collective validation—might be posited as pillars of this sort of activist research, together yielding its principal methodological advantage.

At the same time, the process was rife with tensions and contradictions. Leaving aside the more mundane logistical and organizational problems that always arise in collaborative research endeavors, I have identified five contradictions, presented here as questions or quandaries, each deeply embedded in the activist research method itself:

1. The research was predicated on a close alliance with OFRANEH, which represented the Garífuna communities. How comprehensive and uncontested was that representation?
2. The research yielded sensitive data, which if publicly aired at the wrong moment could have damaged the embattled political effort. How should such data be handled?
3. The research generally validated the territorial claim, but certain findings stood in tension with OFRANEH's overall political strategy. How should such tensions be mediated?
4. This political strategy quite likely would have been best served by research viewed as having unimpeachable scientific rigor. Yet one pillar of activist research is the direct involvement of the interested parties. Can both goals be achieved?

5. The study placed the researchers in a position of power in relation to the organizing effort. How can this sort of unwelcome power be reconciled with activist anthropology's egalitarian principles?

With a list of quandaries this weighty, even when the activist research project was designed with careful methodological and theoretical forethought, one might well think twice before embarking on such an endeavor. Counterintuitively, I contend that these are quandaries no scholar of Central American cultural politics, or of parallel topics in other places, should want to be without. To be sure, the particular approach to activist research described here would not be appropriate for all topics at all times. There must be room for a plurality of approaches and for flexibility in their application, depending on circumstances. Moreover, not all these quandaries have satisfying responses that are appropriately aired in academic venues such as this book, especially when the research is still under way. For example, this is not the time or place to scrutinize OFRANEH's legitimacy with the community, and for the time being, any data that could reasonably be thought damaging to the organizing effort will not see the light of day. I can only affirm that the research team discussed both issues extensively and that the study was generally informed by these discussions, even if the details are omitted in public writing.

Whereas conventional research methods regularly generate sensitive data and ethical dilemmas over how to handle it, the situation is different in activist research for two reasons. First, because the research agenda is collectively established, the researcher will gain a much greater degree of access and insight into the inner workings of the organization, and second, the dialogue prior to the establishment of this research agenda will, almost by necessity, result in some ground rules for the handling of sensitive data. In short, activist research methods oblige us to confront these dilemmas head on, together with the people with whom we are in collaboration. The same goes for the last three quandaries: activist research brings these questions to the fore, even if reportage on the deliberations that follow must at times be partial. The wager is that even with these constraints, such deliberations will enrich the research immensely.

The third quandary, concerning tensions between the political process and the research findings, opens onto examples of the way activist research methods can provide an added measure of analytical depth and sophistication. In our land rights mapping research, one such tension revolved around the political drive for collective solutions for land rights claims versus the established practices of individual and market-oriented resource use. Since the movement leaders were deeply committed to making the collective approach viable, they were especially interested in documenting and understanding individualist aberrations; whole meetings were devoted to exploring the rationale and magnitude of individual land transactions, in order to promote the alternative more effectively. Another tension was focused on OFRANEH's emphasis on Garífuna indigeneity as a rationale for territorial claims, juxtaposed with another strand of cultural-political sensibility in the same Garífuna communities associated with what scholars have called "black modernity."[16] The mapping project brought this juxtaposition to the fore and subjected it to sustained analysis, because it was so crucial to the overall political strategy. Both issues are crucial to any thorough analysis of Garífuna land rights and identity politics; both would surely come up in a study using conventional research methods. Activist research methods assign them greater importance, which in turn offers a reasonable guarantee that the resulting analytical insight will be deeper and more sophisticated.

The fourth quandary, regarding the role of scientific rigor in anthropological research, also receives special attention in activist research methods. Thinking through this quandary obliges us to carefully disaggregate the distinct meanings of "scientific rigor," which often are presented as inextricable strands of a single knot. On the one hand is the claim to disinterested, neutral, objective social inquiry, which has been the subject of so much critique in contemporary social theory and which the idea of activist research plainly rejects. On the other hand is what might be called methodological propriety: careful adherence to established rules for collecting and interpreting research data. Activist researchers must be firmly committed to the latter—perhaps even more committed than conventional scholars, because the direct political stakes of their work tend to be higher. This commitment inevitably introduces tensions, grounded in the different perspectives and positionings of researchers and activist-intellectuals. The wager of activist research is that these tensions are more likely to be mediated successfully, precisely because the activist scholar has rejected the first strand of established notions of scientific rigor (distanced neutrality) and has an established relationship of mutual confidence with the protagonists.

An example from our land rights mapping project again helps to make this point more concretely. During the marathon meeting with community leaders held to scrutinize the preliminary results of our mapping research, one principal OFRANEH leader made a forceful initial intervention. She did not believe in objective research, she said; in the past, science had been used mainly to the detriment of Garífuna people, in defense of the powerful. Anthropologists had played the role of *antropófagos* (literally, cannibals, who suck you dry and give nothing back). Although she did see our study as an exception to the *antropófago* rule (indeed, she had participated fully in its design), this did not completely lay the science question to rest. She insisted, with our hearty consent, that Garífuna researchers play a central role in the study and that the research must, at each juncture, be oriented toward the broader needs of the Garífuna people. Yet during that "validation" meeting she also acknowledged that the powerful institutions OFRANEH confronted daily were deeply invested in the idea of scientific rigor, understood as both detached, objective inquiry and methodological propriety. That acknowledgment led to a long discussion about how to write up the results and to an eventual decision that the research would yield two complementary documents: one with CCARC as principal author, emphasizing the deployment of expert knowledge in accordance with the rules of methodological propriety, and the other with OFRANEH as principal author, highlighting the political objectives of the study.

This was far from an ideal solution: it could be seen by some as a capitulation to oppressive definitions of science and by others as a corruption of scientific rigor. Yet it had a strong rationale in the political exigencies of the Garífuna struggle, and it offers a window onto one of the most challenging epistemological questions of our time. How do we disentangle our critique of science as serving elite and oppressive interests from our deep, ongoing responsibility for methodological propriety? How should principles of methodological propriety be conceived and practiced in the context of "situated" objectivity? Activist research offers no easy answers, just a guarantee that the question will be posed, under conditions propitious to moving the discussion forward.

This wager seems especially well founded in the case of the final quandary, regarding the unwelcome power that activist research methods can bestow. A lot rode on the results of our ethno-mapping study, which had the potential to become a primary point of reference in the legal-political battles that were sure to follow. This imbued the research process and findings with high-stakes political significance, something that in turn risked giving the researchers undue power and influence. But what do conventional research methods offer as remedies for this problem? One response would be to sidestep it altogether, making sure the research topic and writing style are esoteric enough that any results will be largely irrelevant to the political stakes at hand. A second response would be to tell all, accepting the role of powerful interlocutor, and avoid future contact with those involved in the organizing effort, who might demand accountability. Although both paths are relatively common in anthropology today, neither is satisfying; both disengage through a retreat into academic parochialism.

Activist research, by contrast, with no pretense of resolving the problem, keeps the research subjects' demand for accountability at the center of the scholarly agenda and establishes a relationship with a reasonable chance of sustaining the negotiations that follow. However uncertain the outcome of such negotiations, it is clear that some effort along these lines is the only way to confront this quandary. Indeed, once the conventional researcher rejects the opposite responses of esotericism and exposé and moves toward a middle ground, the activist research principle of negotiating accountability with the subjects of research becomes the only credible way to proceed.

To summarize, when we downplay difficulties such as the five I have listed and briefly analyzed, we inadvertently undermine one of the strongest arguments for our distinctive research methods. The reasons that one might downplay the tensions are clear: the case for activist research appears more compelling when we emphasize its positive and synergistic advantages. This reasoning, in turn, tends to lead to a defense of activist research around the ethical-political imperative and around the work's practical-political contributions. I do not wish to discount either of these factors in the least. They were central motivations for my own decision to embrace activist anthropology some two decades ago, and they have kept me committed to the endeavor. In a previous moment they might have played a prominent role in my efforts to explain and justify these choices: reference to the critical importance and urgency of black and indigenous struggles for land rights in Central America, for example, and to the key contribution that well-trained anthropologists can make to these struggles.

I now believe these are not the appropriate arguments—or at least lead arguments—to be made in dialogue with our university-based interlocutors. Ethical-political appeals (especially regarding faraway peoples) are not especially persuasive in this milieu. They also have the potential to leave the listener feeling uncomfortable or judged, and they inevitably reinforce the perception that one has traded scholarly objectives for commitment to the cause. "Practical effects" arguments play differently, but with equally problematic results. They may have a residual appeal to administrators' cost-benefit sensibilities, and if the results are dramatic they will be impressive and interesting to all.

But more commonly, the complex balance sheet of advances, setbacks, new problems, and unintended consequences will deaden the dialogue, convincing our university-based colleagues that we have "gone applied." Especially if the ultimate goal is to challenge and dislodge the applied-theoretical binary, the practical-effects argument falls short. It leads activist anthropologists to turn inward, defending what they do in terms that—at least for the foreseeable future—will keep them fighting the good fight from the margins.

In Praise of Reckless Minds

This "from the margins" position is not inevitable. Especially by detailing contradictions to the full extent that political conditions allow, activist research methods can yield sophisticated understandings of social processes that conventional methods cannot provide. This is because most activist anthropology projects engender collaborative and confidence-laden relationships between researcher and subject. Even more basically, they require the researcher to be present, as an active participant, in contexts from which he or she otherwise would likely be barred. The more politicized the process in question, the greater the potential gap between activist and conventional anthropologist, in access, insight, and understanding.

Yet this argument for the advantages of activist research needs to be pushed further still, to encompass unique opportunities to rethink received theoretical understandings and even epistemology. My cautious hypotheses along these lines are also provoked by the counterarguments of scholars such as Mark Lilla (2001), who asked why intellectuals, when they meddle in politics, so frequently end up defending ideologies of absolutism, intolerance, and ultimately "tyranny." The very qualities that facilitate their brilliance as purveyors of new understandings of the world, he argued, make them ill-suited for political engagement. If they abandon the space of arm's-length contemplation for political alignment, without first having mastered "the tyrant within" (2001: 226), Lilla concluded, their brilliant minds turn reckless.

My purpose here is not to engage in a detailed refutation of Lilla's argument but rather to use it as a foil for my own. Lilla was certainly correct to assert that scholarly work and political engagement involve very different training, disciplines, and dispositions and that crossing over from one to the other can be hazardous.[17] But are there conditions under which the inverse proposition might prove valid? Are there contexts in which political engagement has been crucial to the development of new theoretical ideas, which in turn have significantly transformed our understanding of the social world? In a trivial sense, the answer is a tautological "yes." Once we have acknowledged that all intellectuals are positioned social actors, making all knowledge production, in the last instance, political, then we are all, always, already "politically engaged." With a more focused framing, however, the question generates an intriguing proposition. I contend that key clusters of ideas that today circulate in the academy as theory originated in "activist research" settings.

This proposition begins with the assertion, made by Robin D. G. Kelley, Donna Haraway, George Lipsitz, S. P. Monhanty, and many others, that subordinated social actors, especially when they are engaged in collective struggle to confront their subordination, develop unique and acute insights into the world around them.[18] A second assertion follows. Often such insights stand at odds with existing representations of these very social conditions. The political struggle in question is waged against structures of inequality and at the same time against received understandings that make the struggle itself appear untenable or misconceived. More often than not, the protagonists themselves have partly internalized these premises and understandings, making "decolonization of the mind" the third task in this logical chain.

Effective political struggle under these conditions involves and requires theoretical innovation: forging alternative representations of the world that can offer clarity and guidance, both in depicting the adversary and in imagining the social transformations for which the struggle is waged. The activist researcher has an especially important role to play in this process: engaging in dialogue with the organized group in struggle, offering research skills that might help advance the group's efforts, and participating in the "rough cut" process of theory building that is already under way. This proposition—involving the ways in which organized people in struggle produce knowledge and the ways in which activist research can play a part in that process—adds up to an explicit counterpoint to the Lilla thesis. Rather than decrying the reckless minds positioned at the fertile meeting ground of political struggle and intellectual production, we need to praise and encourage them. With no pretense of complete substantiation, let me ground this proposition with two examples—those of cultural Marxism and black feminist notions of "intersectionality"—and then, in a modest and preliminary way, offer a third example from our group's work in Central America.

In any discussion of the relationship between theoretical innovation and political struggle, Antonio Gramsci's re-visioning of Marxist theory comes immediately to mind. As Walter Adamson's careful intellectual biography makes clear (Adamson 1980), Gramsci grew increasingly critical of standard interpretations of Marxism proffered by orthodox Communist party intellectuals, and his involvement with the Turin workers council, the Communist party newspaper, and other direct organizing efforts fed his critiques. By the time he was incarcerated, Gramsci had logged an intense two decades of frontline experience attempting to organize workers for collective action, with numerous frustrations and outright failures. This experience led him to shift the center of gravity of Marxist analysis away from structural determinism and toward a much more nuanced understanding of workers' acute (theoretical) knowledge, gained through praxis. It also led to his central preoccupation with the pervasive workings of hegemony in relation to the workers' consciousness.

This moving of Marxist theory into the realm of signification—the broadening of the notion of class conflict to encompass struggles over meanings, symbols, and representations—has been enormously influential in anthropology, literary and cultural studies, and related fields, to the point of becoming a well-established, completely legit-imated component of the theoretical repertoire of cultural critics and many others. Despite the indisputable "activist" origins of Gramsci's theoretical revisionism, an academic today can use his ideas with no commitment whatsoever to activist research methods.[19] Perhaps this disarticulation, this erasure of the social conditions of the emergence of theory, is one reason the position Lilla defends has gained such widespread acceptance within the academy. Otherwise, all those who work, broadly speaking, in the Gramscian tradition would be tainted by the "reckless" genesis of the theory they deploy.

Scholars working in traditions of black and third world feminism, by contrast, are much more likely to affirm the activist origins of their key theoretical ideas and to seek ongoing connections with these social conditions of theory creation. Black feminists invariably register the deep formative influence of the "Combahee River Collective State-ment," which is part political manifesto and part revisionist theoretical intervention. Robin Kelley's (2002: chap. 4) review of the twentieth-century history of black women's organizing in the United States gives further substance to the message that the Combahee statement itself clearly transmits: that existing (theoretical) representations of the social world, and forms of political struggle associated with these representations, have failed to capture the complex "intersectional" character of inequality that black women experience. The entwined and inextricable axes of oppression—race, class, gender, and sexuality, for starters—must somehow be grasped simultaneously as mutually constitutive features of the social conditions that we wish to understand. Anything short of this intersectional approach is bound to be analytically reductive and, by extension, politically regressive.

Audre Lorde, another voice situated in spaces of intellectual production and political struggle outside the academy, was deeply influential in giving substance to this theoretical-political intervention with her ground-clearing calls for "third wave" feminism, her early insistence on sexual orientation as part of the intersectional analysis, and her tracing of the implications of intersectional theory for a radical rethinking of the political.[20] That adherents of intersectionality theory tend to acknowledge much more readily the activist origins of the ideas they use is surely related to their daily struggles against marginalization within academic institutions that remain bastions of white and male privilege.[21] To the extent that these struggles against marginalization meet with success, we can expect the activist tracks of intersectional theory gradually to be erased as well, just like those of Gramsci's cultural Marxism.

With regard to our group's activist research on land rights, I have no desire or basis to claim any major theoretical breakthrough. A modest research outcome in support of the basic proposition involves our effort to rethink demands for rights grounded in cultural difference, in conjunction with multiple claimants (distinct Afro-descendant and indigenous groups), such that the idiom of the claim does not unduly privilege one group or pit one group against another. This has focused our attention on a comparative discussion of the ways in which culture is deployed in such struggles and on the patterned differences in the place of culture in, for example, black and indigenous Central Americans' notions of their own identities. This comparative inquiry, grounded in the politically motivated need to establish bridges between black and indigenous struggles, also yields a critique of the existing literature on indigenous identity politics on related grounds: they tend to downplay processes of racialization (common to both black and indigenous people) and work with notions of indigenous culture and identity that privilege roots (nationlike authenticity) over routes (fluid boundaries and horizontal connections).

This has given rise to a preliminary, alternative theoretical formulation for claims to ancestral or traditional occupancy, which are crucial to any land rights struggle. Rather than asserting the isomorphism of culture, identity, and place, we have been trying to think in terms of a "social memory of struggle" that links members of a collective in the present to their antecedents—a historical consciousness that creates a common political genealogy without asserting strict boundaries between "us" and others engaged in parallel struggles with convergent political ends (Gordon, Gurdian, and Hale 2003). The proposal is cautious for a number of reasons. It has been introduced and developed mainly by those directly involved in the research, with less evidence of broader endorsement among the political movements in question. And it is unclear whether such an approach, theoretically resonant as it may be, would win the day politically in struggles and negotiations with dominant institutions (courts of laws, state bureaucracies, etc.). But the grain of theoretical insight, emerging from a political process in which existing portrayals fall short, beckons further elaboration.

Conclusion

An influential interlocutor in a recent workshop devoted to these topics listened quietly to two days of papers and commentary and then, in the wrap-up session, put forth a disarmingly modest critique: "I worry that this kind of anthropology is arrogant: who are we to come from the outside and presume that we can engage politically in their affairs? We are there to listen, to learn, to be instructed, as their respectful guests, rigorously trained to have shed the arrogance of knowing ahead of time what is to be done." In one concise intervention, she both cast serious doubt on the leading rationale for activist research and reinstated the key premises on which conventional anthropology always has rested.

On one hand, she was of course right: there is nothing more harmful to activist research than the image of anthropologist as Rambo, barging into a fraught and complex political thicket, pen and notebook in hand, with showy proclamations about how his anthropology will liberate the subaltern. This kind of reckless mind (and I can think of a few) needs neither praise nor encouragement.

On the other hand, behind her "arrogance" argument lies an equally dangerous image, that of a serene "field" of subjects who gladly welcome their naive but well-trained and quick-learning guest, asking only that he or she represent them appropriately to the outside world. It is not so much that anthropologists can no longer pull off this trick, although I believe the minimal facilitating conditions are rapidly fading; more importantly, the image expresses a nostalgia for macro relations of neocolonial compliance between anthropology and its subjects. It was precisely this illusion of anthropology's powerlessness—of our informants really "running the show," of fieldwork taking place in a Habermasian ideal speech community among equals, and of the anthropologist as well-intentioned scribe and cultural translator—that the cultural critique so effectively called into question beginning two decades ago. That this arrogance argument remains strong, and indeed may even be returning to the fore, means that the dilemmas of ethical-political engagement are still likely to be framed as a debate between conventional anthropologists and rebel cultural critics.

Herein lies the predicament for activist research. Cultural critique has been a central force in opening the space for and bolstering the legitimacy of activist anthropology, contesting the gatekeepers of the time. But ultimately it has become an impediment to further development and institutionalization of activist anthropology. To the extent that proponents of cultural critique argue that the historic task of decolonizing anthropology can be achieved principally through a new politics of representation—a revised tool kit of textual and narrative strategies and theoretical positionings—the potential to undermine the impetus for activist research will remain strong. To make this a leading point in a case for activist research, however, seems needlessly divisive and, ultimately, a serious diversion from efforts to overcome common threats that loom larger by the day. Moreover, given the correlation of forces, the structure of rewards and opportunities in the academy, I suspect this would doom efforts to institutionalize activist anthropology.

The alternative strategy proposed here is to abandon efforts to justify activist anthropology within the academy on the grounds of ethical-political principles or efficacy of research outcomes. Instead, I propose that we highlight the inherent contradictions of activist research methods, thereby deflecting concerns about the sacrifice of analytical complexity, and justify activist research methods in terms of the privileged knowledge gained—both empirical understandings and theoretical insights. This strategy makes cultural critics into allies and key interlocutors in the academic arena, even if on methodological grounds (and ultimately, perhaps, on political priorities) we continue to disagree.

Although I favor this approach over previous ways of making a case for activist anthropology, I would be remiss to conclude without noting the principal drawback: it is exhausting. The strategy asks that we remain engaged on two fronts simultaneously: carrying out activist research with our allies, attempting to produce the practical results required according to the ethical-political guidelines established with them, but also producing research results that fully circulate in the legitimated realm of academic knowledge. I am convinced that special insights do result from these alternative methods, but I am much less sure that the conditions exist for activist scholars to carry out such commitments *and* produce legitimated intellectual products for the academy. Younger scholars, even if they share this conviction about the fruitful synergies of the two worlds, are generally forced to choose the latter as a matter of career survival. Tenured faculty members who endorse activist research are also inclined to become involved in collective efforts to transform the university, which represent a third pull on an already taut wire.

I do not want to reduce the entire flow of arguments in this essay to the mundane question of time, energy, emotional disposition, and life cycle—there is plenty to discuss before getting there. But these issues cannot be ignored, especially in relation to the question posed at the outset: Why has so little progress been made toward activist anthropology, especially when a preponderance of the discipline is politically sympathetic to the endeavor? This final point, about time, energy, and life conditions, must figure prominently in the answer. The only way I can imagine to overcome these obstacles is significant progress toward the institutionalization of activist anthropology, so that the alternation between the two distinct worlds is more fully acknowledged, valued, and rewarded. This, in my view, is the principal challenge that lies ahead.

Notes

1. Traditions of politically engaged anthropology, following in the spirit of the Barbados declaration, have developed with vibrancy in various Latin American countries and in other world regions. A comprehensive treatment of the central question driving this chapter would require comparative analysis of these traditions in relation to their respective mainstreams. Although I suspect that much of the analysis developed here would be applicable in this broader frame, in order to avoid unwarranted (and ultimately US-centric) generalizations, in this chapter I refer solely to the United States.

2. I also draw on diverse experiences over the past twenty years that involve some attempt to practice activist research: a role in two research projects involving indigenous and non-indigenous intellectuals, one with the "red *indígena*" of CLASPO, a University of Texas–based project that I coordinate, and the other called "Gobernando (en) la Diversidad," coordinated by Xochitl Leyva, Araceli Burguete, and Shannon Speed, for which I serve as a senior consultant; a Social Science Research Council project on "activist scholarship"; and efforts, along with colleagues at the University of Texas, to institutionalize an "activist anthropology" track in our graduate training program and to widen the legitimated space for activist scholarship in the university. The website of the activist anthropology track can be visited at http://www.utexas. edu/cola/depts/anthropology/activist/.

3. This account has been worked out through extensive dialogue with colleagues at the University of Texas, especially Edmund T. Gordon, João Costa Vargas, Shannon Speed, and Richard Flores. I have also refined my thinking through engagement with many graduate students who are developing their own distinctive approaches to activist anthropology. I have published one brief summary of these ideas (Hale 2001) and drawn on a number of published works, including Benmayor 1991, Fals Borda and Rahman 1991, Field 1999, Gordon 1991, Greenwood and Levin 1998, Naples 2003, and Smith 1999.

4. A fuller development of this point would note that, ironically, the basic principle is forcefully present in Weber's classic essay on objectivity in the social sciences (Weber 1949), which generally has been appropriated to argue against activist scholarship. Unfortunately, I do not have the space to develop this argument here.

5. The program for the 2007 (fourth annual) Activist Scholarship conference can be found at http://www.utexas.edu/cola/centers/caaas/.

6. The UNC program is called the Center for the Integration of Research and Action. Cornell has an "action research" program, and at Toronto it is the Social Justice Cluster, http://www.socialjustice.utoronto.ca.

7. For an especially influential work in this line of analysis, see Rose 1999.

8. See Plattner and Gross 2002. But interestingly, the National Science Foundation has also become increasingly insistent that the research it funds have some sort of practical or policy relevance beyond the realm of academe. This is a prime example of the contradictory spaces of "audit cultures" alluded to earlier.

9. My substantiation for this point is primarily ethnographic, not textual. That is, it is based primarily on discussions I have had with proponents of cultural critique and on a general sense for the feel of their response in various discussion forums. I know of relatively little literature in which cultural critics directly engage with proposals for activist research; the much more common

tendency is for such proposals simply to be ignored. A partial exception might be Orin Starn's smart and critical essay "Rethinking the Politics of Anthropology" (1994).

10. I explore the relationship between activist research and cultural critique in greater detail in an article *Cultural Anthropology* (Hale 2006a).

11. For one candid and probing example, see Foley 2000. Another is Gordon 1998.

12. See Fals Borda and Rahman 1991; Horton and Freire 1990.

13. See, for example, Gordon et al. 2004; Hale 2006a.

14. For further information, see the CCARC website, http://ccarconline.org/.

15. Core members of the research team were Luis Velásquez, Jennifer Goett, Christopher Loperena, Horacio Martínez, Heriberto Arriola, Roxana Ordóñez, Megan Chávez, Marlon Martínez, Selvin López, Peter Dana, and Gianluca Gaia.

16. With regard to the Garífuna, the key work is the research of Mark Anderson and Sarah England (1998). See also the broader comparative analysis of Gordon and Anderson (n.d.).

17. Even if some of Lilla's interpretations of specific cases—Foucault, Heidegger, Derrida, and others—are disputable, and even if his choice of cases seems quirky and one-sided, it would be silly to contend that the kinds of disaster scenarios he sketched never occur.

18. See, for example, Haraway 1988; Kelley 2002; Lipsitz 1998; Mohanty 2000.

19. For one especially striking example along these lines, see Laitin 1986.

20. See, for example, her essay "Uses of the Erotic: The Erotic as Power" (Lorde 1984).

21. For a detailed analysis of this problem, see Harrison 1999.

What Do Indicators Indicate?

Reflections on the Trials and Tribulations of Using
Food Aid to Promote Development in Haiti

Drexel G. Woodson

What does it mean to "work" anthropology to understand the human spectacle and support efforts to change the human condition? Cultural-social anthropologists have good reasons to ask.[1] In most nation-states, politicians, policymakers, and "influentials" (idea-mongers and intellectual trend-setters), along with John Q. and Jane Q. Public, still turn to economists, historians, and psychologists for fact-based analysis of the world's ways. Practitioners of "old" social science disciplines and "new" interdisciplinary fields do ethnography, appropriating the cultural-social anthropologist's traditional turf. Funding for long-term, intensive, empirically grounded ethnographic fieldwork in one place diminishes each year. Publishers solicit theoretically "cutting-edge" but "readable" books and articles—short works minimally concerned with the complex lineages of ideas (concepts, methods, or previously "worked up" facts) that canalize knowledge production in any discipline.

Cultural-social anthropologists, responding to ambient conditions, question the epistemological moorings, conceptual and procedural guardrails, and political relevance of their pathways to and from knowledge. Activist, engaged, and public anthropologies independently contest and intermittently illuminate terrain demarcated by labels that once fitfully identified fields of inquiry: kinship, descent, and alliance; religion; law; development; cultural and political ecology; economic, political, and symbolic anthropology. Under new labels, cultural-social anthropologists busily pluralize subjects, fragment subject matters, and multiply fieldwork sites. Borrowing theoretical gazes from philosophers and literary critics (preferably Continental ones) rather than disciplinary ancestors' stances, they "acknowledge," "address," "engage," "transcend," and "critique" nearly everything under the sun.

Such disciplinary self-interrogation is not new. Over thirty years ago, Clifford Geertz heralded the interpretive anthropology era, scrutinizing, criticizing, and seeking to improve (largely US American) studies of culture by working (fashioning) an empirically oriented rapprochement of Max Weber's sociology, Kenneth Burke's literary theory, and, among other philosophies in new keys, Alfred Schutz's phenomenology. Geertz's "Thick Description: Toward an Interpretive Theory of Culture" chided colleagues for allowing arguments about what anthropology is to deflect attention from what anthropologists do. "Interminable, because unterminable, debates," he noted, and "mutual exchanges of intellectual insults—'idealist!—materialist!'; 'mentalist!'—'behaviorist!'; 'impressionist!—positivist'"—discouraged investigations of culture as a publicly acted document and of behavior as symbolic action (Geertz 1973: 10).

In "They Divide and Subdivide, and Call It Anthropology," Eric Wolf (1980) explained to general readers why and how anthropologists study human affairs. Intellectual sniping between "materialists" and "mentalists," he observed, evaded critical-constructive examinations of anthropology's concepts and methods amid the real world's wars and power differences. Wolf (2001 [1984]) subsequently argued (worked the insight) that Marxian tenets could be wedded to lessons from anthropological fieldwork to forge historically grounded understandings of the way sociocultural microcosms and political-economic macrocosms interact to reproduce violence and inequality.[2]

Associating Geertz with Wolf—contemporaries on opposite sides of intellectual and political barricades—may seem as odd as contrasting them with their successors. (Today's cultural-social anthropologists are suspicious of binary oppositions and insult one another in different terms.) Yet Geertz and Wolf couched disciplinary self-interrogations in dialogues with common frames of reference: one an anthropological canon (a flexible but recognizable assemblage of scholars, texts, and positions on intellectual problems), the other a conviction about the canon's reach. Canonical grounding was a purchase for studying the world scientifically and, with mandatory awareness of extradisciplinary factors (e.g., other people's nonscientific concerns), for acting in it. That way of working anthropology has given way to parallel monologues about multipurpose, direct worldly action, in ever-narrower intellectual *demimondes* with few common frames of reference.

Applied anthropologists, having worked the discipline outside the academy long before the discipline's institutionalization within it, differ from activist, engaged, and public anthropologists (Chambers 1987; Ervin 2000). "Policy-relevant" research on peoples, places, and practical social problems is the stock in trade of anthropology's "fifth subfield" or "crosscutting research focus." Critics find applied anthropology theoretically unappealing (if not null), the practice of researchers for hire by the rich and powerful. Admirers emphasize the generation of theory from "policy-relevant" research and extol applied anthropology as the entire discipline's future, if it is to remain useful in a rapidly changing world.[3]

Communication among the world's development stakeholders increasingly centers on indicators—symbols of quantitative or qualitative information that represent existing conditions and establish benchmarks for evaluating, even measuring, change—even though their meanings may be unclear.[4] Having defined indicators for one country, programmers or researchers routinely export them to other countries, where colleagues use them without the requisite ground-truthing. In program offices, staff members and consultants speak of "collecting indicators" to monitor progress toward achievement of program objectives rather than investigate the conditions that indicators symbolize.

These communicative practices beg several questions. Are indicators integrated within an information infrastructure for research and policymaking, or are they separate from it? Which aspects of cultural, social, ecological, and political-economic conditions do indicators represent (that is, depict and present a second time in different form)? Does a given indicator point to the same structures and processes for all development stakeholders? Such questions force cultural-social anthropologists to inquire about connections between basic and applied research and to think critically about the role of social science in public policy.

Since 1990, bilateral or multilateral agencies, international nongovernmental organizations (NGOs), and the Government of Haiti (GOH) have sought to reorient food aid programming from humanitarian assistance to development intervention. Their efforts, replete with heady talk about indicators, prompted my essay's title and my attempt to answer the question "What do indicators indicate?" in ways that illustrate anthropology at work and as work.

Baseline Studies of Livelihood Security in Rural Haiti

During 1994–96, the Bureau of Applied Research in Anthropology (BARA) at the University of Arizona, with which I am affiliated, coordinated three diagnostic baseline studies of livelihood security in rural Haiti, working with some fifty Haitian field researchers trained in various disciplines to design appropriate research instruments and gather the necessary information (BARA 1996a, 1996b, 1997). The Cooperating Sponsors of the US Public Law 480, Title II Food Program in Haiti—namely, USAID, along with CARE, Catholic Relief Services (CRS), and the Adventist Development and Relief Agency (ADRA)—initiated the baseline series.[5] Their immediate goal was to upgrade the information infrastructure for food aid programming while laying the foundation for an eventual reorientation of food aid programming from "relief" to "sustainable development."

This policy agendum, including plans for diagnostic baseline studies, was approved before the Haitian Army's coup d'état on 29 September 1991 against the democratically elected government of President Jean-Bertrand Aristide provoked Haiti's most serious political crisis since the fall of the Duvalier dictatorship in 1986 (Trouillot 1990). The Cooperating Sponsors temporarily postponed the policy agendum's implementation to manage international humanitarian assistance under crisis conditions (Berggren et al. 1993). They resumed the work in October 1994, when President Aristide returned from exile. Although they have continued the relief-to-development transition, progress has been slowed by Haiti's ongoing crisis, coupled with the emergence of other world crises. Both circumstances have diminished interest in indicator development and complementary research that might be pursued even under crisis conditions.[6]

BARA's mixed methods approach to diagnostic baseline research in rural Haiti treated food security as a dynamic output of livelihood system performance, rather than a result of the volume and targeting of foreign food aid commodities. The baseline research methodology focused on the household as the pivotal component of rural livelihood systems, emphasizing the collection, description, and analysis of household-level qualitative and quantitative data. BARA adapted a survey research methodology originally designed for Chad (west central Africa) to distinctive features of the Haitian setting: a spotty information infrastructure, difficult fieldwork logistics, and the time and budgetary constraints of the Cooperating Sponsors, which had resumed regular programming activities by 1996.

BARA tailored each baseline study to the physical, cultural, socio-economic, and political characteristics of one international NGO's primary zone of operation, generating a minimal data set for randomly sampled rural localities and households in each zone for a single reporting year. BARA's analysis of each data set was the simplest yet most thorough consistent with a general understanding of factors that promote or inhibit household food security. The series of studies produced the largest data bank of its kind for Haiti's nine contiguous administrative departments, profiling conditions experienced by 23,365 individuals, heads or members of 4,022 households in 119 rural localities.[7]

I can start with a simple ethnographic fact: stakeholders (organizations and individuals) working to create more abundant and accessible supplies of high-quality food in Haiti speak three mutually unintelligible languages—Haitian Creole, French, and English. The main stakeholders are, lest we forget, Haitian men, women, and children, especially *moun andeyò* ("country folk") and *abitan* ("peasants").[8] Next come local civic and religious organizations, as well as *gwoupman,* development-oriented groups composed of five to fifteen persons (Mondé 1980; Smucker and Noriac 1996). Last but, given decision-making power, not least are comparatively well-fed folk: the personnel of donor agencies, the staffs of their international NGO partners, GOH officials, and members of Haitian civil society organizations (e.g., professional associations and church groups).

Language differences among these stakeholders precipitate semantic disparities such as the one between the Haitian Creole term *lamanjay*— sundry things having to do with *manje* ("food" or "victuals"), namely, production or trade, cooking, and eating—and *food security* or its French part-cognate, *la sécurité alimentaire* (Woodson 1997). Amid the mountains of problems that hamper Haiti's fledgling democracy-building (Fass 1988; Fatton 2002; Trouillot 1997), miscommunication and noncommunication cast especially long shadows. With regard to ideas, talk, and action concerning food, the shadows obscure the necessarily slow organizational work required to enhance food security based on sustainable livelihood security (cf. Brinkerhoff and Garcia-Zamor 1986; Maguire 1984, 1997).

Adopting an ethnographic perspective on indicator development, I turn to the character of individual baseline indicators as a step toward assessing the integrity and utility of indexes (that is, packages composed of different types of indicators). My aim is to elucidate indicator development as a process, aspects of which we too often take for granted or consider settled. Indicator development warrants closer processual examination because it is critical for applied anthropological research projects in the wake of a diagnostic baseline study. Such post-baseline projects would utilize stratified samples of Haitian rural localities and households to analyze the most significant production and consumption variables, including the resource management capacities of specific institutions. An applied research agenda that builds on diagnostic baseline studies might induce powerholders to implement equitable and sustainable livelihood security policies that assist rural Haitians to meet food needs.

Indicators: A Rapid Conceptual Overview

Indicators are supposed to facilitate the collection, analysis, and dissemination of reliable, statistically representative data on agroecological, socioeconomic, and nutritional conditions in a given area (Maxwell and Frankenberger 1992). That area may be an entire country, one of its political-territorial-administrative subdivisions, or a region of a subdivision. Moreover, indicators presumably offer cost-effective and scientifically valid means to identify vulnerable areas and groups and to determine the effects of food programming or development intervention. Indicators thus symbolize a broad range of data pertinent to livelihood security and food security, and they become foci for program or project targeting, monitoring, and impact evaluation. Applied researchers, especially applied anthropologists, must subject this symbolic function to critical scrutiny.

The CARE, CRS, and ADRA baseline studies raised questions about how well indicators used in Haiti actually serve either function. BARA's analysis of the baseline data sets suggested that the indicators might be too general to capture critical forms and levels of variation in factors that promoted or inhibited livelihood security and food security in rural Haiti. The indicators simultaneously appeared to be too complex for policymakers to integrate into routine decision-making protocols. In other words, using any baseline indicator entails collection or collation, analysis, and summary of a vast amount of information. Moreover, it is usually necessary to repeat phases of baseline research to examine any indicator's performance in a new social-spatial setting.

Haiti's natural resources and, some observer-analysts argue, human productivity have steadily declined for at least sixty years (Lundahl 1979, 1992). Yet there is remarkable regional and local diversity in the Haitian countryside, and poor households improvise highly complex livelihood strategies to balance sporadic incomes against steady expenditures to meet food needs and fulfill social obligations. Diversity and complexity prompt questions about the integrity and representativeness of indicators. An especially significant baseline finding was that the range of variation in any socioeconomic variable increased as one descended the ladder of descriptive and analytic units toward the basic unit of study, the "household" (*ti lakou,* or "individualized house-yard complex"). Variation was greater among the thirty to thirty-eight households sampled in each locality than between two localities in an agroecological zone or between two agroecological zones in a department. Consequently, BARA's analysis of the baseline data made less progress toward indicator development than anticipated.

The Cooperating Sponsors and BARA expected the baseline series to identify distinct factors or conditions that determined location-specific levels of food insecurity for discrete household types and reliably predicted changes in insecurity. Yet the baseline indicators— agroecological zone, household socioeconomic status, and child nutritional status—were neither simple nor distinct. Moreover, to date, no Haitianist has attempted to verify their predictive value. The baseline indicators are static, or, more precisely, the currently available information pertinent to their interpretation is static. Minimally, one more round of data collection would be necessary to determine the reliability of indicators for prediction. In the best-case research scenario, third-round data collection would permit analysis of three separate observations for each indicator. This complicates the construction of reliable livelihood security or food security indexes, which collate subsets of agroecological, socioeconomic, and child nutritional baseline indicators.

A Panoply of Baseline Indicators Pointing at Different Things

State-of-the-art reviews in the early 1990s maintained that baseline indicators anchored a wide-ranging set of concepts, methods, and objectives in livelihood security and food security research (Frankenberger et al. 1994; Hutchinson and Hall 1993; Maxwell and Frankenberger 1992). Those indicators, still used in Haiti today, are diverse: direct (or "genuine") indicators nestle alongside proxies; some indicators concern current phenomena; others disclose past conditions or predict future conditions.

The most significant point is that indicators, like symbols generally, stand for other things.[9] Indicators represent—select, depict, condense, and summarize—conditions, processes, relationships, structures, and other phenomena. Yet indicators differ from other symbols in that their representations are putatively more accurate and efficacious. Deliberately constructed by experts (researchers in the best of circumstances), indicators incorporate and convey information about a limited set of phenomena construed as variables in a data set. Consequently, an indicator brackets a portion of phenomenal reality, on the presumption that cohesiveness marks what is bracketed. This also means that any indicator is only as "good" or "strong" (read: accurate and reliable) as the information it represents.

A direct indicator represents a single phenomenon or points to a set of phenomena either closely related in theory or so related by the analysis of empirical data. Thus, household income represents a production-consumption unit's earnings or revenues for the previous year—in cash and in kind, for all members and from all sources. Income becomes a direct indicator of livelihood security and food security because it directly supports household expenditures for food, other necessities (including reproduction of the means and relations of production), and perhaps a few luxuries.

Proxy indicators, by contrast, substitute for indicators that directly represent phenomena. A household head's gender, for example, represents that person's sex (a biological phenomenon), his or her status and power positions, and the roles he or she performs in a production-consumption unit. Therefore, gender of household head is a proxy indicator of household resource endowments such as landholding size, livestock value, the availability of labor, and, ultimately, income level.

Five broader types of indicators emerge from the foregoing discussion:

1. Current indictors represent significant relationships among various conditions, material or social, at the time the pertinent information is collected. If they could speak, these indicators would say, "Here are the major variables right now, and this is how they are patterned."
2. Output indictors tally the quantities of resources, material or human, that a program or project allocates within its zone of operation or that a target beneficiary utilizes to achieve a beneficial outcome. For a food aid program, examples are tons of commodities distributed, number of distribution centers, and person-days devoted by field staff to commodity distribution or to animation and training sessions with beneficiary groups. For target beneficiaries, examples include increases in cultivated land, agricultural laborers employed, and crop harvests.
3. Predictive indicators embody reasonably well-founded speculations about future conditions. They project the likely outcomes of event

sequences that have not yet occurred—say, the reproduction of a structure or the repetition of a process—on the basis of existing circumstances.

4. Retrospective indicators disclose past conditions. "Retrodictive" is perhaps a more appropriate adjective, because these indicators specify only those past conditions that account for and presumably caused the intensity or array of phenomena observed when indicators are "read" (that is, when relevant information is collected, analyzed, and summarized).

5. Impact indicators, the foci of program or project evaluations, capture changes in the behavior of target beneficiaries, which program or project resources—tangible or intangible—presumably bring about.

Given space limitations, one illustration of problems with proxy indicators must suffice.[10] The household head's gender indicates (represents) a production-consumption unit's typical characteristics, including resource endowments. Women tend to head smaller households than do men, but their households often have higher dependency ratios (consumers to producers) and own less land or fewer (and less valuable) livestock. Usually, therefore, female-headed households are in a relatively weaker position to farm than are male-headed ones, and they are more susceptible to recurrent crises that hamper farming. Note here the conceptual transformation of the indicator "gender of household head," read as female. In synchronic survey research, a proxy indicator of current conditions is quickly transformed into both a predictive and a retrodictive indicator.

Agroecological Zone

Agroecological zones furnished the first level of livelihood security and food security indicators in BARA's baseline research. The physical environment influences settlement patterns, as well as the economic organization of farming and other revenue-generating activities. A search for environmental indicators might have focused on ecological zones to capture the environmental contexts of all revenue-generating activities in rural Haiti—agricultural, semi-agricultural, and nonagricultural—and their environmental effects (e.g., soil erosion, deforestation, water pollution). However, the term *agroecological* underscores the importance of farming as a livelihood in BARA's baseline research methodology. The differential organizational demands of rainfed and irrigated agriculture, along with their differential risks and rewards, were of particular interest.

Definitional criteria for agroecological zones conventionally include altitude, annual rainfall, soil type, predominant mode of intercropping (French, *association de cultures*), and presence or absence of irrigation (Anglade 1982: 50–54; Moral 1978 [1961]: chap. 2; SACAD and FAMV 1993–94, 3: chap. 3). As Haitian agronomists and agricultural economists emphasized, topography (especially the slope of land), air temperature, and seasonally variable exposure to sunlight (that is, hours of sunlight per day) are supplementary definitional criteria. Unfortunately, for most rural Haitian localities (as opposed to their communes or departments), little reliable information exists about the four basic definitional criteria, and none exists for the supplementary criteria.

As a result, BARA and Haitian baseline researchers relied on approximations—relative positions within a range—to classify an entire locality in a single agroecological zone. Relative moistness or dampness versus dryness substituted for rainfall data measured in precise intervals. Relative elevation and distance from a seacoast substituted for altitude. Soil quality became land quality as subjectively assessed by household heads—namely, "good," "passable" or "average," and "bad" land. Likewise, typical crop associations sufficed to define modes of intercropping, rather than the specific agronomic or economic interactions of cereals, legumes, root crops, and fruits in discrete inventories. Thus, the process of classifying localities by agroecological zone generated incomplete replicas of proxy indicators.

Even price information does not reduce the hazards of classifying a locality in one agroecological zone, given microenvironmental variation and the fact that most households manage small landholdings, their plots dispersed among different agroecological zones and cultivated under different tenure arrangements. ADRA baseline data on landholding size and dispersal are instructive (BARA 1997: 102–9). The 1,166 households held, on average, 2.7 plots totaling 1.4 hectares. Houses were a 45-minute walk from plots (some 3.75 km), with mean walking times of 15 minutes to an hour for 36 localities and a maximum of 9 hours. Walking 3 or 4 kilometers in any direction took a person out of the locality where he or she began and often into another communal section.

Education

Education, policymakers and program managers assume, expands a rural household's general fund of knowledge, enabling farmers to cultivate land more efficiently and effectively or to take advantage of nonagricultural employment opportunities. Education also putatively promotes enlightened use of household resources, because educated people presumably devote greater attention to dietary issues such as the nutritional balance of meals than uneducated people do.

Few researchers would question the general benefits of education (especially basic literacy and numeracy), and baseline household heads made considerable sacrifices for their children's schooling. However, the reliability of education as an indicator of a production-consumption unit's relative livelihood or food security depends on analysis of exogenous factors (Locher 1991a, 1991b). Rural primary schools—national (that is, public), congregational, or private—omit lessons about food acquisition and preparation or nutrition. Moreover, labor-market conditions make connections between education and employment problematic, given the specific skill sets and skill levels that available jobs require. Most agricultural tasks involve manual labor, which neither requires nor rewards high levels of formal schooling, and nonagricultural employment opportunities are few in rural Haitian localities and small towns.

Religious Affiliation

As a proxy indicator, religious affiliation represents notions about how beliefs or moral-ethical tenets influence thrift and saving and how Christian congregations foster and reinforce social networks. BARA considered Sèvis Lwa ("Voodoo" ceremonies) performed in conjunction with family ancestor cults or temple-centered devotion functionally analogous to Catholic and Protestant rituals. Consequently, this proxy indicator suggests, religiously based social networks channel resources insofar as ritual sponsorship or participation affects household production and consumption.

Although many policymakers and social scientists maintain that "traditional" religious rituals drain household resources, little ethnographic research supports this proposition. Gerald Murray (1977: chap. 11; 1980) demonstrated that fulfillment of ritual obligations in the family ancestor cult acted as a "motor" for land transactions in Kinanbwa, a lowland locality in Haiti's Department of the Center. Karen Richman (1992: 11–18, 67–70, 109–12) explored ritual praxis associated with pwen (French, pointe), or "points"—ideas, words, acts, or images that capture a complex situation and reformulate it for easy remembrance. Pwen, she showed, punctuated remittance flows within a "transnational

Haitian community" stretching from Ti Rivyè, a coastal locality in the Department of the West, to the United States.

The CARE baseline study's Haitian field researchers estimated the cost of a *fèt gonbo* ("okra thanksgiving feast") sponsored by one household in the Northwest but involving four branches of an extended family. The nine-day feast, part of a series of devotional acts, cost G107,000 (roughly US$7,000), excluding the sale of seven *kawo* (approximately nine hectares) of land and numerous animals over several years (BARA 1996a: 116–17).

Tantalizing evidence aside, no cultural-social anthropologist has *systematically* studied the way resources mobilized and reallocated by a rural household to organize *Sèvis Lwa* flow to and from neighboring households, among rural localities, between the countryside and towns or cities, or from Haiti to foreign countries (and back). The requisite microlevel fieldwork and library research, which only ethnographers would undertake, entails tracking funding sources for ritual and ceremonial expenditures in cash and in kind.

Migration

Migration serves as an indicator because it constitutes a mode of access to off-farm income from agricultural day labor or nonagricultural employment. When adult household members emigrate to Haitian towns or cities or to foreign countries, it is presumably advantageous, because the household simultaneously loses one consumer and gains access to remittances (Locher 1984; Stepick 1984, 1998). Two qualifications must be noted. First, someone must cover the emigrant's transportation costs or travel fees, and he or she incurs living expenses before and after employment. Second, depending on the jobs that emigrants find, the income differential between agricultural and nonagricultural employment may neither cover new living expenses nor permit remittances. I consider this issue in the discussion of household income later.

Child Nutritional Status

In the early 1990s, experts considered the nutritional status of neonates and toddlers a strong indicator of household food security, because these most vulnerable household members have time-sensitive needs for nutrients to support mental and physical development (PAHO/WHO 1994). Anthropometric measurements match children to international standards for physical growth: height for age (stunting), weight for age (wasting), and weight for height. Deviance from the standards establishes levels of malnutrition.

The three anthropometric indicators measure two different things, however, and neither of them is predictive. Height for age and weight for age are retrospective indicators, revealing the child's access to nutrients and the incidence of childhood diseases since birth. Weight for height is a current indicator, suggesting access to nutrients during a relatively brief period, usually the six months prior to measurement.

Food aid programmers and some researchers maintained that the child nutritional status indicators disclosed the quantity of food available to rural Haitian households. It was more likely, BARA discovered, that the indicators revealed dietary composition—proportions of empty calories (that is, sugars), carbohydrates, proteins, and vitamin sources (BARA 1996a: chap. 7; 1996b: chap. 7; 1997: chap. 7; cf. Alvarez and Murray 1981). Given that food quantity and quality differ, the relationship between child nutritional status and household food security status appears more tenuous than "strong indicator" suggests.

Household Vulnerability Status

Household vulnerability status, the most complex baseline indicator, directly incorporated information about household resource endowments and indirectly incorporated information about household composition. Although I must omit background discussion, the elicitation and analysis of this "incorporated information" illustrate how applied anthropologists work their discipline.[11]

BARA utilized four vulnerability status categories—extreme, high, moderate, and low—thereby documenting food insecurity and, to a lesser extent, livelihood insecurity. The categories were derived analytically from household data on owned assets, annual per capita income, and income-expenditure balance. To determine the value of land as an asset, BARA calculated the land area from which households derived cash or in-kind income during the reporting period. Land prices were unavailable, and it was impossible to elicit reliable figures during rapid fieldwork. Key informants reported asset values for livestock: cattle; donkeys, mules, and horses; pigs; goats; sheep; and fowl (that is, chickens, guinea fowl, turkeys, and ducks). Although retail consumer prices determined the monetary value of livestock assets in the first three baseline studies, BARA attempted to capture potentially significant value fluctuations in the ADRA study.[12] Haitian field researchers elicited four price observations for each locality—high and low prices during the reporting year, the price at the time of the household survey, and the price before the US-UN embargo of September–December 1991.

The household sample was first sorted into quartiles based on sample means to determine the range of asset values and incomes for each vulnerability status category. Then, households were assigned to one of the four categories by applying an "or statement" to asset-value and income data. Households with a range of very low assets or incomes entered the Extreme category, and households with increasingly higher ranges of either resource entered the High, Moderate, and Low categories.

BARA did not attempt to include several types of assets in the vulnerability categories. For example, in Haitian farming systems, there is good reason to consider perennial crops—coffee, plantains, and certain fruit trees such as mango, grapefruit, orange, and soursop—as assets. The point also holds for root crops such as yams and sweet potatoes that have long growing cycles, high prices, and stable market outlets. BARA also ignored personal belongings and movable property such as jewelry, furniture, cooking utensils, and tools. During rapid baseline fieldwork featuring single-shot interviews and relying on respondents' self-reports, there was no time to assess the monetary value of such assets or to refine understandings of short-term benefits when households liquidate or pawn them as a maneuver in livelihood and survival strategies. In post-baseline applied research, this shortcut would be unacceptable.

The income data captured irregular remittances and gifts. However, BARA did not treat social networks as household vulnerability indicators. Haitian researchers conducted baseline fieldwork on a tight schedule, ranging from two and a half days per locality for the CARE study to four and a half days for the ADRA study. This left little time to pursue leads about socioeconomic and political relationships linking a locality's thirty to thirty-eight sample households. Such relationships, formed within and across class lines, make resources differentially available and accessible to households.

Membership in traditional labor associations affects interhousehold resource flows. Examples include salaried squads—known regionally as *èskwad, mera,* or *ranpanno*—and invitation work parties (*konbit*), about which anthropologists and other social scientists have written extensively (Métraux et al. 1951: 68–86; Moral 1978 [1961]: 190–93; Woodson 1990: 495, 620–29). Membership in church groups affords households certain welfare or investment benefits, whereas *gwoupman* membership provides both. Since the 1970s, residents of many rural Haitian localities have formed *gwoupman* in explicit opposition to community councils (*konsèy kominotè*), which are organizational nodes of state-sponsored "community development" methodologies. *Gwoupman* supply credit on reasonable conditions and terms, to subsidize consumption, finance investment, and promote civic education (Locher, Smucker, and Woodson 1983; Lowenthal and Attfield 1979; Mondé 1980; Smucker and Noriac 1996).

BARA's analysis of household vulnerability status revealed a potential conflict between livelihood security and food security. Liquidating assets when a crisis occurs enables a household to meet current food needs, but unless the household can replace the liquidated assets, it will be unable to resume livelihood activities. A household that sells agricultural land no longer owns land to farm and must resort to leasehold, sharecropping, or gifthold. These modes of access to land are, assuming equality of all factors other than tenure, more costly and less secure than ownership.

Conclusion

Indicators make sense in and of a confused and confusing world. Yet if indicators are symbols that bracket, compress, and simplify selected segments of phenomenal reality, then applied anthropologists must probe and unpack the orderly sensibility that indicators create. These are the only ways to prevent repeated eruptions of mistaken identity between indicators and the conditions they represent. Indicator development is an ongoing process in which the results of baseline surveys and other kinds of research—historical, political-economic, ecological, and ethnographic—continuously confront one another, and applied anthropologists must continuously sift and evaluate the outcomes of confrontation.

Haiti is exceptional among the world's nation-states for historical, sociocultural, and political-economic reasons. The country exhibits a high degree of microenvironmental variation (physical and sociocultural), its livelihood systems are complex, and Haitians exploit them by creatively pursuing intricate livelihood or survival strategies. Moreover, anyone attuned to media reports knows something of Haiti's compound crisis—a seemingly intractable concatenation of social, economic, ecological, and political problems.

Acknowledging that Haiti is exceptional, however, does not mean embracing exceptionalism as a framework of anthropological understanding. The Haitian situation is instructive for work on indicators elsewhere. Growing populations, rising standards of living (however modest, uneven, or slow), and increasing awareness of injuries caused by locally inflected global pathways of power intensify pressures on the natural as well as human resources of most nation-states. Development intervention contributes to those pressures. Hidden economies, black markets, and massive "informal" institutional sectors that swamp "formal" ones abound. And this merely hints at the rethinking and repositioning of constraints, opportunities, identities, needs, wants, rights, entitlements, and duties that today's cultural-social anthropologists associate with various "posts"—post–Cold War, postmodernity, postcolonial, postfeminist, and postsocialist, to name a few, or, for Haitianists, post-Duvalier and post-Aristide. Absent serious work to fortify information infrastructures in developing countries and to resist the temptation to mistake indicators for things they represent, the symbolic efficacy of indicators will diminish, along with their utility as guides to sound development policy.

Cultural-social anthropologists, applied and basic, have useful intellectual tools with which to investigate the world's unswept corners at close range without losing sight of the buildings that have corners or the human settlements—villages, towns, cities, and megalopolises—where buildings are located. Personal experience puts me in a nontranscendental mood, and anthropological work discourages me from jettisoning the applied-basic dichotomy in research. Instead, I insist that basic and applied cultural-social anthropology are sides of a single path, across which some of us zigzag depending on the character of research projects. Basic research addresses fundamental questions about the structure, organization, and effects of culture, history, society, economy, and polity, taking into account similarities and differences among human beings across space and time. Applied research appropriates basic concepts and methods, first, to define practical human problems in temporally and spatially restricted settings and, second, to propose effective, efficient, and equitable solutions for those problems. Productive feedback loops link basic and applied work in cultural-social anthropology, or anthropologists can create them.

What do indicators indicate? What good cultural-social anthropologists have known since they began to "work" anthropology. First, contextualization makes all symbols meaningful. Second, theory is neither the sole nor always the primary objective of anthropological work. Method matters, as do training students in the crafts of anthropology and communicating anthropological knowledge to non-anthropologists. Third, ideas have lineages. Tracking concepts and methods, along with *good for career skills –*

conclusions and generalizations, is the best way to determine which aspects of anthropological thinking and practice to retain, transform, or jettison. Finally, understanding the human spectacle and supporting efforts to change the human condition require discipline—indeed, a discipline—as well as a division of labor. Who better to seek answers to modest questions that shed light on big issues than cultural-social anthropologists?

Acknowledgments

Wenner-Gren Foundation International Symposium number 134 was the most constructive conference I have attended since escaping from graduate school. The point holds for the formal sessions, informal conversations over delicious food and ample libations, and a memorable evening of great jazz. I thank the co-organizers, Les W. Field and Richard G. Fox, Wenner-Gren president Leslie Aiello, and conference program associate Laurie Obbink. Good company aside, I am grateful to the other participants for their stimulating interventions, especially when we discussed our disagreements. Coping with formidable constraints on a social science research organization at a public university in financial difficulty, the Bureau of Applied Research in Anthropology has created a supportive intellectual environment for my work on this essay's ideas. Haitians (intellectuals and "ordinary" folk) have so thoroughly informed the way I work anthropology that naming them is impossible. Richard G. Fox, Robert A. Hackenberg, and Brackette F. Williams offered useful criticisms of an early draft of this chapter, some of which I heeded in my own way.

Notes

1. Four-field anthropology—archaeology, biological-physical, linguistic, and cultural-social—thrives at Yale University, where I was an undergraduate, and at the University of Arizona, my employer since 1990. My doctorate is from The University of Chicago, which offers but does not require all students to master four fields. I write only about cultural-social anthropology, applied and basic, resisting the misleading practice of allowing one subfield to metonymize anthropology.

2. Wolf 2001 [1984] includes a description of the 1980 *New York Times* article.

3. The University of Arizona's Bureau of Ethnic Research (BER), founded in 1952 by Emile Haury, Edward Spicer, and William Kelly, investigated the practical social problems of American Indians in the southwestern USA until the 1970s. During the following decade, the organization's intellectual horizons and contract research portfolio expanded and diversified to address problems of sociocultural, environmental, and political-economic change, including their differential outcomes for diverse collectivities in the Southwest, along the USA-Mexico border, and in Mexico, Central and South America, the Caribbean, Europe, the Middle East, and Africa. BER became BARA (Bureau of Applied Research in Anthropology) in 1983. The name change reflected "unity within diversity" of applied anthropological interests and shifting sources of research funding.

4. By "development stakeholders" I refer to donor agencies (single-country, bilateral, or multilateral), governments (national, state or regional, and local), international or national nongovernmental organizations (NGOs), community-based organizations (CBOs), and target beneficiaries involved in processes of directed or guided change.

5. The Cooperating Sponsors also established two organizations, the Haiti Monitoring Unit and the Interim Food Security Information System (iFSIS). From 1992 to 1996, USAID's *Monitoring Unit Report* compiled national information on food prices, child nutrition and health, and electric power from observations in regional marketplaces and selected health care facilities. During 1994–96, iFSIS reconstructed part of the Haiti Area Sampling Frame, created in the late 1980s under the auspices of the second phase of the USAID Agricultural Development Support Project (ADS II), and hired private consultants to conduct a two-season national crop and livestock survey. As an information conduit for the Cooperating Sponsors, iFSIS monitored crop and livestock prices in selected regional marketplaces and child nutrition and health indicators in selected healthcare centers. It also facilitated BARA's execution of the last two baseline studies (see BARA 1997: chaps. 1–2 for an overview of these activities).

6. Haiti's second most serious post-Duvalier crisis is the one current at the time of this writing. On 28 February 2004, President Aristide resigned under pressure from the United States, France, and Canada, after a six-week armed rebellion by former Aristide supporters and former Haitian Army soldiers and in the wake of widespread opposition to Aristide's policies and style of governance since his reelection in 2002. Haiti's interim government managed to organize presidential elections in early 2006. "Crisis" remains the appropriate term for the transition, because, first, Haitians still face serious economic, ecological,

and social problems. Second, Haiti's national leaders (backed by powerholders in the international "community") may use populism's failures as a pretext to undermine the Haitian progressive movement's constructive efforts to uproot dictatorship since 1986, once again ignoring or circumventing the multifaceted challenges of democratic institution-building.

7. The CARE study investigated conditions in the Department of the Northwest during 1993–94 (BARA 1996a). The CRS study did so for the Departments of the South, Southeast, Grande-Anse, and the southern part of the West during 1994–95 (BARA 1996b), and the ADRA study focused on the Artibonite, Center, North, Northeast, and the northern part of the West, including La Gonâve, Haiti's largest island (BARA 1997). BARA drew random samples of rural localities, eschewing the common practice of sampling by accessibility to motor vehicles. Haitian baseline researchers often walked from a tertiary road for four and a half hours to reach a locality. See Oriol 1994 on Haiti's administrative and political subdivisions and their institutional weaknesses.

8. Gérald Barthélemy (1989) reminded Haitians and foreigners who ignored or dismissed cultural-social anthropological research of this simple fact. Haiti's national majority—peasants, other rural dwellers, and working-class or lower-class residents of cities and towns—are mostly monolingual Haitian Creole-speakers. Unless otherwise indicated, italicized terms and expressions are in the official Haitian Creole orthography (see Savain 1993; Valdman 1988).

9. For simplicity, I use "symbols" rather than "signs." Clifford Geertz (1973, especially the essays on ideology and religion from his "as a cultural system" series), Edmund Leach (1976), Marshall Sahlins (1976), and Victor Turner (1975) discussed signification rigorously but accessibly. On metaphor, see Lakoff and Johnson 2003.

10. Glenn Smucker and Nina Schlossman (2001) analyzed impact indicators and field data on education, health and nutrition, infrastructure projects, and social safety net institutions. Elsewhere (Woodson 2001), I grappled with defining appropriate impact indicators for food-for-work construction projects.

11. Chapters 3, 4, and 6 of each baseline study report (BARA 1996a, 1996b, 1997) discuss the elicitation and analytical procedures for household composition and household resource endowments.

12. JoAnn Jaffe (1990) showed why fluctuating livestock assets were critical variables in the performance of one rural locality's livelihood system in the Department of the South.

Working Anthropology
A View from the Women's Research Arena

Linda Basch

My voice comes from the borderlands of mainstream anthropology. I have worked as a research director at the United Nations and as an academic dean and vice president, and at the time of this writing I direct a national nonprofit network of 110 women's research and policy centers, two-thirds of which are located on university and college campuses. These are all places outside of what is typically thought of as the anthropological mainstream, and certainly outside of academic anthropology. Nonetheless, in all this work I have identified myself as an anthropologist, and the lens through which I view my work has been informed by anthropological theories, perspectives, and methodologies. I have been influenced by anthropological understandings and analytical frames such as power, border crossing, and coalition building; the politics of globalization, neoliberalism, transnationalism, race, and class; and the challenges and contradictions of connecting theory and action and of understanding the contingent nature of subjectivities.

The goals of the network I direct are to encourage and produce research that will improve the lived experiences and status of women and girls and advance equality and social justice; to raise public awareness of these issues; and to ensure that public debates and policies on critical issues are informed by a gender lens. In this work I interact and collaborate with a variety of constituents or partners—academic researchers and faculty from a diversity of disciplines including anthropology, activists and advocates, funders, policymakers, and corporate and academic leaders.

Although on the face of it this work might seem to build on an applied and practicing anthropology, I think my work has also benefited from a critical and empirical anthropology that is concerned with understanding the world "as it is" (Cowan 2006) and with understanding the intellectual histories in which empirical realities are grounded. In this chapter, through two case examples, I want to show how my work oscillates between a critical engagement with issues in which knowledge is used instrumentally to further aspirational goals such as economic justice and a recognition of the value of a more descriptively empirical understanding of the landscape in which I work. These two thrusts and the tensions between them have been seen in various contexts and at various moments in anthropology as opposed or as potentially complementary (Goodale 2006). They have also framed the work of a number of anthropologists concerned with animating social change (see Basch et al. 1999), such as Arjun Appadurai (2002), Franz Boas (1945), Jane Cowan (2006), Les Field (1999), Mark Goodale (2006), Dell Hymes (1972), Louise Lamphere (2004), Margaret Mead (1928), Sally Engle Merry (2003), James Peacock (1999), Peggy Reeves Sanday (2003), Terrence Turner (1997), and Eric Wolf (1999). As I show in this chapter, both approaches inform and influence my work, although at times the tensions between them seem irreconcilable.

In the following pages I first briefly describe the perceived role and goals of the research network I direct and then examine two seemingly very different projects as examples. One is focused on issues of human security in a globalizing world and follows on earlier work in which I explored the ways in which global capitalism creates, shapes, and is further shaped by fields of transnational social and political relations (Basch, Schiller, and Szanton 1994). The other addresses corporate women and their efforts to navigate the uncertainties and insecurities of a "new economy" (Fisher 2004) shaped by the changing conditions of global capitalism. Both projects are influenced by my anthropological grounding. Both are concerned with expanding understanding and knowledge of certain social phenomena, but they also have "political" agendas aimed at effecting change through the instrumental use of this knowledge. In both cases my anthropological perspective helps me to see, and weather, the contradictions inherent in trying to reconcile these at times seemingly opposing goals. Ultimately that perspective buttresses my view that an ecumenical approach (Goodale 2006) is possible.

Both projects are interdisciplinary and premised on the importance of collaboration in achieving the projects' goals. Here, my anthropological lens has enabled me to deal with the ontological challenges often posed by interdisciplinarity (Tickner 2004). It also helps me to be aware of and address the challenges of collaboration, including the pitfalls of potential complicity.

The Council, an Anthropological Lens, and Human Security

The National Council for Research on Women was founded in 1981 as a network of twenty-eight diverse research and policy centers, differently structured, with the broad goal of producing feminist research to improve the lived experiences and status of women and girls and advance equality and social justice. Created with funding from the Ford Foundation, the network was based on the view that in the increasingly conservative political and economic climate being shaped by the administration of President Ronald Reagan, the fledgling women's research centers would be better able to flourish if they were connected through a knowledge- and resource-sharing network. This network continues to grow: we admit about 6 centers a year, are now at 110, and have a large pool of centers interested in joining.

The centers share progressive missions and forms of analysis and are variously concerned with issues such as economic security, violence against women, reproductive rights, and gender and racial inequalities within institutions and communities. Some have a global thrust to their work. Grounded in a belief that academic researchers and advocates can productively work together to shape an informed activism in order to influence social change, Council members consist of both academic and policy research centers, some with explicit advocacy agendas. In the first decade of the twenty-first century, with gains achieved by women and girls under broad attack almost everywhere and with serious structural discrimination against women and girls continuing unchallenged in many parts of the world, it is felt that this research network has a real potential to make a difference.

The Council often plays a catalytic role in identifying new areas for research and change efforts while providing channels through which centers can develop collaborations. It aims to work across disciplinary boundaries and divides, in the belief that such hybridity can create fresh approaches to understanding and addressing the world in which we live. Increasingly, the Council and its members have been concerned with incorporating a more global focus in their work. A project focused on human security in this era of globalization seemed to address many of these goals and concerns.

The impetus for the project, which we called "Facing Global Capitalism, Finding Human Security: A Gendered Critique," was the emergence of a new discourse in the international community—that of human security. The focus on "human security" represented a shift in the paradigm of global security held by international organizations in the mid-1990s, away from a singular focus on the protection of national security and boundaries and toward the security of individuals during a moment of intense globalization, privatization, political conflict, militarization, and geopolitical border crossing by almost half the world's population (Basch 2004). A broad construct, human security, as defined by some, was seen to encompass human rights, economic development, and social activism. We applied for and received a Rockefeller Humanities grant to undertake this work.

I found that an anthropological lens helped not only in shaping the project and the questions we asked but also in analyzing and understanding the dynamics at play in carrying it out. Our goals for the project were at base the production of knowledge, which included an analysis of the value and meaning of a human security framework in the early twenty-first century, its contradictions, and the implications of this knowledge for the kinds of activism that could enhance human security. We also wanted to examine human security as a discourse, to understand whose security and rights were being served in the discourse, and to understand the larger relations of power and knowledge within which the discourse was being framed. And as in much of the anthropological and feminist work on human rights, which has critiqued the normativity of the white, heterosexual, European male as the liberal subject (Cowan 2006), we wanted to understand why a recognition of the multiple ways in which gender, racial, and class diversity affect security was largely absent from the framework.

Another important goal of the project was to create a space in which academic and policy researchers, as well as advocates in nongovernmental organizations (NGOs), could together problematize this construct and produce knowledge to enable actors to intervene in shaping both the discourse and activism around human security. We also thought this was a topic that would interest several of our centers and enable them to engage with global issues, and in fact we partnered aspects of the project with some of them.

A centerpiece of the project was a biweekly interdisciplinary seminar held over a three-year period at the City University of New York (CUNY) Graduate Center, in partnership with our member center at CUNY. We worked hard to include policy researchers from the United Nations and other international organizations and activists from NGOs and community-based organizations in our meetings, along with an interdisciplinary group of scholars, researchers, and graduate students— all people we wanted to engage in the critique process. The seminar consistently attracted a core of thirty to forty people, and it garnered a cachet and reputation as a place to debate critical global issues. While the seminar, through its readings, presentations, and discussions, was the site of much of the knowledge production generated by the project, it was also the site of multiple contentions and differences.

Beyond giving shape to the overall project, an anthropological lens helped influence many of the understandings that emerged. Because of the ontological and epistemological differences between political and feminist theorists and anthropologists and between academic researchers and activists, at many points in the seminar we seemed to be speaking past each other. Co-theorizing, a goal of the project, was often challenging. For example, the political and feminist theorists often focused attention on the principles, norms, and procedures associated with justice and with universalistic and ethical approaches to security and rights. The social anthropologists, in contrast, often anchored the discussion of security and rights in particularistic, empirical situations. Drawing on their empirical analyses, for instance, they were able to show the potential dangers of a hegemonic human security or rights regime and point to the ways in which many people, often the most marginalized, are excluded from this formulation. An anthropological lens also enabled anthropologists in the group to challenge assertions by some policy researchers who located the problems of establishing security in cultural practices that were seen as fixed and static; we argued for a contingent understanding of culture.

The first year of the project, during which we addressed security issues in the immediate aftermath of the attacks of September 11, 2001, was marked by frequent and heated challenges, debates, and expressions of multiple tensions. It was during this year that the opposition Mark Goodale (2006) described for anthropology, between an emancipatory cultural politics concerned with making knowledge instrumental and effecting change and an empirical anthropology skeptical of normative claims and concerned with unintended consequences of action, seemed to erupt. At many points in the seminar the force of critique stymied discussion of potential activist strategies, in particular, and had an immobilizing effect, leaving the impression that action in any direction had too many pitfalls. Consequently, although academics, including anthropologists who disagreed with some of the silencing that seemed to occur, continued to be regulars in the seminar, and although participation rates remained high, the participation of many activists and policy researchers from the United Nations and NGOs—those most concerned with effecting change—fell off, diminishing the co-theorizing and collaborations we had envisioned.

The Challenges of Collaboration

Anthropological research and theorizing also influenced both my analyses of and my efforts to address the challenges of collaboration that arose in the human security project. In a paper focused on locating public anthropology within the larger field of anthropology, Louise Lamphere (2004) discussed the necessity for and the challenges of creating meaningful collaborations when doing anthropology and the issues of power among participants that need to be addressed and negotiated. Issues of collaboration and power have in fact been addressed by many anthropologists concerned with social change, and they have helped me understand some of the dynamics in our human security project. For example, some anthropologists at the University of North Carolina (UNC) have created a context in which differently positioned actors—activists and academics, public intellectuals and community leaders—come together in symmetrical alliances to reflect on their experiences and generate new frameworks and strategies for creating and fostering social change (Fox, Powell, and Holland 2004).

The UNC efforts built on the work of Arturo Escobar (1998), Gustavo Lins Ribeiro (2004), and the World Anthropologies Network, who call for denaturalizing the dichotomies between academic and non-academic knowledge and for a simultaneous valuing of both local knowledges, gained through life experiences, and university-based knowledge in order to do social justice work. This reading of collaboration argues that everyone has valuable and only "partial perspectives" (Haraway 1991: 196) to bring to the discussion. Yet initial reports from this project cite the challenges of engagement across these differences.

Collaboration across disciplines and nationalities and among academic and policy researchers and organizational activists was central to the human security project. Yet as the project unfolded, we saw that there were challenges to collaboration that we needed to problematize and address. During the first year of our seminar, we were surprised at our inability to successfully engage the diverse participants in building new models of theory and action for addressing security issues. We had purposely reached out to academic scholars and feminist activists working with NGOs and the UN on global projects linked to issues of human security—all of whom shared substantive interests and political commitments.

The way scholars in the seminar responded to a guest expert who came to discuss the International Criminal Court as a potentially important site for addressing the security of women offers insight into the specific challenges posed to our envisioned collaboration. In our discussion, academic theorists put forth a critique that implicated human rights discourse in the power relations of global capital, which they depicted as inherently Western in genealogy. This analytical trajectory led to a questioning of the ethical morality of many NGOs as well as international organizations such as the International Criminal Court, given their locations in political spaces dominated by hegemonies of global capital.

What was missing from the discussion, and what became increasingly difficult to insert into the seminar, was a drawing of connections between the knowledge and analyses produced in the seminar and activist strategies. We were unable to move from an analysis of the dangers of co-optation and complicity to one in which we could see institutions such as the International Criminal Court and NGOs as emergent sites of intervention and resistance in which activists could and did struggle to disrupt and revise human rights strategies (see Cheah 1997). It was at this point in the seminar that many activists and policy researchers from the UN dropped out.

How can we understand the scholar-activist disconnect that seemed to fester early on in our seminar? This is a challenge that others have also experienced in different ways and have addressed. Les Field (1999), writing about the complicities and collaborations of anthropologists working among tribes in California, also drew attention to the difficulties of trying to speak both to politically concerned groups engaged in struggle and to one's more formally academic anthropology colleagues. He raised question about the different methodologies and commitments that guide such theorizing and action. It seems that in order to go forward with this kind of work, we need to develop a firmer understanding of these differences.

Dorothy Holland (2003) has raised questions about the ways in which identity shapes participation in hybrid networks. Reflecting on the identity politics that often underpin collaborative efforts, it seems that our seminar, especially in its early phases—given the way it was constructed—was perhaps destined to have the outcome it did. In order to provide everyone with a common baseline, we assigned a series of critical feminist readings, without also explicitly creating space for discussion of the diverse experiences activists brought to the group. We had expected that accounts of personal experiences would flow from the discussion, but the frames provided by the readings gave the meetings a distinct academic cast, precluding the kind of cross-border sharing of knowledge we had anticipated. Rather, cross-border engagement seemed to be trumped by identity and experiential factors, which precluded the development of the trust that might have facilitated such exchange.

Peggy Sanday has discussed how, in some cases, theorists "construct a formal theoretical language, which seems primarily designed to keep the uninitiated out and produce intellectual hierarchies" (Sanday 2003: n. 4). The fetishizing of knowledge that first emerged in our seminar, with its privileging of theoretical "thinking" over strategic policy and activist work, might also have been anchored partly in the disciplinary structure of the academy and its reward system, which by and large neither values new forms of collaborative knowledge production nor provides spaces for its emergence.

At the end of the first year of the seminar, to try to reflect on and understand what had happened to our interactive model, we held a series of discussions in which we confronted questions about the power dynamics in the seminar and about differences in the styles in which academic and non-academic identities were performed. These discussions led us to revise the structure of the meetings during the second and third years of the seminar to encourage the presentation of activist experiences, which became an increasingly important focus of our discussions. The participation of activists and policy researchers, however, remained sporadic and limited. At the same time, several in the seminar reported missing the sharp edge that had come from the more critical readings and analyses. Bringing together the sharp critiques of academic research with analyses of activist efforts remained elusive, even in the seminar's third year.

A Corporate Circle, Gender, and the New Economy of Uncertainty

The National Council for Research on Women has a diversity of projects in its repertoire, all aimed at understanding and addressing various types of gender discrimination. In 2001 the Council initiated a Corporate Circle, a network of approximately twenty companies, the majority of them situated in the financial services, pharmaceutical, and cosmetic industries and in law. The basis of the relationship between the Council and these corporations is the research and information the Council provides to the companies to enable them to create greater gender diversity at senior levels, for which they pay an annual fee. The Council views the corporate arena as a new terrain for women's work and activism, one in which women's advancement into key decision-making positions is severely limited. The participants in the circle's activities are primarily senior women and some supportive men, who are intent on changing these relations of power.

As in the human security project, the vision and shape I have brought to this project as the Council's director, and the research issues it addresses, draw heavily on anthropological understandings and analyses. A major dynamic of the project is the knowledge and information provided to senior women that enables them to examine both their circumstances and strategies for change as they try to navigate the "new economy" of uncertainty and insecurity generated by frequent mergers and acquisitions, downsizing, rapid changes in work structures and environments, and the changing composition and demographics of the workforce (Fisher 2004). Toward this end, the Corporate Circle draws on research examining the brittle structures that envelop these women and that cannot accommodate their life-cycle experiences and needs, as well as the cultural attitudes that support these structures and make negotiating advancement difficult. Here, too, as in the human security project, there is a concern with making knowledge instrumental. But there is also a concern to help these actors understand the ways in which issues they deal with in the corporate arena are related to larger social and cultural issues.

Senior human resource professionals charged with recruiting and retaining a diverse and talented workforce predominate in the Corporate Circle. Along with researchers who produce the knowledge and information, they shape the circle's agenda. Programs have focused on work/life balance issues, strategies for working across racial and ethnic differences, the complexities of crafting diversity and gay-lesbian-bisexual-transgendered practices and policies in global companies, and ways to address thorny issues such as religious and gender expression in the workplace given legal and cultural constraints. A particular contribution of anthropology has been the analysis of how power works, so that the research can lead to strategies that go beyond mere window dressing to identify ways to change structures and supporting cultural assumptions, even though this is knowledge that only some actors can use, and only in limited ways.

An anthropological lens also places in relief the contradictions that inhere in a collaboration between corporations and a network of academic and policy research centers, given the different interests, ideologies, and positionings of women in the two arenas and their potential to collide. Many researchers in our member academic centers have examined and are concerned about the negative effects of expanding neoliberal economic practices and policies, unbridled capitalism, and privatization on social injustice, growing economic disparities, and continuing inequalities of race and class. To some researchers in our network, corporate women inhabit a space that is implicated in generating these inequalities. Corporate women, for their part, "don't get" the relevance of much of the Council's research agenda outside the corporate arena—for example, our focus on human security and a project that has examined the ways taxes negatively affect whole classes of women. One of the challenges for the Council is to find ways for these differently positioned women to begin to understand each other's circumstances and challenges and to see the connections between the different kinds of discrimination they confront.

Collaboration or Complicity?

In both the human security and Corporate Circle projects, questions have been raised about where collaboration veers into complicity. In the human security project, for example, diasporic scholars in our seminar with roots in the global South expressed concerns about their complicity in maintaining the global hierarchies of power that constrain both their countries of origin and themselves in their current locations in a racially structured society. Similarly, collaborations between academic researchers and corporate women have the potential for complicity in a number of situations, most imminently in constraining researchers' ability to speak out publicly about how their research shows that tax cuts on wealth translate into service cuts that negatively affect most middle- and low-income women. And along these lines, although corporate women will collaborate with anthropologists in unmasking a system that limits their advancement, the collaboration thins when it comes to analyzing how that system intensifies wealth disparities between rich and poor.

Here, too, however, anthropology provides useful analytical tools. In analyzing complicities and collaborations among anthropologists and the "unacknowledged tribes" of California, Field (1999: 193) drew on a maxim developed by Audre Lorde, that "the master's tools will never dismantle the master's house," insinuating that these tools are complicit in sustaining entrenched hierarchies of power. Yet Field also raised questions about how these tools might change, depending on who wields them and for what purpose, suggesting a more contingent relationship between the tools and the house.

Field's observation has relevance for both the human security and Corporate Circle projects. A growing literature has begun to address the ways NGOs, by virtue of funding by governments and foundations, become stakeholders in current neoliberal policies (Charkiewicz 2004; Yuval-Davis 2004). As the argument goes, NGOs can become so subsumed within frameworks of power that they no longer see the inequities in the larger institutions in which they have become enmeshed—often the very institutions that need to be transformed. But as Field asked in his analysis of anthropology's tools, are they merely the tools of the master or might they, in the hands of others, be able to undermine the master's house?

Although it is true that the Council receives funding from foundations and corporations, each with its own agenda, the Council is also potentially in a position to wield tools, with some reflection, that bear its perspective. Indeed, a question for our organization is whether we can collectively engage women who occupy multiple positions and are at different economic levels—academics, activists, policymakers, and corporate leaders—who are represented in our broad network. Can we, for example, help them to recognize the stakes for all women in issues of human security, tax policy, diversity in higher education and corporate arenas, and other areas of social justice that we address? And how can we avoid getting drawn into their interpretations of the world and their priorities?

In Sum

In addressing the ways anthropology as a field has expanded beyond academe and other more "traditional" settings, I have highlighted a new site for anthropological work—a network of women's academic and policy research centers organized as a nonprofit organization. On the face of it this network, in its concern with fostering social change and justice that addresses gender discrimination and in its work with diverse partners such as academic researchers, policy advocates, funders, and corporate leaders, might seem to speak exclusively to and draw upon methods from an applied or practicing anthropology. I have tried to show, however, that many of the projects in the network's repertoire have been shaped not only by a strand of anthropology concerned with developing knowledge that can be used instrumentally to foster change but also by a critical anthropology grounded in empirical investigation and undergirded by particular intellectual and social histories.

Two examples illustrated the way these two anthropological approaches can be complementary despite contradictions that must be addressed. Those examples were a project focused on understanding the meaning and value of a human security framework under recent conditions of globalization and a project concerned with shaping a circle of women corporate leaders who could go beyond addressing their own particular circumstances to seeing interconnections with other kinds of discrimination. This analysis and work have benefited from the work of anthropologists engaged in the human rights arena and of those attempting to speak from their locations within mainstream anthropology to and for groups engaged in political struggle.

An organization located at the nexus of a network of diverse constituents both enjoys possibilities for and faces challenges to collaboration. Anthropological analyses have expanded my understanding of ways to negotiate and also forge collaborative connections in a sea of complex differences, interests, and epistemologies. Anthropological analysis additionally has helped me understand the dangers posed by potential complicities but also to consider the ways different methodologies and approaches can address and mitigate these complicities. In sum, I have described, at mid-course, a new type of work drawing on anthropological theories and methodologies. The challenge will be to see whether these methods and approaches can continue to productively infuse the organization's diverse agendas.

Potential Collaborations and Disjunctures in Australian Work Sites

An Experiential Rendering

Sandy Toussaint

I travel 4,300 kilometers north of Western Australia's capital city, Perth, to undertake fieldwork in the remote Kimberley, a region renowned for its sparse population. Most of that population is made up of Indigenous women, men, and children who live in small, scattered towns and communities or on large cattle stations. The landscape is characterized by red earth (or "pindan"), sand hills, and dense clumps of low-lying eucalyptus trees. Intertwined river systems that rely for their survival on annual rains known locally as "the wet season," along with a rich spectrum of unique native flora and fauna, add to the biodiversity of the region.

It can take four or five days to drive from Perth in the south of Western Australia to the Kimberley in the north. This time I take three hours to fly by plane to Broome, on the west coast, a seaside town that increasingly attracts national and international tourism. From Broome I hire a four-wheel-drive vehicle to cover another four hundred kilometers inland to the Fitzroy Valley in the Kimberley's heartland. It is "hot weather time," several months before the anticipated rains. The daily temperature averages 45 degrees Celsius, resulting in a dry environment that I am now accustomed to working in, having done so for several decades.

Like other anthropologists who retain long-term relationships with the people with whom they work, I am returning to familiar places and faces, sounds and smells. An affectionate, interactive process of news exchange takes place in settings that include people's homes, riverbanks, dry creek beds, the roadhouse, or garage (where petrol, cool drinks, and food can be purchased), the local art center, bush camps such as Moorgoomoorgoowidi and Jiliyarti, cattle stations, and shady roadside byways. Conversations focus on newborn infants, an innovative pottery making center, the diminished state of the local Fitzroy River, the extent of fish catches, progress on the latest native title land claim, and the content of a meeting on economic and environmental issues that I have come to attend.

Our interactions also focus on sorrowful and tragic news: the suicide by hanging of an eleven-year-old boy, the death due to renal failure of a middle-aged man, and the senseless bashing of a woman by her inebriated and violent husband. Several communities have houses in urgent need of repair, and a bore-water pump requiring maintenance floods at least one family's home. I learn, too, that without adequate funding, an Indigenous organization has relocated its office to Broome, leaving local groups without their own resource center to facilitate, on their behalf, matters such as resource exploration and native title land claims.

I remain in the Kimberley for four weeks, participating in meetings and carrying out ethnographic work related to a collaborative research project about the use and management of water sources. The Kimberley is one of four Australian locations where this research is being undertaken. After a month, I return to another work site. This one is at a Perth university where I have a tenured academic position. I lecture, tutor and mentor students, carry out reviews of research grant applications and manuscripts, and attend to far too much administration. I check emails, correspondence, and phone calls, mark honors papers, and prepare an exam for a social theory course. I consult with students aspiring to become professional anthropologists and deal with requests from the administrative unit within which anthropology is situated to quantify workloads. I am advised that from now on, research for lecture creation and presentation is to be counted as equivalent to two hours only for one lecture and as one hour only for a tutorial or seminar.

I attend to a range of other matters, including information that the ethnographic museum for which I am a board member is to extend its membership to include business personnel, so that the museum's financial potential can be better realized. Like other academics, I am encouraged to apply for research grants to enhance school and faculty budgets and individual "teaching buyout" possibilities, so I peruse the literature directed to me. A journalist from a national radio station makes contact to organize an interview about the water research project, as does a senior adviser from a government department who wishes to arrange a meeting to discuss the project's findings.

Several days after being back in Perth, I contemplate the vastly different work sites in which I am involved, pondering the geographic, economic, and intellectual distances between them. I also receive a phone call one evening from a Kimberley family member who tells me that another death has occurred. I am at home at the time, still grading honors essays. I replace the receiver and reflect on the deceased person's life and death, the enormous loss to loved ones, and her family's situation. I also find myself reflecting on being a working anthropologist in the twenty-first century.

At a time when interest in anthropology is growing in countries such as Australia, the variegated demands that shape anthropology's adaptive practices generate both promise and contention. Inspired by the emergence of a range of "world anthropologies" (Ribeiro and Escobar 2006; see also Toussaint 2006a; World Anthropologies Network 2003), in this chapter I explore, from an experiential vantage point, the way anthropologists both within hegemonic anthropology and as critics of it might endeavor to communicate more effectively with people who are unfamiliar with the discipline's ethos, etiquette, and expertise. I treat "work" primarily as research but also as a range of other labor-oriented tasks. I consider anthropology as a culturally convenient product and look at the multiple sites in which anthropology increasingly is done.

Focused on Australian settings and offered as a multilayered and interwoven rendering, my approach to this timely topic is largely reflexive and descriptive. I concentrate on two examples from Australian work sites: a legal controversy surrounding the estate of an Aboriginal man who died intestate, and a cross-disciplinary cultural tourism project. Both work sites are situated in the remote Kimberley region of Western Australia, Australia's largest state.[1] My concern is with what these examples, on their own and in conjunction with each other, reveal about anthropology both at and as work.[2] I am especially interested in exploring the richness, the limitations, and the cultural convenience of working anthropology's expansion. In a less pronounced way, and consistent with the opening paragraphs of the chapter, I contrast the two examples with experiences at the university work site. I begin by outlining the scope of Australian anthropology at the time of writing and recent changes in its practice.

The Work of Australian Anthropologists

Australian anthropology, like anthropologies elsewhere, is an increasingly diverse field of inquiry. Although my experience, hardly unique in the history of Australian anthropology, has been primarily with Indigenous groups (e.g., Toussaint 1999a, 2001, 2003),[3] academic interest has grown to include settler societies and non-Indigenous topics both inside and outside Australia—and somewhere in between, as in the plight of Indonesian fishers caught fishing off Australia's northwest coastline. Research and teaching are carried out with regard to a spectrum of Asian contexts such as Bangladesh, the Philippines, and Indonesia, European settings such as Italy and the Balkans, and locations in the Middle East and North Africa. Subject matter varies greatly and includes refugees and migration, environmental studies, the anthropology of disability, musicology, gender and sexuality, governance, healing rituals, textile practice, globalization, and the politics of health.

Alongside this rich expansion of topics has come a marked shift in the extent to which applied or practical anthropology is being done. The main reason for this development is a 1992 decision by the Australian High Court in the case *Mabo v. Commonwealth (No. 2)*, generally known as the "Mabo decision" or *Mabo*. This ruling resulted in passage of the 1993 Native Title Act and the establishment of a process whereby Indigenous people could lodge claims for land in a national tribunal. This process necessitates anthropological input, and *Mabo* has generated substantial employment for anthropologists as full-time or part-time researchers for Indigenous land councils, government agencies, nongovernmental organizations, and sectors of industry (see Toussaint 2006a). It has also facilitated the introduction of expensive, fee-paid courses in Australian universities in which students are specifically trained for work in multidisciplinary native title research projects. It is less clear that Indigenous claimants and their families have benefited from *Mabo* in the way the original decision foreshadowed. Few claims have been wholly successful, and mediation to resolve claim disputes is often lengthy and costly, tending to privilege the laws of the Australian state over customary land tenure laws (Ritter and Flanagan 2004).[4]

For anthropologists, native title claims represent a work site that draws on manifold aspects of anthropological research—conducting fieldwork, analyzing ethnographic data, recording oral histories, preparing and reviewing claim reports, researching and producing genealogies, filtering archival material, and so on. These activities take place in different settings (on-site at specific locations, in university, government, and tribunal offices, in federal or high court, in museums and libraries) and with different persons (claimants, lawyers, administrators, archivists, geographers, and so on). Work on native title cases also requires anthropologists increasingly to reflect on how best to serve a range of clients and to explain the benefits of anthropological inquiry to non-anthropologists.

Although native title work regularly highlights the type of communication possible between anthropologists and lawyers (a point expanded on in Trigger 2004), other aspects of Indigenous life, in addition to title recovery, are likely to benefit from anthropological knowledge and practice. These include health, healing, and mourning, where possibilities for enhancing knowledge and ensuring appropriate care for ill or bereaved persons are likely to arise if discursive engagement between medical practitioners (nurses, doctors, specialists, counselors, therapists) and cultural or medical anthropologists takes place. Moreover, constructive rapprochement between anthropologists and environmental scientists can facilitate greater understanding of human-habitat relationships.[5]

The sort of multifaceted, multisited anthropology I have just outlined encompasses, of course, far more than just native title, health, and environmental studies. The outline does, however, introduce the complex of issues I pursue in this chapter. To illuminate those issues, I examine two projects focused on Indigenous Australian settings, with the university work site as backdrop. My aim is to show how the two kinds of sites can be distinguished from each other, a distinction that brings into sharp relief working anthropology's rich potential, as well as its limitations. It is these "twin peaks" of potential and limitations that ensure anthropology's working future: there is promise to be better realized, obstacles that warrant further anthropological engagement, and pathways that should be approached with caution.

Describing and analyzing anthropology both as and at work embodies, not surprisingly, a range of inquiries, perspectives, and experiences, some of which I cannot explore here. The exclusion of, for example, settler and environmental issues in Australia and the complex relationship between Australia and its neighbors does not minimize their importance to working anthropology in particular and to Australian anthropology in general. My concentration on Indigenous Australians undoubtedly raises concerns that anthropologists who work with other groups do not regularly have to take into account. It is no secret, for instance, that Aboriginal and Islander women, men, and children continue to suffer the highest rates of morbidity and mortality in Australian society. This shocking situation complicates the ways in which anthropological work with Indigenous groups takes place, a reality evident in the opening paragraphs of this chapter and threaded throughout the rest of it.[6]

Kumunjayi's Estate

"Kalyeeda," a member of the Walmajarri language group, whose homelands are in the southwest Kimberley, called to say that one of her uncles, a man in his sixties whom I refer to here as "Kumunjayi" (an Indigenous term for a recently deceased person) had died. As a young man in the 1970s, Kumunjayi had suffered a mental illness and been removed by health department authorities from his family and community to an institution in Perth. He lived at the institution for almost three decades, unable to return to visit his Kimberley kin. Family members kept in touch with him by sending cards and parcels of clothing and by making phone calls. They also visited him whenever they traveled the long distance to Perth.

In accordance with local custom and law, Kumunjayi's body was returned to the Kimberley. Extensive arrangements for the burial were made by close family members. After the funeral, mourning activities, including ritual wailing or keening, a smoke ceremony, and the enactment of dietary restrictions for kin, especially restrictions on the consumption of beef, took place among his closest relatives.

Several months after the funeral service, a social worker from the Perth institution where Kumunjayi had resided for so long contacted the family to advise that because Kumunjayi had died intestate, the staff was unsure what to do about the funds that remained in his bank account. Kumunjayi had accumulated a sizable amount of money as a result of social security (or "government welfare") entitlements he had received. The cost of his institutionalization had not consumed all of his fortnightly disbursement, nor had these funds been used for other purposes, primarily because Kumunjayi's absence from his community meant that he had been uninvolved in the usual cycle of economic exchange and reciprocity in the Kimberley. Without a will, the social worker advised Kalyeeda, the institution had to direct the matter of Kumunjayi's untouched funds to the state government's Public Trustees Office. Once this occurred, the legal and administrative arrangements could be worked out.

Upon contact with the Public Trustees Office, Kalyeeda called me again. She said that the office and a genealogical services organization had been briefed to work on Kumunjayi's case. Personnel from these offices had stressed to Kalyeeda, as the family's representative, that various pieces of family information were missing. Because Kumunjayi and his siblings were of the generation for which being born in "the bush" and not in a local hospital was common, certificates to confirm their births and birthdates did not exist. Of less importance, but also at issue, was that the state had never issued a certificate showing the legal marriage of Kumunjayi's parents, who had been betrothed and married under the Indigenous system of religion and customary law.

From the perspective of the state, no official documentation existed to show that Kumunjayi was who he was said to have been.[7] The problem that arose for the family, therefore, was that of demonstrating his existence and their heritage to the Public Trustees Office and the genealogical services office. How could the family show its relationship to Kumunjayi in a way that would be acknowledged outside their own system of religion and law? On behalf of Kumunjayi's family, Kalyeeda asked whether I could provide some assistance. In particular, the family thought that the family tree on which I had worked with them for many years (and in which Kumunjayi had automatically been included) might help to explain their circumstances.[8]

My initial response was that the state personnel involved should understand that Indigenous testimony was sufficient to support the family's claim, especially because historical problems associated with customary-law marriages and the use (or misuse) of certificates had been dealt with in findings of the Australian Law Reform Commission (1986) and the Royal Commission into Aboriginal Deaths in Custody (1991). But Kalyeeda's response and, to a lesser extent, the responses of people in the Public Trustees Office and the genealogical services organization was that the genealogy was crucial to revealing how Kumunjayi had been connected to past and present kin, especially grandparents, parents, siblings, and the offspring of siblings.[9]

Staff at the Public Trustees Office and the genealogical services organization also made it clear that genealogical data could assist them in "filling in the historical gaps" where birth and marriage certificates should (from the vantage point of the state) have been.[10] Similarly, Kumunjayi's family made the point that the genealogy could now be used for a purpose that had not originally been envisioned, and although they felt some reluctance to provide information to an unknown group of government officers, the genealogy had the potential to enhance their claim as beneficiaries. The family believed that communicating such data could also help to educate non-Indigenous people about the structure and the affective content of Indigenous family relationships.

Taking into account the concerns of all parties, but still ambivalent about the use of anthropological work in circumstances where Indigenous testimony should have been all that was needed to prove the case, I agreed to extract the relevant information from the large genealogy on which I had been working. I also prepared a letter explaining how to interpret the material and sent both documents to the staff working on Kumunjayi's case. This action, unfortunately, did not end the matter. Although Kumunjayi's mother, father, siblings, and maternal and paternal grandparents were all located in the genealogy in accordance with the information I had collected, the extract seemed to complicate things in ways we had not anticipated.

For one thing, officers at the genealogical services organization asked me to clarify Kumunjayi's "biological" and "blood" relationships, because these were the most important ties with regard to current policy and legislative requirements.[11] My task then became one of trying to explicate the way in which Indigenous families are constituted, which includes a complex mix of social and biological classifications wherein "blood" ties are not necessarily privileged. In Kumunjayi's case, his biological father was not the man who lived with his mother. Nor was he the man Kumunjayi called father. The man Kumunjayi called father, a man widely recognized by members of his extended family and the local community as Kumunjayi's "proper father," was the man who lived long-term with his mother and with whom she had two other children. These children were regularly referred to and treated as Kumunjayi's sister and brother, although within the government's purview they were regarded as half-siblings.[12]

Although I was able to explain to Kumunjayi's family the need to have "white fella" documentation to verify to the state who he and his descendants were, I was less successful in persuading either the genealogical services organization or the Public Trustees Office of the importance of understanding the social and cultural implications of Kumunjayi's situation. Staff at the two offices had indicated in our initial discussions that Kumunjayi's case would benefit from cultural analysis and anthropological input on some of the kinship issues, but as a more complex interpretation emerged, this position shifted to one focused on the reporting of biological ties in the terms required by relevant policies and legislation. A letter I received from the genealogical services organization, dated 7 April 2005, said, "For the purposes of inheritance under intestacy laws ... we are only interested in biological relatives, not cultural ones."

This statement stifled communication, revealing that although at one stage it had been culturally convenient and perhaps thought of as expedient for each party to draw on anthropological work, this was no longer the case. The family's major concerns included its desire to have its social and cultural (as well as biological) affiliations with Kumunjayi recognized and the ambivalent status of Kumunjayi's father rectified. What constituted evidence to demonstrate kin-based relationships became a major issue.[13]

At the time of writing, Kumunjayi's case remains unresolved, and it is unclear whether or not his descendants will benefit from his estate. The hope that some of the more complex issues that guide and make meaningful contemporary Indigenous sociality and cultural life and the aspiration that future claims will not be denied in the same way continue to be unfulfilled. The usefulness of anthropological work in the case also remains unclear, despite that work's being based on long-term engagement resulting in, among other things, a detailed and potentially useful genealogy, and despite the opportunity of cultural translation for each party. Such knowledge and expertise were undoubtedly limited by the legal, historical, and structural domains in which attempts to resolve Kumunjayi's legacy were made.

I worked on the case in multiple ways familiar to most anthropologists— as researcher, interlocutor, expert witness, advocate, and interpreter— and at many different sites, including Kumunjayi's home community and government and university offices. I was also required to explain knowledge and information in different communicative formats— translated conversations, emails, faxes, phone calls, correspondence. I explained a complex system of kinship and customary law to one party and an equally complex system of evidentiary issues to another. Questions of kinship resulted in a distinction's being made with respect to family members related through biological descent, or "blood ties," and those related through "social kinship." This distinction was a key issue, one likely to arise again in Australia, where Kumunjayi's case highlights the difficulty for Indigenous persons of dealing with jurisdictional intestacy laws.

Several significant issues arise from this example. How can anthropologists more effectively put to work the knowledge that emerges in very different ethnographic sites and as a result of cultural translation and interpretation? How can the results of our practices be translated into structural change? In this case, how can the principles of Indigenous kinship be formally encoded in relevant policies and laws? How useful was the anthropological work when, with its focus on the social and cultural rather than biological requirements of kinship, it had the potential to work against the interests of Kumunjayi's family?

Indigenous people are increasingly being advised by lawyers who work in organizations such as the Aboriginal Legal Service (a service now available in every Australian state and territory, although its offices are widespread and not always funded adequately) of their entitlements with regard to the writing of wills and the consequences of dying intestate. Consequently, the situation that arose for Kumunjayi's family is likely to be repeated. Demands for the kind of anthropological work I have described are likely to increase, so it is an area that requires attention to ensure its effectiveness. But such effectiveness has to do not only with anthropologists, whose power and authority will always be constrained by forces outside their sphere of knowledge and control. I was unable to assist Kumunjayi's beneficiaries, despite the fact that the genealogy and the translation of Kumunjayi's family's information contained vital evidence to support their case. The question that arises, therefore, is how the process and results of anthropological work can be transformed from being conceptualized as convenient or muted to being seen as a vital resource.[14]

A Cross-Disciplinary Cultural Tourism Project

This example, too, involves a Kimberley work site, and the community is again one with which I have worked as an anthropologist for many years. We were therefore "known" to each through decades of work and other experiences. For example, we shared family interests, regularly stayed at each other's homes when either party was in the Kimberley or in Perth, tutored each other about cultural beliefs and practices, and enjoyed fishing and camping excursions when northern seasonal conditions allowed.

Several community family groups were committed to developing a cultural tourism project on their homelands, a location adjacent to a unique series of limestone caves and river systems. A place of refuge during harrowing colonial encounters, it also figured prominently as a significant site in local trading routes and song cycles. The traditional owners, or senior custodians (the persons who retained cultural and religious authority over the site as ordained by customary law), asked whether I could work with them to record ethnographic data that could be written up into a booklet to be sold to tourists. The aim was to make available unrestricted (publicly available) information about their beliefs and practices as these related to the landscape and frontier history, bush food and medicine, mythological accounts, and historical events.

The land (also referred to by Indigenous groups as "country") on which the community had lived and worked for countless generations was positioned between a national park and a cattle station. It was the type of location that tourists increasingly wanted to visit, partly because of broader interest in Indigenous cultures and reconciliation in a post-Mabo era. The Indigenous owners were happy to share some of their knowledge and were enthusiastic about constructing an enterprise that might enable them to be economically independent. Without such opportunities the community, like many others in Australia, remained dependent on government-issued social security entitlements. The venture was therefore conceptualized as one that could not only provide education for people visiting the site but also generate employment for current and future family members.

I readily agreed to work alongside the community, a strong, cohesive group of families with a desire to maintain a viable living and working place on their own land. After some preliminary research, and mindful of the site's geological, geographic, environmental, and archaeological qualities, I raised with the community the possibility of having a scientist work on the project.[15] There were several reasons for this suggestion. First, such involvement might produce research results that I could not provide. With the kind of "hard" scientific data promised by another researcher complementing the ethnographic data I would produce, the evidence might appeal to a number of audiences in addition to tourists. These included scholars in Indigenous and environmental studies, colleagues in cognate disciplines, and future funding agencies.[16]

The second reason was that as a full-time academic who regularly undertakes applied research, in part to retain a grounded perspective and to support community aspirations, I wanted to foster cross-disciplinary work that might "add value" to future research grant applications. Another important dimension was that such collaborative research might help to generate a new, unique, substantive body of knowledge. My interests could therefore be described as encompassing a variety of work sites and a complex mix of intellectual, practical, ethical, and economic motives.

After lengthy communication that included conversations at the site, a meeting between the scientist and the family groups involved, and follow-up phone calls and faxes, the community indicated a willingness to have another researcher work on the project. With support from the community and in receipt of the required ethics approval, my colleague and I then applied for and received a grant to undertake the research.

As the project proceeded, my work extended to keeping the scientist and the community informed about each other's situation—for example, by contextualizing the cultural environment and local history for the scientist and explaining the actions and priorities of the scientist to the community. It seemed likely in the early stages that the project would be a rewarding one with the potential to promote practical ideas for cross-disciplinary work in similar situations. Although the project was built on an Indigenous initiative, an additional aim became that of constructing a "working model" for cross-disciplinary collaborative projects involving diverse researchers and community groups elsewhere.

Over eighteen months, research was carried out intermittently for several weeks at a time both at the field site and at our respective work-places. Guided by members of the community, especially the senior custodians and a local liaison officer, the project team was able to produce extensive cultural and historical documentation about the place, including significant ethnographic, historical, environmental, and archaeological sites, one of which revealed thousands of years of human occupation. The project also resulted in community agreement to nominate the area for inclusion in a national heritage register and produced material for the preparation of a cultural tourism booklet.

At the outset, the aim was for the community to be involved in training and on-site research methods, such as recording interviews, cultural mapping, photographic work, and digging. A further aim, as I mentioned, was to identify a model that might be useful for cross-disciplinary work in similar projects and in the human and other sciences more generally. But during fieldwork it became apparent that the scientist and I had quite different emphases and worked in very different ways. What seemed to matter most for my colleague, as far as I could gauge, was physical evaluation of the site and the recording of material items. What mattered most to me was understanding the community's representations of its cultural attachments to persons and place.

Tensions between my co-researcher and me began to become apparent in the mornings, when we visited the community on the way to particular work sites or where we planned to work on a certain day. This kind of ritual visiting usually involved several hours of conversation and negotiation with the project collaborators, often while drinking cups of strong "billy tea," eating home-baked bread (known as "damper"), and talking about matters of relevance to the community. As an anthropologist, I regarded these times as crucial to the project's success. Conversations and spending quiet or noisy time together not only elicited data but also generated substantive debate related to cultural history and matters of interest to the families. These times, which for any anthropologist could be referred to only as "work," also involved an assessment by senior women and men regarding who was best suited to work as paid assistants on the project that day—collecting species examples, explaining cultural data, tagging samples, tracking, and so forth. Such time, too, opened up valuable opportunities to discuss people's questions or concerns about a project going on at the community's home, a place it had occupied for thousands of years.

The scientist, however, became increasingly agitated and expressed irritation about "too much time being wasted" at the community each morning before traveling to the actual work site, a distance of approximately ten kilometers across difficult terrain in a four-wheel-drive vehicle. A number of fractious moments arose that affected us in different ways. The scientist expressed urgency to collect and bag as many samples (charcoal, plant species, etc.) as possible, whereas I was keen to build on and interpret the ethnographic and historical data. I was also concerned to maintain the kind of sociality I had established with the community over several decades and was mindful of the social and economic circumstances in which they lived.[17]

Things worsened after the field component of the research was completed and the scientist and I returned to our respective work sites. Difficulties arose when certain items were not returned to the community within a required time frame, despite an earlier agreement that the items would be removed only temporarily and had to be returned. From the scientist's angle, these items could be usefully employed in teaching students, a judgment I regarded as a divergence from our original work plan and one that a lawyer later advised was a breach of confidentiality.[18]

An added concern was that whereas we had both agreed not to write about the research project or our findings before conferring with the community and each other, the scientist overlooked this and wrote about the project without prior consultation. When I became aware that an article had been submitted for publication, it was too late for it to be withdrawn. The response from community members on hearing this news was one of anxiety, as expressed by one of the custodians: "But everyone will know about us now ... we're worried ... we don't want television cameras out here." In light of the difficulty of securing the return of the items to the community, the publication of the article, and a number of related concerns, support for the scientist was withdrawn in a letter sent by the traditional owners, a request with which the scientist eventually complied.

The community and I were both distressed by this unanticipated series of events. For different reasons, it is likely that the scientist felt similarly disaffected. Despite all original intentions and a continuing interest in having a "different" kind of knowledge infused into the project, I sustained a terrible unease and came to regret facilitating the involvement of someone unknown to the community.[19] I looked for ways to try to reconcile the situation but was not particularly successful, except that the community and I continued to collaborate on the cultural tourism booklet. Our joint endeavors resulted in its realization.

This example raises a number of issues that demand anthropological contemplation. Although in a variety of ways the cultural tourism project could be analyzed as an endeavor in which ethical and political conflicts were amplified, with some distance from the project it seems clear that certain problems arose because each researcher approached the work situation from a very different experiential dynamic. We also came from very different educational and socially attuned cultural backgrounds. It was not that we were unable to understand the possible contributions of each other's discipline; before the fieldwork, the emphasis was on collaboration. In the field, different priorities emerged, and after the fieldwork, they intensified. The scientist, for instance, felt pressured to produce the kinds of results that are increasingly encouraged in Australian universities—grants, publications, prospects for further research. Anthropologists are similarly encouraged, but most of them, I suggest, continue to put the communities with which they work first when a conflict of interest arises. It also appeared that the scientist, unfamiliar with local faces and places and the sounds and smells of the work site (and as someone not "known" by the local community), had tried to optimize a culturally opportune means to gain access to a site and community otherwise inaccessible.[20]

Cross-disciplinary work was unsuccessful for any of the parties on this occasion. Although I believe anthropologists need to be cautious about cross-disciplinary work, primarily because the uniqueness and integrity of anthropological work may be diminished under such arrangements, there is clearly room for such work to be effective in research and teaching. A perennial epistemological and ethical problem for all anthropologists, especially those in similar situations, is how to ensure that anthropological work, experience, and knowledge are fruitfully sought and acquired. At present, as the examples discussed here represent, anthropology's contribution remains contested or ambiguously understood. In Australian settings, circumstances for anthropology and related disciplines are often affected by structural and economic changes in the university sector and the effects of technology in increasingly global contexts.

Discussion

The experiential character that forms the core of my two examples contrasts starkly with the character of a university work site. But although the environment, aesthetic, methods, and purposes of the two sites differ—as in the use of participant-observation fieldwork in one and the preparation of lectures in the other—they parallel each other in that each is a location in which different kinds of anthropological work take place.

For a number of reasons, the distinction between work sites is widening, a phenomenon that necessitates an exploration not only of anthropological practice but also of the teaching, research, and ethical implications for anthropology's working future. One reason underlying this phenomenon is that, as a result of government policies aimed at commercializing the tertiary or university sector, academic anthropologists have been drawn into a situation in which competition for research grants and consultancies is regularly encouraged. In some projects, the inclusion of anthropologists might add a convenient edge in terms of expertise in social or cultural issues. A corporate-like structure is emerging in Australian universities, bringing with it a managerial style some intellectual distance from academic research and scholarly expertise (Strathern and Stewart 2001). A second reason is that the Australian federal government has introduced industrial reforms that have the potential to further diminish the working entitlements of all academics, including anthropologists. New contracts referred to as "Australian Workplace Agreements," or AWAs, threaten to abolish protection for unfair dismissal, change the ways in which minimum wages are set, diminish the role of tertiary sector unions, and remove the powers of an independent industrial relations commission (Allport 2005).

The third reason is that the use of technology in global contexts has added to the complex demands made on and by university staff, including anthropologists. As I have discussed elsewhere (Toussaint 2006b), although the Internet and cyberspace facilities can produce the conditions for productive engagement—such as for communication among members of the World Anthropologies Network—in local circumstances such technology can weaken collegiality. For example, expedient email exchanges may replace more discursive and informative corridor conversations.

The work sites discussed here provide, at one level, unique case studies, but they also reveal striking resonances and reflect changing social, economic, and political circumstances, including those within the discipline of anthropology. When the layers of each work site are unraveled, it is clear that a multitude of complex issues is in need of further inquiry, discussion, and debate. Anthropologists are best placed not only to undertake such discussions but also to educate future generations about their epistemological, methodological, and ethical importance. A range of working pathways is clearly emerging, alongside questions surrounding how, what, where, and by whom such work will be done.

Anthropologists who do not work with colonized communities (sectors of which remain severely disadvantaged) might tell a different working story of Australian anthropology. But I believe the experiential rendering I have offered reflects practical, intellectual, and ethical concerns that will be recognized by, if not directly understood or experienced by, many kinds of anthropologists. Communicating among ourselves, creating room for multiple anthropologies to emerge, and investigating a transparent means to explain the potential of anthropology as working "product" represent manifold possibilities. But these possibilities will always need to be balanced alongside the social and cultural complexities that filter and sometimes stifle the lives and aspirations of the people among whom anthropologists work.

Epilogue

The Australian academic year is drawing to a close. University staff are now heavily involved in marking exams, organizing and ranking scholarships, thinking about teaching requirements for the next year, and preparing coursework outlines and reading lists. Writing projects remain half-finished, giving way to more urgent tasks such as dealing with students who failed essay and tutorial papers, final exam meetings with colleagues, administrative demands, and the preparation of referee reports for students about to enter the "real" world of work. Email exchanges are at a premium, often replacing what might have been more immediate and fruitful conversations but sometimes enabling aspiring international students to make inquiries they would have been unable to make ten years earlier. A rally to protest the effects of AWAs on university staff is widely advertised, and there is a general mood of unease about future working conditions, especially for less senior contract staff.

I start to prepare for a return trip to the Kimberley, where I will attend the funeral I have been told about. "We have some more bad news," the caller had said. Although the news was hard for me to hear, for the families it means a time of prolonged anguish. Referred to locally as "sorry business," an expression that eloquently conveys the distress of all-concerned when a death occurs, the process has become unrelenting, so that now "too much sorry business" is regularly exchanged.

Traveling north to the Kimberley, again by plane, I contemplate the different work sites in which I am involved, work sites that are not unusual for anthropologists with knowledge, backgrounds, and histories similar to mine. I realize that the lived experience, the questioning, and the critique I have learned by being an anthropologist and working as one embody a certain practical and symbolic inspiration. This rigorous practice and unique ethos nurture a belief in the possibility of change and the uniqueness of cultural difference. A different vision—one without anthropology—is a much darker and less vital vision of working anthropology's future and of the human situation.

Notes

1. A brief selection of publications focused on Indigenous groups in the Kimberley location discussed here includes Blundell and Wooloogoodja 2004, Crough and Christophersen 1993, Hawke and Gallagher 1989, Jebb 2002, Lowe and Pike 1991 and Toussaint 1999a, 1999b.

2. This chapter builds on the paper I originally presented at the Wenner-Gren symposium convened by Richard Fox and Les Field (New York, 2005). I thank the conveners, as well as each of the other symposium participants, for creating such a discursive, collegial, and inspirational environment in which to discuss issues of vital importance to present-day working anthropologists.

3. Many Australian-based anthropologists who have worked with Indigenous groups could be cited here; some of them are Ian Keen (2004), Francesca Merlan (1998), Howard Morphy (1998), Deborah Bird Rose (1992), Peter Sutton (2003), Robert Tonkinson (1991), and David Trigger (1992).

4. The Australian High Court's Mabo decision represented the first time a form of land title had been constructed around Indigenous meanings of

property ownership. Indigenous peoples now have to prove, with supporting evidence from anthropological data, that they have a right to claim native title. It is essential to the requirements of native title law that an individual or group show a continuing connection with the land consistent with traditional Indigenous use, show that rights in land have been conferred by customary law, or both.

5. For more on native title claims, see, for example, Toussaint 2004. Although I have indicated caution about the value of cross-disciplinary work to anthropology, it is discussed in an increasing number of examples. See, for instance, Milton 1994 for a general discussion. For a collection focused on Australia, see Minnegal 2005. The URL for the collaborative water project I mentioned is http://www.anthropology.arts.uwa.edu.au/home/research/under_water, which provides an outline of a three-year, Australian Research Council–funded research project grant awarded to the environmental anthropologist Veronica Strang and me. Titled "Under Water: A Comparative Ethnographic Analysis on Water and Resource Management in Queensland and Western Australia," the research concentrates on the social and cultural uses and management of water in four contrasting locations.

6. Australian Bureau of Statistics and Australian Indigenous Health and Welfare 2001 and Anderson 2003 are among many texts that provide critical and substantive insights into the state of Indigenous health.

7. Archival material in "Native Welfare" government records indicated that members of the family were known to have lived during the 1940s, 1950s, and 1960s on certain reserves and pastoral stations, but these data were regarded as insufficient because they failed to clearly indicate descent. It was birth and marriage certificates that mattered most to the state authorities.

8. I worked on Kumunjayi's case because I had known the families involved for several decades and wanted to support their aspirations. I did not undertake the work as a consultancy or contract, and I was paid by none of the parties involved. This type of situation is not unusual for anthropologists in similar circumstances and helps to illustrate the diverse ways in which anthropological work is done—in this case as a kind of voluntarism, equivalent to the pro bono work undertaken by some lawyers. That I have chosen to write an academic paper about Kumunjayi's family's situation also makes plain another category of "work."

9. A further issue that arose was that some family members did not know that the man Kumunjayi had called father was not his biological father. It was only during discussion for the purposes of the will that a senior man clarified the situation. Family members accepted this clarification as a statement of fact, but it in no way affected the father-son relationship established by Kumunjayi and his "social" father.

10. The Public Trustees Office advised that cases such as Kumunjayi's were on the increase. Before this time (a moment undoubtedly influenced by the Mabo decision and the subsequent Native Title Act, which had resulted in broad recognition of Indigenous land tenure law and often necessitated the production of genealogies to support claimants' evidence), when Aboriginal and Islander people died intestate, leftover funds were usually diverted back to the state. Lawyers with the Aboriginal Legal Service were ensuring that as many people as possible were informed about their rights in this regard.

11. Kumunjayi had no children, but within the requirements of customary law, he did have family members who referred to him socially as "father" and "grandfather."

12. Not all family members were interested in inheriting money through Kumunjayi's estate. Of greater importance for some people was the failure of the Public Trustees Office to recognize their identities and relationships to each other. From their point of view—one given authority by a different legal culture—it was incomprehensible that the absence of relevant certificates could cause such problems.

13. Keen 1988 provides a detailed overview of Australian Indigenous kinship.

14. This example also reveals the importance of genealogical work in anthropology, perhaps indicating the need to reintroduce the teaching of genealogical research in universities. In most Australian universities, this field of teaching and learning has become almost obsolete, although in response to *Mabo* the situation is beginning to change.

15. I do not name persons, locations, or disciplines here. My concern is to canvass some of the vexed issues that this cross-disciplinary example prompts rather than apportion blame. The community wishes to remain anonymous.

16. That anthropology sits midway between the humanities and the sciences is generally accepted among many anthropologists, despite some arguing for one emphasis over another. My own practice is situated in the arts-humanities spectrum.

17. Such professional emphases are not unusual, but the overriding cause of my concern was that we had originally agreed to work collaboratively and equally, with neither discipline dominating the other. The fieldwork experience, however, revealed early on that this was unlikely to be the case. The possibility of developing a cross-disciplinary practice model also became elusive, although keeping such a vision in mind highlighted how and when working relations diminished.

18. The items were eventually returned to me and transported back to the community. They are now held by the senior custodians in a "safekeeping place" on-site.

19. I do not mean to suggest that all scientists or research partners would have acted in the same way or that the person concerned would do so again.

20. Approval to work in Indigenous communities is now formally required by local Indigenous organizations and funding bodies, such as the Australian Institute of Aboriginal and Torres Strait Islander Studies, the Australian Research Council, and the National Health and Medical Research Council. The community concerned must provide evidence that it has been consulted about the project and is willing to give researchers access to the community. Research partnerships are generally encouraged, such as between Indigenous communities and universities and between government and nongovernment agencies. An indication of the likely benefits to Indigenous communities is highly regarded. Examples of such benefits include improvements in social conditions, innovative employment strategies, cultural storage (oral history records, artifact displays), and educational programs. Given my long-term involvement with the community, I was in a position to consult regularly with its members and to explain the role of another researcher on the project. I was also able to achieve support from the community on the basis of its having come to trust my judgment. Such community support extended to the unknown researcher. This permission would not have been so easily gained in other circumstances, a point not fully understood by any party at the time.

The Dilemmas of "Working" Anthropology in Twenty-first-Century India

Nandini Sundar

Periodically in the last hundred years or so, anthropologists have sought ways to renew their discipline, to make it both theoretically and practically more responsive to new working conditions. At the beginning of the twenty-first century, such an exercise suffers from at least two problems. First, it presupposes that we know what anthropology is, or the kinds of issues with which it generally deals: it looks to us more like a fried egg with an identifiable core and runny margins than like an amoeba. Second, it implies that we use the term *anthropologist* to refer to someone who has a university degree (generally a PhD) in anthropology, as opposed to an amateur interest, and who deploys that professional expertise to do research. Neither of these assumptions may be borne out in practice as universities suffer from funding cuts, as students move away from graduate programs into corporate jobs or the NGO sector but still identify themselves as anthropologists, and as anthropology is extended into diverse fields. Diverse national histories and traditions of anthropology complicate the matter further.

In the Indian context, the choice of identifying with the disciplinary nomenclature "anthropology"—as against "sociology"—is by itself a research problem, a condition of work that affects what we do and how we might do it (see also Beteille 1993, 2000). Most histories of anthropology published in the "West" (see, for example, Freeman 1999; Hays 1992; Kuklick 1991; Stocking 1986, 1991, 1992; Van Bremen and Shimizu 1999; Vincent 1990) have emphasized British and American scholarship. Asia, Africa, and Polynesia figure merely as "sites" for fieldwork rather than as places with their own traditions of scholarship. When the contribution of Asia or Africa is recognized, it is usually in terms of the challenges that its cultural peculiarities pose for the disciplines: for example, the challenge posed by caste to studies of stratification and social inequality worldwide (on Africa and the disciplines, see Bates, Mudimbe, and Barr 1993).

Because much of this history is written in the United States and the United Kingdom, perhaps it is natural that American and British scholars figure large in it. To some extent, moreover, this imbalance is being corrected by other national histories of anthropology (see Ahmad 2003; Guldin 1994; Kloos and Claessen 1991; Liu 2002; Peirano 1991). Yet we are still some way off from seeing anthropology as a global formation of knowledge, encompassing several distinct subformations among which US anthropology is simply one. Of course the very notion of national discursive traditions may be problematic, given knowledge flows, but the effects on the discipline of differences in emphasis, audiences, and so forth need to be studied further.

One standard history of Indian anthropology-sociology traces it to administrative productions of knowledge in the form of censuses, gazetteers, and the like, which reduced India, culturally speaking, to a land of caste, kinship, family, and village (Cohn 1990; Dirks 2001). Yet there is more to it than that. Indian anthropology and sociology were developing as professional disciplines and coming out of the shadow of government ethnology around the same time Malinowski was introducing his fieldwork revolution. The first departments of sociology and anthropology were established in Bombay and Calcutta as early as 1919 and 1921, respectively. Although the anthropology taught might be said to have been derivative—insofar as anthropologists were trained by the British and read British and American anthropological literature—these early Indian anthropologists were not and could not have been mere clones, considering their position as colonized Indians in a nation struggling for independence. And in the 1950s it would have been impossible for an anthropologist teaching in India to ignore the background of nation-building in any discussion of caste or family. Indian anthropologists-sociologists such as Irawati Karve, N. K. Bose, and G. S. Ghurye took up studies ranging from temple architecture to city planning and the displacement of people by large dams, from the working conditions of clerks to the sexual habits of the middle class. All this was done long before such topics became fashionable in the anthropology or sociology of India in the West.

Like Westerners, when Indians studied themselves, they called the discipline by which they did it "sociology," even though, largely due to the anthropological training of the "founding fathers" in the United Kingdom, their research was largely anthropological—that is, it depended on ethnographic observation rather than large-scale surveys (see Desai 1996). The bulk of the work was on kinship, religion (mainly Hinduism), and caste, although, as the work of M. N. Srinivas and others shows, it was often concerned with the transformation of these institutions by colonialism and modernization.[1] In certain parts of the country, anthropology continued to be the disciplinary name, with a four-field representation.[2] The relationship is far too complicated to be explained in a few sentences. In the department of sociology in which I work, for example, what we teach has much in common with the subject matter of sociology departments elsewhere in the world (e.g., stratification, the sociology of work and leisure, industrial conflict, theories of organization). But we also teach traditional anthropological subjects such as kinship, and in terms of research method, the majority of faculty and PhD students do ethnography. My own training has been in a US department of anthropology. In this chapter, therefore, I use the terms *sociology* and *anthropology* interchangeably to reflect this mixed experience.

Having listed a set of caveats, I offer one particular take on anthropology's future preoccupations. Within the international political context of the beginning of the twenty-first century, I look at some of the different arenas in which anthropological dilemmas of "engagement" are played out. Anthropologists, especially university-based academics, face these dilemmas both as a social class and as a special category of "intellectual." Although my focus is on India, I believe the situation is sufficiently similar elsewhere (or the dissimilarities sufficiently striking to serve as points of reflection) to lend this chapter wider relevance. I argue that anthropologists concerned with "relevance" must necessarily perform a balancing act—for instance, while setting "standards" of anthropological excellence in a universe divided by language and experience, or when combining academic research and activist work at a time when activism is no longer confined to the left. Looking back at the ways in which earlier generations of anthropologists dealt with the problems of their times, problems that were no less urgent than ours seem now, often helps in looking forward.

The University as a Site of Knowledge Production: Debates over Credentialing

Within anthropology, the distinction between applied and basic research has long been contested. However, the central problem in

understanding, maintaining, or negating the basic-versus-applied distinction is a dilemma that is not peculiar to anthropology but relates to
the university as a site of knowledge production. As Bourdieu showed us,
universities by their very nature are part of the way in which the modern
state (and status quo) is constructed. Exams, degrees, and credentials
are all ways in which a class system reproduces itself, under the guise
of "meritocracy." The emphasis on the importance of certain kinds of
knowledge, scholarship, and "academic manners"—Bourdieu's academic
habitus—enables the remarkable feat in which scholars performatively
re-create structures of class even while, as individuals, they simply
uphold "standards" in scholarship (Bourdieu 1996).

Several studies of intellectuals as a social class have attributed their
power to their position in the occupational structure. This power is
thought to have grown with the rise of a "knowledge economy" (see
Gagnon 1987; Robbins 1990). It is clear that getting university degrees
is an important part of the acquisition of power. The role played by
"credentialing," however, is not straightforward, in terms of the kind
of capital represented by "cultural capital" (versus financial capital),
the kinds of people who might have benefited from this strategy
(women, some minorities), or who it excludes (see Dupuy 1991: 77).
Anthropological credentialing at the beginning of the twenty-first
century is no longer what it was in the mid-1950s, the field having
rapidly expanded to include feminist anthropology, queer anthropology,
and similar subdisciplines.

Yet even as post-sixties scholars sought to make the university more
radical through "action research," "engaged anthropology," "concerned
anthropology," and so forth (see *Current Anthropology* 1968; Huizer and
Mannheim 1979; Hymes 1972), they had to struggle for acceptance
of this scholarship as legitimate (see Gramsci in Forgacs 1988 on the
need for knowledge to appear "disinterested"). The struggle, then as
now, was to simultaneously challenge the structure and rationale of
universities within a wider scheme of class reproduction and yet rely
on universities' professional power to legitimate one's findings. Today,
given the fractured nature of the academic elite and the fact that people
on both the right and the left deploy the power of professionalism,
producing good "basic" research has become a more strenuous exercise.
Whatever one's concerns with the elitism of scholarship or anthropology,
there seem to be few practical alternatives to having one's conclusions
legitimated through the skein of peer review and other forms of scholarly
certification. On the other hand, because of the multiplicity of journals
and theoretical and political perspectives, peer review is a problematic
notion.

Scholars who do wish to intervene in the "real" world are widely seen to have three choices open to them: detached analysis and its attendant powerlessness, service for the state or those in power, or alignment with forces seeking to challenge the status quo (see Flacks 1991: 3; Gagnon 1987: 3). Yet as Dick Flacks pointed out, salvation is hard to come by, whether in the state, in political parties, or in university halls:

> Intellectuals seeking connection to potentials for social change thus have found available avenues for relevance to be dead ends. Both party and state require acceptance of the logics of domination, power, organisational aggrandizement. The academy and the professions require acceptance of the logics of disciplinary specialisation, peer review, competitive achievement. The hope for a public as a sustaining framework for politically engaged intellectual work seems implausible, indeed chimerical. (Flacks 1991: 13)

One arena in which the question of subaltern versus dominant forms of "knowledge" has been posed sharply is the debate over indigenous knowledge (see Agrawal 1995 and the September 2002 issue of *International Social Science Journal* on *Indigenous Knowledge*). But the problems of how and which kinds of indigenous knowledge to "validate" are immense (see Sundar 2002). For example, in 1992 in India, "Hindu" *kar sevaks*, or "volunteers for god," under the leadership of the Bharatiya Janata Party (BJP) and other fronts of the Hindu chauvinist organization Rashtriya Swayamsevak Sangh (RSS), demolished the Babri Masjid, a sixteenth-century mosque in Ayodhya, sparking a round of violence across the country. The perpetrators claimed the mosque had been built over an earlier temple commemorating the birthplace of the Hindu god Ram. Arguably, the destruction of the mosque could have been treated simply as a question of vandalism of historical monuments. However, the case rapidly became a debate over historical "fact" and over the professionalism of university historians who dismissed the BJP claim as a myth versus the faith and folk knowledge of the public (for a history of scholarly debate over the site, see Lal 2003: 141–85). Although he clearly does not come from the perspective of the Hindu right, the subaltern studies historian Dipesh Chakrabarty argued that the attempt by historians at Jawaharlal Nehru University (JNU) to educate the public about "truth" and "myth" in Ayodhya amounted to an attempt to civilize the natives. Even if one were to accept his patronizing argument that "you have to be a certain kind of literate and educated person even to be interested in any abstract formulation of the distinction between myth and history" (Chakrabarty 2003: 136), the consequences of abandoning that distinction and the notion of the university as a place that enables one to make this distinction would be even direr.

Ironically, the distinction between myth and history was recognised by the BJP when it was in power in the federal government from 1998 to 2004. The BJP, having harnessed "faith," soon moved to wrest away the ground of professionalism as well, by positioning its own ideologues in national educational bodies such as the National Council of Educational Research and Training (NCERT), the University Grants Commission (UGC), the Indian Council for Social Science Research, and the Indian Council for Historical Research. In September 2003, the government-run Archaeological Survey of India issued a report suggesting that the mosque had indeed replaced a temple. University archaeologists described this report as biased and unprofessional, pointing out several flaws in methods and interpretations (Sahmat 2003). With a change of government in 2004, the issue was put on a back burner, but it is always open to resuscitation by the RSS. To take a parallel example, the rise of creationism, or intelligent design, in the United States reflects a certain kind of public skepticism about scholarly professionalism. Yet there are few alternatives with which to challenge creationism other than the internally argumentative grounds of professional biology.

The notion of engagement with "communities" as a sign of anthropologists' political commitment is problematic, considering the diversity of publics and communities. The issue takes on a different hue if one stops assuming, first, that the default political position of university scholars, especially anthropologists, is left or liberal, and second, that the communities they engage with are always subaltern groups rather than right-wing, racist, or xenophobic organizations. The idea that "communities" should decide what counts as good or relevant research needs to take into account the campus "watchdog" role played by organizations like the David Project and Accuracy in Academia. According to some of its well-known right-wing promoters, the latter is "shining a light on the continuing depredations of leftist thugs at our universities." Accuracy in Academia does much more than complain about the leftist, statist, and Marxist biases on American campuses. It promotes "awareness and understanding of our genuine political tradition; it puts young Americans back in touch with their ancestors. This noble mission deserves the support of everyone who treasures liberty" (http://www.academia.org/about.html).

Campus Watch, according to its website, is "a project of the Middle East Forum [that] reviews and critiques Middle East studies in North America, with an aim to improving them." Problems allegedly calling for improvement include "analytical errors" (having different views about militant Islam from those of Campus Watch), "extremism" ("Many U.S. scholars of the Middle East lack any appreciation of their country's national interests"), "intolerance," and "apologetics," such as having a conference with 550 papers in which only one dealt with Al-Qaeda. And for all one knows, even that solitary paper was anti-national enough to note that Osama Bin Laden was first promoted by the United States to battle the Soviets in Afghanistan (http://www.campus-watch.org/about. php).

A report by Thomas Bartlett in the *Chronicle of Higher Education* of 18 April 2003 described Columbia University anthropologist Nicholas De Genova as the "most hated professor in America." De Genova's views, expressed at a teach-in at Columbia University against the invasion of Iraq in 2003, resulted in death threats against him, denunciations in newspaper editorials and on television programs, alumni threatening to withhold donations until he was fired, and Columbia's phone lines being jammed with angry callers. More than one hundred members of Congress petitioned Columbia, demanding that he be fired. De Genova was forced to leave his home and employ security guards (chronicle.com/ free/v49/i32/32/5601.htm). Another Columbia University professor, Joseph Massad, has been targeted by the David Project for his views on Palestine (www.columbia.edu/cu/mealac/faculty/massad).

Had it been left to some "community" or "public," both these men's academic careers would have ended. However, it is still possible to argue that anthropology has a natural and historical affinity with groups that have historically been discriminated against, though what the contours of this affinity should be is difficult to define.[3] At the very least, what anthropology offers, and which by itself is a stand, is a distinctive challenge to the positivist meta-theorizing of other disciplines—a closer attention to contexts and pluralities of reasoning—even as it engages in comparison (see Fox and Gingrich 2002).

In the following sections I look at the ways in which generations of anthropologists in India have dealt with the issue of social engagement, teetering between professionalism and practice. The first section is focused on the benefits and costs of professionalizing anthropology, and the second and third on problems in the practice of a socially engaged anthropology.

In the Cause of Anthropology?

I will pay my debt to society through research in my subject. And beyond this, I owe no other debt to society.

—Irawati Karve, quoted in Vidyadhar Pundalik, "Irawati Karve"

I told him [Mahatma Gandhi] how scientific research was my true vocation [*swadharma*], while serving in the political campaign, even when it was by intellect, was no more than an emergency duty [*apadharma*].

—Nirmal Kumar Bose, quoted in Pradip K. Bose,
"The Anthropologist as 'Scientist'?"

In India, anthropology has long existed in arenas outside the university, particularly in government, and it continues to do so in the Anthropological Survey of India. Several early anthropologists, such as Patrick Geddes, S. C. Roy, and Verrier Elwin, came to the discipline through their involvement in urgent social issues. Geddes, for instance, who set up the Bombay Department of Sociology, was a town planner (Munshi n.d.). Roy, who started the journal *Man in India,* became interested in *adivasi* (scheduled tribe or indigenous peoples) issues by fighting legal cases for them (Dasgupta n.d.), and Elwin, who wrote numerous monographs on *adivasi* communities, started off as a missionary, Gandhian, and social worker (Guha 1998). These were self-trained anthropologists who believed that anthropology could make a difference in the way society, particularly a society struggling for independence, could constitute itself. What was missing in this early period was not engagement with the wider world (far beyond a narrow, applied sense) but the professionalism of a university discipline.

It was in this context that anthropology as a "discipline" became itself a "cause." For instance, Irawati Karve (1905–70), India's first woman anthropologist, decided early on that her best contribution to society could be made by practicing and institutionalizing her discipline.[4] For someone married to the son of one of India's most famous social reformers at a time when independence and social change were in the air, this was by no means an easy decision. For scholars like Karve—self-conscious pioneers in establishing the discipline in university departments in India—the question of what a "working anthropology" might mean revolved centrally around the contributions that "science" could make to Indian society and the emergent Indian nation. This did not necessarily mean promoting policy-relevant research, although they did some of that, but it meant promoting basic research in anthropology as an activity of social value. From the 1920s through the 1940s, universities (at least in the modern sense) were new, students had to be attracted to a fledgling discipline, and sociology-anthropology had to be popularized as a professional "career." Entrenching anthropology and disseminating its importance to a wider world was work enough. In addition, there was so much to study, document, and research (albeit much of it in "salvage" mode) that an inquiring mind could not but feel itself to be doing something useful.

The desire to secure a footing for anthropology in universities as well as in the wider public image was of course not unique to India in that period; virtually any biography of Malinowski, Mead, or Boas deals with his or her conception of the usefulness of anthropology as an academic discipline or branch of knowledge. What was different about Indian sociologists-anthropologists was their concern with the specifically Indian nature of Indian sociology and anthropology, an issue that continues to animate discussions in the discipline today (Uberoi, Sundar, and Deshpande n.d.).

The first generation of scholars might have been less successful than they wished in "Indianizing" the discipline, whether in terms of concepts or of texts, but at least the number of anthropology-sociology departments has grown in India. Although economics and history are still the most popular social sciences for undergraduate degrees (if less popular than science and professional subjects such as medicine, engineering, and accounting), sociology-anthropology is no longer seen as an unusual career choice for a young person. Nor is it seen as requiring any great "commitment."

The professionalization of anthropology within the university has had its advantages and disadvantages, Much that is relevant and contemporary in society and that should be incorporated by sociology-anthropology is written in other forms, notably literature. For example, the Marathi essayist Anil Awachat, writing about ecological problems in Marathi, Dalit writers describing their experiences as "untouchables," and Maoist guerrillas debating with the government (see Committee of Concerned Citizens 2002) often bring out contemporary social issues more sharply than do scholarly debates about caste, class, or ecology. Yet little effort is made to incorporate such writings into syllabi or, even more importantly, to revise our notion of what sociology or anthropology should be about in India. That certain anthropological ⟨ debates may make little sense to underprivileged students may have to do with the poverty of the concepts themselves rather than the quality of the students. "Neutrality" in this context can be a way of suppressing social contradictions and internalizing "disciplinary concerns."—a way of excluding lived experience. When those disciplinary concerns are "international" (read Western), there is a further worry about intellectual colonialism (see Uberoi 1968).

What young people will get out of their careers also varies widely, depending on which department they are in, their social and economic background, and their knowledge of English. Although a few "centers of excellence" produce scholars whose work has a global effect,[5] in many parts of the country teachers suffer from a "vicious circle of non-challenging syllabi, heavy teaching loads, absence of original textbooks and dominance of guidebooks, lack of library resources, widespread resort to coaching classes and the politics of boards of studies and examinations" (Shah 2000: 48).

Problems of differentiation within a university system are common to many countries, though the particular form of this differentiation varies (between the *grandes écoles* and universities in France, between Ivy League and state schools in the United States, and between metropolitan, centrally funded and mofussil, state-funded universities in India), as does the relative position of professional (medical or law) versus general degrees (see Wacquant 1996: xiv). What makes the Indian condition particularly problematic is the colonial context in which university disciplines were instituted and in which they continue to function, with English the language of learning and knowledge and all other languages secondary.

For the pioneers of Indian sociology-anthropology, many of whom wrote in both English and their own vernaculars, anthropology was what they did in English with "scientific tools." In fact, what they wrote in their own languages, which they themselves regarded as popular literary writing, would be more readily accepted as ethnography by today's standards (Bose n.d.; Sundar n.d.). Today, teachers talk in private about the problems their students face in understanding English texts, the students' humbling diligence as they translate dense theoretical essays line by line, and their frustration at pitching classes to students of widely different linguistic capabilities and social backgrounds. In discussing ways for anthropology to enter new arenas, it is essential to address the question of translation, both into and out of non-English languages. Writing in the vernacular, for non-university audiences, and having one's books translated (keeping aside money in research budgets specifically for this) would inevitably invite new forms of intellectual collaboration, to the extent that perceived audiences would determine much of what we write and how we write.

Indian anthropology, unlike "Western" anthropology, also faces a problem in reconciling "concerned" anthropology with disciplinary self-confidence. Unlike in the United States, where anthropological advocacy, or activist anthropology, has usually meant acting with and for third world citizens, in India there has been far too much concern with the problems of Indian society. The paucity of Indian scholars studying other countries, especially those of the "West," although a mark of their engagement with their own society, is also a signifier of academic colonization (see Roy-Burman 2000; Sundar 2004; Sundar, Deshpande, and Uberoi 2000; Uberoi 1968).

Without addressing the material context—the funding, libraries, availability of literature in the vernacular, outdated syllabi, recruitment practices, historically inherited nomenclatures and disciplinary traditions—it is hard to fashion a way forward for Indian anthropology that simultaneously recognizes social contradictions and provides a disinterested perspective. The problem, of course, extends beyond anthropology. Yet anthropologists-sociologists seem to be more concerned about these issues than professionals in many other disciplines. The reasons for this may vary, from informants who "talk back" to the feeling that nothing is beyond the purview of sociology. In India, every ten years or so, sometimes in conjunction with and sometimes independent of "international" angst fests, anthropologists get together to debate how their discipline might be made more relevant, more "urgent," better, brighter, and newer (for a discussion of fifty years of anthropological worrying in India, see Uberoi 2000).

Reconciling Anthropology with Activism?

Madam,
I was very happy to receive your mail. I plan to meet you very soon to discuss the progress of my research. Nowadays I am really under tremendous pressure as the progress on my PhD front is not satisfactory. I do not understand how to do justice to my academic work as in spite of all my promises and commitments I always get motivated by different social issues. I sincerely hope you do not mind my telling all this to you.

—email to me from a PhD student

Generations of students (and some teachers) in India have felt torn between lives of activism and lives of research. In 1921, during

Gandhi's noncooperation movement, Nirmal Kumar Bose, who was later to become one of India's most famous anthropologists, wrote in his dairy, "In our national life we feel the arrival of a great period! ... I do not know whether we are going to attain *swaraj* [independence] within a year only on account of leaving schools and colleges. But it appears to me that these movements are going to arouse our national consciousness and life, and many of us would wake up and start thinking" (quoted in Bose n.d.). He quit work on his master's of science degree to set up a night school and a spinners' co-operative in a slum. In the late 1960s, many college students became "Naxalites," or Maoist guerrillas, going underground and suffering huge privations for their politics. In the mid-1970s, others joined Jai Prakash Narayan's Sarvodaya movement for rural reconstruction work (though the numbers were greater in his "Total Revolution" movement against corruption).

Student idealism faded with the years and the absence of any stirring ideological politics. Now, with the efflorescence of nongovernmental organizations, students with a conscience (and many without) are more likely to join the "voluntary sector" and seek satisfaction in work that addresses social issues than to join the mainstream corporate sector or choose what they see as a sterile academic life. Yet for many, as for the young lawyer-activist who wrote me the preceding email, the dilemma of combining activism and academic life remains.

People have dealt with this dilemma in different ways. Nirmal Kumar Bose saw his political work as distinct from his anthropological work—as an "emergency duty"—and each period of political involvement meant a clean break from the university. He was arrested twice and the second time was jailed for three years. In 1946 he accompanied Gandhi on a tour of Noahkali, which had seen some of the worst pre-partition violence, on Gandhi's condition that "you sever your connection with the University and ... risk death, starvation etc." (Bose 1974: 44, cited in Bose n.d.). In between, Bose wrote on the structure of Hindu society, the relationship between anthropology and architecture, associational life in cities, and a variety of other subjects.

Ramachandra Guha (personal communication) has argued that combining activism with academic life and claiming the label "activist-academic" constitute an insult to both professions, because both require full-time commitment (though he himself manages serious scholarship and public writing). He cites the examples of N. K. Bose and E. P. Thompson, who, while combining research and activism over the course of their lives, did only one or the other at any one time.

There is much to this point of view, but the problem goes beyond the mundane question of juggling timetables and schedules to thinking of time and location. E. P. Thompson's (1993) distinction between pre-capitalist and industrial time provides a useful point of departure; one might ask whether there is a similar disjunction between "academic time" and "activist time," especially when it comes to human rights work. Academic time is intensely subjective and personal (the time it takes to write a paper, for example) and in many of its stretches and cadences is closer to precapitalist time. Yet it shares a certain rhythm with industrial time—there are classes to be taught relentlessly week after week during term time, papers to be published for tenure, conference deadlines to be met.

Activist time, especially in human rights work, is also slow on occasion but desperately frenzied when press releases have to be written, authorities contacted, and statements made on the basis of limited information. Nicholas De Genova (personal communication) has suggested that the pace of both academic and activist time is speeded up precisely when they come into contact with regimes of capital or power and lose their autonomy either to think or to plan for an alternative world. Yet there may be serious differences between the two kinds of time and the kinds of work they imply. Absorbing ethnographic information takes time, against the activist need to get information out fast. Audiences and styles of writing differ; for scholars, it is often as important to under-stand perpetrators and those in power as it is to talk to victims. Often, moreover, scholars face a basic ethical dilemma: taking an activist stance may jeopardize future research that may have greater value in the long run, but this can often seem, to the scholar concerned and to others, a feeble excuse for not taking a stand.

Location also matters, as was particularly obvious in different resp-onses to the pogrom against Muslims in Gujarat in 2002, organized by the BJP-ruled state of Gujarat (see Varadarajan 2002). At the time, some forty citizens' reports giving victims' testimonies were produced, in many of which university teachers participated. Such reports have value in mobilizing public opinion and serving as a record of violence. But from the perspective of the victims themselves, what was required was a different sort of activism, which university teachers were unable to provide, such as helping victims file compensation claims, attending court hearings with them, and ensuring witness protection. A small group of feminist activists took up the rape case of one victim and worked with her to collect evidence and sustain her morale. Others, lawyers and Gujarat-based activists, provided legal aid, monetary support, and moral assurance to victims. But by far the maximum work of rehabilitation was done by Muslim organizations and other members of the community who survived. In other words, whereas anthropologists and others can act in support roles, they need to qualify their claims to be human rights activists (see for example, some of the claims made in Sluka 2000: 12–13), given the scale of what human rights activism ideally involves.

The point is not that anthropology cannot or should not be taken to arenas outside universities or that we should not write for nonspecialist audiences, but that we should be modest in our understanding of what we have achieved or can achieve. Anthropologists face an additional problem that other, seemingly more useful disciplines do not face. Economists in India, for instance, have always worked in policy arenas. Activist economists such as the Marxists of JNU and the Belgian-turned-Indian citizen Jean Dreze have used their skills to put issues such as education and employment in the public eye. But anthropological research rarely speaks in the number-crunching register required by policy, and much applied anthropological research is often simply ignored.

To accommodate real social concerns in a university setting requires more than just the formal recognition of engaged research. The Institute of Economic Growth in Delhi, for example, set up in the "socialistic" 1950s, states in its memorandum of association that one of the objects of the institution is to "conduct ad-hoc investigation at the request of governments, organizations of employers, workers and peasants or of other bodies or persons interested in promoting a study of economic questions" (IEG 1952). Fifty years on, no one seems to remember this clause, and most research is done at the behest of the government, the World Bank, or other funding organizations. Whereas it would be legitimate for an anthropologist to list a World Bank–funded report advocating large dams or structural adjustment as part of his or her work in an annual report, bringing out a research pamphlet for an anti-dam peasant group or for a worker's union showing the problems of retrenchment would be dismissed as "mere activism." In any case, neither type of contracted research is a substitute for peer-reviewed academic research.

Balancing Act: Is There a Role for Anthropology in "Development"?

Let us look at the problem from another angle. If anthropologists within the university are unable to do more than dabble in activism, perhaps we should encourage activist research in other spaces, particularly in nongovernmental organizations (NGOs). Indeed, this was the inevitable direction in which the emphasis on action research, advocacy, and development anthropology, which gained currency in the 1970s, was bound to lead.

From the point of view of society and of funders, there are many advantages to research being funded outside universities. For one, NGOs are often able to identify new issues when academics are bound by the conventions of their field or by whatever theory is fashionable at the moment. In India, ecological anthropology, feminist studies, philanthropy, urban planning, and legal anthropology are all fields in which academic research has piggybacked on activist research. NGOs are also often quicker to produce results and to produce them in forms that can be used by practitioners.

Increasingly, however, there are dangers in letting donors and NGOs define what proactive research is and in restricting it mainly to research that feeds directly into development projects. First, research done ostensibly in collaboration with the subjects in pursuit of a particular agenda is glorified with the name "participatory research," without questioning whether the agenda itself, such as participatory forest management or family planning, is something that was developed in participatory fashion. Second, once a subject becomes fashionable, there is a tendency for people to jump on the bandwagon and produce endless case studies, many of which have limited value. Often, little justifies the funding that goes into such case studies, for which consultants charge huge fees.

Third, the money that goes into so-called research consultancies undermines research in third world universities (although it may help universities in the West, from which the consultants are drawn). In places like India, it is hard for universities with comparatively limited resources to retain people, and besides, the pressure of having to compete with NGOs for funds means that much research in universities tends to become project driven, short-term, and powered solely by whether or not it has policy implications. Finally, what tends to result from such donor-driven research is an excessive focus on the poor to the exclusion of the rich, and on the presence or absence of social capital among the poor instead of on how the practice of capitalism impedes development in a systematic manner.

Even where research done outside the university suffers from none of these problems, there are ways in which a university-based researcher can address an issue differently from the way an NGO-based researcher might. For anthropologists, this necessarily involves new forms of collaboration. It requires them to sharpen their theoretical perspectives and information in conjunction *with* other people as against simply *on* them (see Field 1999; Rappaport 2005). Addressing the contradictions between the constructionism of social science and history and subjects' essentialist representations of themselves, Les Field laid out a range of possibilities that require "an overt commitment on the part of the anthropologist to tribal strategies rather than to current academic theories and trends" (Field 1999: 199). As he himself pointed out, though, tribal strategies are divided, creating further questions for anthropologists.

The problem of conflicting positions has great resonance in the Indian context, particularly in light of recent controversies over legislation involving scheduled tribes' rights to land in the form of the Scheduled Tribes (Recognition of Forest Rights) Bill of 2005.[6] The roots of the bill lie in the colonial appropriation of forests from tribals (indigenous peoples). In the absence of proper land surveys, many families who had been cultivating forest land for generations were legally reclassified as "encroachers." A large number of others—including people displaced by "development" projects such as dams and industries—broke fresh ground in forest land, because they had no other means of subsistence. Over the years, this has created huge tensions between the forest department and tribals, with foresters resorting to forced evictions, the burning of crops, and the razing of houses.

In 2003, several tribal organizations came together on a platform called the "Campaign for Survival and Dignity." Through a fortuitous combination of having the right officers in the newly created Ministry of Tribal Affairs (MOTA) and a political party in government that was keen to regain the tribal vote, the campaign was successful in pushing a bill aimed at redressing the "historical injustice" done to *adivasis* by recognizing their existing cultivation. The bill soon ran into trouble from conservationists, and the debate came to be posed as one of tigers versus tribals, ignoring the loss of forest land due to large industrial and hydroelectric projects and the multiple reasons why tiger conservation was not working. Both the conservationists and the Ministry of Environment and Forests (MOEF), which was losing some control to the Ministry of Tribal Affairs, argued that if the bill was passed at all, then benefits should be extended to nontribals. Although this had always been a demand of the Campaign for Survival and Dignity, identifying suitable nontribals who were genuinely eligible proved difficult. Opening up forest land to nontribal communities as a whole would have meant allowing a range of large business and commercial interests onto that land.

In terms of current understandings in both history and anthropology, a sharp distinction between tribals and others living in the same area is impossible. A focus on tribal communities as wholes also ignores the internal differentiation that has taken place within tribal communities. Yet the category "tribe" is embedded in a range of official practices and laws in India, and the power of state categories is such that even movements fighting for rights against the state are trapped in its discourse.

Collaborations with anthropologists' interlocutors and with social movements are not the only forms of collaboration anthropologists may be engaged in. Increasingly, as research tends to be conducted through large-scale projects, understanding intellectual negotiations within such projects becomes critical to understanding their outcomes. In the 1990s, a great deal of research took place in India (and indeed worldwide) on new, participatory forms of forest management. The Ford Foundation funded a "support network" of groups working on joint forest management (JFM) in India, which included NGOs, donors, forest officials, consultants, and a few university- or research institute–based economists. Many of the NGOs were doing their own research into whether and how JFM could be made to work to satisfy the needs of local communities and regenerate the forests.

In late 1994, I began work at the University of Edinburgh as a research fellow. My task was to manage a large research project on JFM in India.[7] The project involved research in sixteen villages in four states, as well as in the multiple institutional locations in which JFM was constituted as an object of study, policy, and practice: the policymaking arenas of the four states, the Ministry of Environment and Forests, donors, forest bureaucracies, activists, NGOs, national advocacy networks, and academic research on forests and ecological history. Our research fed into the same development programs as those of the other actors. We shared questions of methods and objects with them and subjected them to our research gaze.

As the anthropology of policy (see Shore and Wright 1997), or, more specifically, of a shift in policy, this research was consciously aimed at developing new methodological tools: developing both a comparative and a general perspective on a policy and yet retaining the specificity concerning vision and implementation that comes with detailed ethnographic research. Our research emphasized the importance of recognizing variation (Sundar, Jeffery, and Thin 2001), but this was unsatisfactory for policymakers and economists, who wanted to know in yes-or-no terms whether the policy was succeeding or not.

Although the research was deeply anthropological in method, it was also the product of a particular organizational style of doing fieldwork. Such large research projects are inevitably negotiated products—especially when carried out by people from different disciplines, with different objectives and different positions in the research hierarchy.[8] For example, the principle investigators' personal preferences and previous research experience suggested certain field sites, whereas the logic of the research question demanded others. Among the research assistants, those who were forestry graduates claimed a certain kind of expertise while the sociology graduates claimed another. As Jan Nespor noted in her article on bureaucratic research, "instead of simply making research more difficult to practice, these factors alter the constitution of research by creating a situation in which the production of knowledge is tightly interlaced with struggles for autonomy, control and discretion" (Nespor 1989: 326).

Conclusion

I have tried to grapple in this chapter with the different ways in which anthropologists might respond to contemporary working conditions. Some of these situations are not so new, and academics, like others, have often been overtaken, if temporarily, by the demands of citizenship. Yet it is hard to decide when "emergency duty" is required that would involve giving up research and what a suitable response is, as citizen and as anthropologist. In other senses, however, anthropology, especially when it relates to development concerns, has to deal with new ways of doing research—in large teams or in alliances, often shifting, contextual, and tension ridden, with different social and political actors. In both cases, the hard task is to be true to one's self-proclaimed profession as an anthropologist, even as one sees ways in which the discipline is being and should be challenged from without. The practical problems in a country like India are to keep in mind that our salaries are paid by a state that draws on the resources of the poor to subsidize a middle class or elite; to engage in extending the democracy and equality that we routinely learn and teach about; and yet to seize the time and space required for reflection and produce research that is seen to be "disinterested" or at least rigorous and honest enough to be respected by those it displeases.

Acknowledgments

I am grateful to Dick Fox, Les Field, Ramachandra Guha, Nicholas De Genova, and all the participants in the Wenner-Gren Foundation "Working Anthropology" seminar for their comments on this chapter.

Notes

1. This observation is substantiated by a tabulation of articles up to 2000 in the two main Indian journals of sociology, *Contributions to Indian Sociology* and *Sociological Bulletin,* made by Nandini Sundar and Aradhya Bharadwaj, respectively.

2. Vinay Srivastava (2000) noted that there were thirty-three anthropology departments in the country, of which four were composite departments of sociology and social anthropology.

3. For a discussion of the differences between left- and right-wing activism within the academy, see Sundar 2000.

4. Karve, who taught for thirty-one years at the University of Pune, published some one hundred papers on a variety of topics, notably kinship and the family but also caste, urbanization, and displacement. She also wrote prolifically in her native Marathi. Her novel *Yuganta,* based on the Mahabharat, won the Sahitya Akademi Award, one of India's most prestigious literary prizes (Sundar n.d.).

5. The "Subaltern Studies" historians spring easily to mind, although they reflect the long-term strength of Indian history instead of Indian sociology-anthropology.

6. The bill has now been enacted as the Scheduled Tribes and Other Traditional Forest Dwellers (Recognition of Forest Rights) Act of 2006.

7. I coordinated eight research fellows in the field, in teams of one man and one woman per state, and liased with two forest officers in the forest research institute, Dehradun, with which the project was affiliated. I also coordinated four senior academics in Edinburgh, three sociologists-anthropologists, and one historian—altogether a team of fifteen people, including me.

8. As research coordinator, I found it was one thing to study the weapons of the weak in external settings and quite another to have them directed against oneself in the form of unsent field notes and absences from duty, and to have to play the role of overseer in an academic plantation economy.

Ethnographic Alchemy

Perspectives on Anthropological Work from Northern Madagascar

Andrew Walsh

Alchemy was adept at what seem to us unlikely comparisons.

—Gareth Roberts, *The Mirror of Alchemy*

The term *work* is so variously invoked by anthropologists these days that it could well serve as the answer to an alchemist's riddle: What is it in anthropology that is most stressful to those who do not have it, most neglected by those most burdened with it, and most onerous when it is not one's own? As I have heard it used over the years, "work" can cover everything from the employment that anthropologists struggle to find to the research they are forced to put on the back burner when jobs come up and the administrative tasks that take them away from things they would rather be doing. Many of us think of and describe ourselves as working "with" certain communities, "on" certain issues, and "toward" the achievement of certain goals, using insights drawn from our fieldwork to inform the various sorts of written work we hope will be effective. Meanwhile, coursework piles up, even as we juggle committee, collegial, editorial, and advising work in the service of disciplinary and institutional reproduction. Enough griping, though. For those of us lucky enough to have found work in anthropology, there is no doubting that all the tasks listed here come together in at least one sense. At the end of the day, or on the last Thursday of every month at my institution, the product of all of this work is a salary. This is the work that I and others like me get paid to do.

Of all the things that might be said of anthropological work, the fact that it often pays is unlikely to be among the first to spring to most anthropologists' minds. Indeed, some of us are inclined to dissuade others, students especially, from considering our efforts in such crude terms. "Anthropology is a vocation, not a job," James Fernandez wrote in an online editorial intended to turn undergraduate students on to our discipline. "It is something we are called to do, not something we are hired to do" (Fernandez 1987: 1).

In this piece Fernandez offers an appealing vision of anthropological work as something worth believing in. Being an anthropologist, he suggests, requires passion and a commitment to "listening to [other people's] voices." Correspondingly, anthropology is characterized as a "calling" that "enable[s] us to be with others ... to share with them, by listening and negotiating, their preoccupations..., to transcend a too exclusively ethnocentric involvement ... and finally by means of transcendence to formulate the general principles that are discovered as we transcend many particular cases." And through all this, in the process, anthropology "permits us [anthropologists] to realize in some small part our distinctively human potentialities." Calling all this a *job* simply does not do it justice. And yet who can deny that any sort of anthropological work exists at all thanks only to anthropological careers and the institutions that support them? More simply still, who can deny that anthropology is, among other things, something that people are hired to do?

If I am belaboring this last point, it is probably because some of the people with whom I have been working of late will not let me forget it. For them—people involved in the northern Malagasy sapphire trade— the matter of just how someone like me can earn a living from what I do has become a matter of considerable speculation. In conversations they have had with me over the years, and undoubtedly in many more they have had with one another in my absence, they wonder how I am able to transform the seemingly mundane things I write down in my notebooks into valuable, marketable commodities at home. They wonder, in other words, about what I have taken to calling ethnographic alchemy—the mysterious means by which the life experiences of people like them might be transformed into livelihoods for people like me. Some assume that I write articles for sale to foreign magazines. Others are a little more optimistic, guessing that I write wildly popular books about them. Still others are simply puzzled, certain only that the transformation in question *is* actually taking place. It must be. Were it not, how would I be able to afford to return to their community year after year? Having questioned me extensively on the topic, they know perfectly well how expensive it is to fly from Canada to Madagascar and back again.

Shortly, I discuss the complications that can ensue when trying to set the record straight about the connections among research work, written work, and the work for which academic anthropologists get paid. For the time being, suffice it to note that many of the people with whom I have worked recently assume that the central purpose of my work must be production of one sort or another. And in thinking this, they are certainly not alone. Productivity fetishism runs rampant in the institutions that employ anthropologists, as well as in the funding agencies that support our research, requiring working anthropologists to fall, or step, into line if they are interested in continuing their work. Indeed, the push to get things done in and with anthropology has become so engrained in our discipline that, for many, productivity might well be figured among our most deeply felt professional responsibilities. Consider how it is that being *un*productive can affect not just the status but also the internal state of a working anthropologist—that is, being unproductive often involves *feeling* unproductive, as sure a sign as any of our complicity in the reproduction of what one of this collection's editors has called the "productivity regimes" within which we work.

It could be that what is most troubling about doing anthropological work within productivity regimes is that the work we end up doing can so often draw us away from what drew many of us in at the start. For the record, I should state that I agree with much of what Fernandez argued, in the editorial just quoted, about the value of anthropology. Not only is the image of the discipline he promoted the one that attracted me as a student, but also, I admit, I occasionally find myself as prone as many of my own teachers were to "playing the enchanter" in the classroom by presenting anthropology as a particularly engrossing "vocation" in which "work and life form a unified whole" (Lambek 2005: 237). For me, as for many others, what most recommends anthropological work is the processes it involves—the "listening to voices" that Fernandez emphasized, or Michael Carrithers's "engaged learning" (1992), or, most generally perhaps, the "taking people seriously" encouraged by Jeremy MacClancy and other contributors to the recent volume *Exotic No More* (MacClancy 2002).

Less distinctive and engrossing are the products meant to come out of these processes, whether books, articles, reports, or even careers. Over the past ten years I have spent a great deal of time on various sorts of anthropological production, all the while becoming increasingly aware of how poorly anthropological products tend to represent the anthropological processes that drew me in at the start. Unfortunately, representing anthropology is precisely what anthropological products do. No wonder that, as Donna J. Young and Anne Meneley (2005: 13) recently noted, there exists a significant "disjunction between what we think we do and what others think we do." We might think of the "work" we do as a verb, but others think of it as a noun.

The coexistence of these different ways of thinking about anthropological work would not be such a problem were it not that people in the second category play such an important role in setting and maintaining the "benchmarks" (to borrow a key term from productivity-speak) against which the value of the work of people in the first category is measured. Not only must anthropology "accomplish things" if it is to "gain recognition and a valuable identity" (Peacock 1997: 12) in the world today, but also it must *deliver* by accomplishing the sorts of things that others expect of it. Of course the expectations of anthropology's many constituencies are neither constant nor uniform, so inevitably anthropologists sometimes succeed in the eyes some at the cost of failing in the eyes of others.

Anthropologists are certainly not the first researchers to struggle with the disparate expectations and evaluations of others. Alchemists of the sort I discuss in the following pages faced similar problems. Indeed, early modern European alchemy was complex and inherently paradoxical in many of the ways that anthropology is today. It combined isolating yet necessarily engaged pursuits, requiring not only reflexivity but also practical engagement with a wide range of differing perspectives on reality's nitty gritty. It was an ambitiously holistic discipline yet one that saw the route to generalizing in the careful consideration of complex particularities. It generated insights into the world that went misunderstood in ways that frustrated its defenders, yet it was practiced and passed on in ways that confounded those who might have used its findings. Most strikingly, alchemy was, as anthropology is, best characterized by certain processes and yet most often evaluated in terms of production.

That alchemists of the past are today commonly regarded as quacks, charlatans, or, at best, misguided failures is undoubtedly due in large part to their never having been able to produce what their emerging understanding of nature promised was possible—whether gold, an elixir for everlasting life, or the practical knowledge necessary for perfecting matter. The great and lasting significance of early modern European alchemy lay not in what alchemists produced but in the processes by which they went about their work (Moran 2005). Not that these processes always *delivered*, accomplishing the sorts of things that others expected of them. In retrospect, it is more important that these processes were simply carried out and that the diverse people involved in their execution learned as much from their failures as from their successes. As Bruce Moran put it: "Even when [alchemists'] procedures and projects lacked success, [their] involvement with alchemical and chemical processes ... had implications for further knowledge because ... to do and to know what to do were, and still are, connected" (2005: 6).

Although I cannot hope to do justice to the complexity of either alchemy or anthropology in this chapter, let alone to all the similarities and differences between them, I hope that in undertaking the beginnings of the unlikely comparison of these two fields, I might suggest an optimistic, if somewhat disenchanting, vision of anthropology's value and future. Just as Moran presented a retrospective account of alchemy as "never ... something that people *believed* in ... but something that people *did*" (2005: 10), I suggest a more prosaic understanding of anthropological work than many will be accustomed to—a vision of anthropology not as something to believe in but, much more simply, as something to be done.

The problem with seeking to inspire, attract, or inform others by promoting anthropology as a vocation is that it cannot help setting both us and them up for the crippling crises of faith that can so easily emerge whenever anthropological work seems to fail to deliver what is expected of it. Not only is teaching people to do anthropology a great deal easier than trying to get them to believe in it, but teaching those who are considering anthropological careers to accept anthropology as a job that, like any other, will involve successes and failures alike may encourage them to channel their intellectual and emotional energies into processes more useful than self-doubt.

In promoting a vision of anthropology as something that is and should be done, in no way do I mean to suggest that we should stop thinking or talking about what we do and just "'get on with it." Like any other endeavor in which "doing and knowing what to do are ... connected" (Moran 2005: 6), anthropological work, to be effective, must be done reflexively and with an eye to what we and others might learn from both our successes and our failures. Nor, in making this argument, do I mean to suggest that we should focus only on our processes without concern for what comes of them. Like it or not, doing and being able to go on doing anthropological work in the contexts that enable us to do it require that we continue to produce. I see no reason, however, not to try to be productive in ways that will lead those who evaluate our work to better understandings of what it is about this work that is most valuable. This chapter is a modest attempt to do just that. I begin with reference to the sort of work that is perhaps most distinctively anthropological.

Fieldwork

The end result of a day of fieldwork in Ambondromifehy, the center of northern Madagascar's sapphire trade, is usually a number of pages filled with written entries on a wide variety of topics. During my past few visits, I have been especially interested in recording local miners' and traders' thoughts on the significance of local resources to foreigners. Among other things, I have recorded their speculations about the intricacies of the global gem trade, the uses to which foreigners put locally mined sapphires, and the motives of the many ecotourists who pass through their community on their way to visit a local protected area (Walsh 2004, 2005).

I have also recorded their thoughts and speculations about me and my interests. To give just one example, in an entry from my most recent visit I noted a conversation I had with a miner whom I had not met previously. Curious about what I was doing in Ambondromifehy, he asked me about my work. In response, I showed him my notebook, running through the entries from that day to give him a sense of the sorts of things I was writing down. Instead of clarifying the matter, however, this exposition only raised more questions. Why, he wondered aloud, would I want to record the laundry list of seemingly meaningless details found in these entries? Who in *my* world would care about the musings or experiences of people like him?

A trader with whom I had spoken frequently over previous days was listening to our conversation and chimed in with his own opinion. "There are some things that most people don't find essential," he said, "but that are essential to you." Who knows what gets done with the things I write down? he implied. That I had come to Ambondromifehy and was doing what I did was information enough from which to draw certain undeniable conclusions about the sort of work I did.

As this trader understood perfectly well, the work I do in Ambondromifehy is in many ways similar to the work of the many other foreigners who have been drawn to this region throughout history. Particularly obvious to him and others with whom I have spoken over the years is that my efforts are both prospective and enabled by political and economic privilege, a combination of features that makes my research an example of what I have elsewhere termed "deep play"—an investigative endeavor enabled by privilege (Walsh 2005). In acknowledging this point and accepting that anthropological work has more in common than some might like to admit with the work of oil exploration or bioprospecting, it is easy to fall prey to cynicism and lose sight of another point that many people in Ambondromifehy also take to be obvious: that as examples of deep play go, anthropological research is a particular sort.

A trader named Bera once told me that what was most distinctive about the work I did was that it required me to "talk to everybody ... whether they are crazy or not." He continued: "I have met many *vazaha* [foreigners]. What is different [about you] is the conversation. Those [other foreigners], they don't even open their mouths. You don't choose among people [to talk with]." In response to these comments, I reminded Bera of what he already knew about me and my work—that these apparently admirable habits of mine were essential to what I did. I "talked to everybody," or at least to as many people as possible, because doing so helped me do a better job. I also reminded him that inasmuch as this research was something my employer expected of me, "talking to everybody" was part of a job for which I got paid. He countered by stressing that these points did not matter nearly as much as the fact that the two of us were actually having the conversation we were having. As he saw it, whatever else it might be about, my work was valuable for requiring me to engage with people like him in the ways I did. How else would someone like him and someone like me find ourselves in a conversation like the one we were having, if not by virtue of the very work we were discussing?

The simple fact that anthropological work, and ethnographic fieldwork in particular, necessitates conversations and enables collaborations among people who would otherwise have no reason to associate with one another must surely be one of its most valuable and attractive features. Like unlikely comparisons, unlikely conversations and collaborations can bear unexpected fruit. Consider again the case of early modern European alchemy. As Moran described it, alchemy was, as anthropology is, a field that involved "numerous figures across the social spectrum" (2005: 6):

> Some were enthusiastic about making gold and silver; some focused more on making medicines. Still others sought out new procedures in developing a variety of chemical technologies. Some found room to do all these things at once. Some were physicians and philosophers who

enjoyed the privileges of university degrees. Others were artisans who learned their art close to home. Some were itinerant and lived on the margins of society, while others enjoyed civic rights or held courtly appointments. Some were Moslems, and others were Jews or Christians. Some were women, others men; some sincere, others frauds. (2005: 9)

Moran warned against giving too much credence to intellectual boundaries drawn retrospectively in efforts to make the story of the scientific revolution more palatable to "solid citizens of modernity on the enlightenment side of town" (2005: 9). Separating the contributions of some figures and perspectives of this period from others is not nearly as easy as some suggest, nor is the wall that protects the revolution's heroes from the taint of alchemy as well founded as some might like. Indeed, Moran argued, what "woke things up" in the scientific revolution was the "sometimes inharmonious intellectual and social mixture of learned and artisan, of occult, spiritual and mechanical" (2005: 187). The context Moran described was one of unlikely collaborations and conversations, in which "the fuzziness of learned frontiers increased the possibility of social interaction between representatives of ostensibly different intellectual points of view" (2005: 157).

Not that all these interactions ended in agreements or profound new discoveries, of course. What is important, in retrospect, and what precipitated the development of the new, even "revolutionary," ways of doing and thinking that we associate with this period of European history is quite simply that these interactions occurred at all and that those involved learned from them. And so it has continued to be in the centuries since that new ways of thinking and doing in science tend to emerge from the combined efforts of unlikely bedfellows. Andrew Pickering (2001) reported, for example, that organic chemistry would not exist but for the interrelated work of tinkering dye-makers and academic theorists in the mid-nineteenth century. Nor, argued Peter Galison (2003), would the theory of relativity have taken shape without the insights Einstein drew from the work of clock designers whose patents he reviewed while famously underemployed.

Obviously, there is only so far one can take even the unlikeliest of comparisons. In bringing up alchemy in this section, I do not mean to suggest that the actual processes that were essential to alchemical research (distillation, for example) have a great deal in common with those of ethnographic research (but see Shaffer 1994). Rather, my intention is simply to highlight two points about any study, however broadly or narrowly conceived, that (1) requires social interactions of the kind just noted and (2) is premised on the prospective assumption that doing and knowing what to do are connected.

The first point is that such work is collaborative in a way that makes it especially prone to change. Not only does research of this sort entail the participation of a variety of players, but also, thanks to the diverse perspectives inherent in this variety and the complications that can come with trying to accommodate or incorporate these perspectives in the course of research, those involved might learn to do or think differently than is their habit.

The second point is simpler still. If the history of science is anything to go by, research of the sort described here is well poised to contribute significantly to new and potentially influential ways of thinking and doing, whether within the confines of particular disciplines or beyond them. All this put differently, and more in keeping with the central push of this volume, what I am suggesting is not just that anthropological research is inherently collaborative but that it is this aspect of our research that, if given its due, is most likely to ensure the short-term vitality and long-term legacy of anthropological work.

Readers of the last few paragraphs might reasonably wonder whether I am not misrepresenting alchemy for the sake of my argument. Was alchemy really all about unlikely collaborations? Is there nothing to the popular image of the alchemist working alone in the laboratory, secretive in his methods and teachings? Have we really been so effectively duped by Moran's "solid citizens of modernity on the enlightenment side of town" (2005: 9)? The answer to all these questions is no. Alchemists did, in fact, spend a great deal of time on their own, working through their ideas individually, subjectively, and experimentally. Many were also quite secretive, cautious in the way they passed on what they learned in the process of their work, aware of the great value of this knowledge but not wanting it to fall into the hands of those who might misuse or misinterpret it. To suggest otherwise would be misleading. But then so would be suggesting that these aspects of alchemy are without their parallels in anthropology. In the following section, I discuss some of the more isolating tasks involved in anthropological work.

Written Work

Although ethnographic fieldwork and the unlikely conversations and collaborations it entails might be the sort of work for which anthropologists are best known, the work of ethnographic and other sorts of writing—done more or less by oneself and privately—can actually take up much more of a working anthropologist's time. For me, certainly, the major part of any day as an employee of a Canadian university is spent in front of a computer monitor, paper writing, outline writing, proposal writing, review writing, report writing, lecture writing, email writing, reference writing, and so on. Indeed, it bears mentioning that I am working right now as I type these words and that, with any luck, I will be working every time I read, rewrite, speak, cite, assign, or defend these words in the future.

That writing is a big part of my job is certainly not lost on people in Ambondromifehy. Indeed, it has gotten to the point where some people there are more likely to remark on the fact that I am *not* writing something down than that I am. That noted, the connection between the writing I do while in their company and the living I make is unclear to them. Many people I have spoken with over the years assume that my notes find their way into books or articles that will find appreciative, and paying, audiences back home. When I reply that things are not quite as simple as this and explain that, in fact, not only have I never been paid to publish what I write but sometimes I have to pay a fee or take out a paid membership in an association in order to have a manuscript considered by a potential publisher, I am met with puzzled looks. Explaining that I am employed by a university and that I sometimes use the things that I and other people write to help in my teaching can help to clarify matters, but only until I am forced to counter the reasonable inference that Canadian students go to university so that they can study the complexities of life in northern Madagascar. I haven't the heart to tell them that many of my students wish I would stop going off on tangents inspired by my research and devote more attention to outlining what is going to be on the exam.

Any academic anthropologist who has found himself or herself in a conversation about the role of writing in what he or she does for a living knows how quickly a seemingly reasonable career choice can dissolve into a mess of discomforting contradictions. People in Ambondromifehy are certainly correct on one front: the end result of all of my scribbling in their company is meant to be products—tangible, quantifiable, vetted things (papers, books, reports, etc.) that, on bad days, can seem to do little more than establish that I have been suitably productive. I would like to think, as many in Ambondromifehy assume, that my students take great interest in the lectures and papers I write and in the written work of others that I assign, but I am well aware that this is not always the case. The same can be said, of course, for colleagues at my own and other institutions who are as tied up with their own work as I am with mine. With so much time spent on various sorts of writing, who has time to read as much as they should? These points in mind, an obvious question presents itself: Why write? Some might well assume that academic anthropologists write in order to get and keep jobs, to ensure tenure or promotion, to build up track records that will enable them to get funding in the future, and so forth. There are far better reasons for writing than these, however.

Writing is essential to the processes I previously argued are basic to anthropological work. Indeed, writing is a central technique of the sort of research I have learned to do, propelling it from beginning to end. This, too, is a point that Bera and others in Ambondromifehy understand. Sometimes it is they who remind me of it, tapping on my notebook in the course of a conversation, suggesting that I take careful note of such-and-such a point so that I do not forget it. What they understand, ultimately, is that writing and other ways of documenting diverse viewpoints are essential to the sort of deep play I do.

Writing field notes can also be, or at least seem to be, secretive at times. People in Ambondromifehy often remark on the fact that I carry my notebook everywhere with me, guarding it carefully in a pouch that almost never leaves my shoulder. Why? What have I written down that I cannot bear to part with? And then there is the frequently noted fact that I speak Malagasy with people and yet write about these conversations in English. One miner suggested that this strategy ensured that the people with whom I had conversations could not decipher one another's words on the pages in front of me and them. If anyone saw what someone else had said, he suggested, it might lead them to change their answers to my questions. What is more, he added, writing in English allowed me to put whatever I wanted to paper without worrying that anyone would be able to read it. There is much to be said for these observations. For me, as for many others, I am sure, writing field notes is often the solitary, selective, and even secretive process that some in Ambondromifehy imagine it to be. If only these observers were also right about what becomes of all these notes in the end; if only the written works that come out of the notes were as prized by audiences outside of Madagascar as some there assume.

Deep play being what it is, much of what I write down in my notebooks is lost in the process of the writing I do at home. But what becomes of the products of this process? Who actually reads what is written in the end? More importantly, who reads it in anything but the "least charitable way possible" (Graeber 2005: 191)? Thankfully, in my experience at least, the answers to these questions are not as disheartening as some might fear. Anyone who has engaged in and learned from reading anthropological work understands full well that reading is as much a way and part of doing anthropology as is ethnographic fieldwork and that creative reading can be as innovative and insightful as can creative writing.

These points in mind, a significant and familiar possibility suggests itself. If anthropology is something to be done, and if reading anthropological work is a good way of doing it, then perhaps the best way to get more people doing anthropology is to get more people reading the products that come out of anthropological work. Achieving such a goal would require writing more strategically, with the diverse audiences we hope to reach with our work in mind. Or perhaps our work would be more accessible to different audiences if communicated through media other than writing. In any case, the task at hand is not simply a matter of rethinking how anthropological work gets presented but of reevaluating how we ourselves evaluate different products of anthropological work. Working anthropologists play no small part in reproducing existing institutional prejudices regarding what "counts" as anthropological production, and we will have to take the lead if these prejudices are to change.

Arguments for and against more accessible anthropological writing have been made many times before, so my concerns will be familiar to most. At what point does accessibility preclude communicating the complexity that anthropologists try to study? How much is too much catering to the existing assumptions, interests, and tastes of potential audiences when the goal is to change those interests and tastes? Ultimately, what becomes of the things we write but others get wrong?

I am hardly the first to fret over questions of the clarity or obscurity of a body of written work. Sherwood Taylor, commenting on the "maddeningly and deliberately obscure" rhetoric of alchemists (1952: 13), noted their deep concern over the ways in which the results of their work might be used and abused by unscrupulous and untrained others in the pursuit of immoral ends (1952: 178–79). Writing obscurely ensured that only worthy adepts, people committed to the goals, procedures, and underlying philosophy of the authors of alchemical texts, could benefit from the insights that the work of alchemy produced. As disturbing as such thinking might seem to some working anthropologists, to others who find themselves complaining from time to time that the relevance of their work goes unappreciated or underappreciated by nonspecialists, there may also be something disturbingly familiar about this logic.

Of all the figures in Bruce Moran's revisionist account of alchemy (2005), the most intriguing to me is Andreas Libavius. Moran first refers to Libavius' book *Alchemy* in illustrating the very practical nature of early modern European alchemy. Here was a practical and accessible guide, intended for students, concerning alchemical processes that might be used in the study of nature. But Libavius was more than just a textbook author. In a collection of letters written in the last years of the sixteenth century, he lashed out at the status quo in his field, giving a sense of the profoundly different understandings of what alchemy was and should be about. There is no doubting where Libavius stood and what he made of the secretive, purely contemplative, and intentionally obscuring ways of many of his contemporaries:

> [W]hat aid is he to humanity who only delights himself by thinking up images in his head and contriving things which cannot be put to use? ... Although we think that the pleasure of chemical contemplation is special, ... this art also demands working [with the hands], both to strengthen theory (since theory can be deceived by the vanity of opinions) and also that something beneficial to all might result. (Moran 2005: 106)

Libavius made a case for a discipline that would serve much more than just the whims, curiosity, and interests of individual researchers and their sponsors and in which secrecy would have no place. Particularly concerning to him was the tendency among some of his contemporaries to condemn "all the writings, assertions and deeds of the past" (Moran 2005: 101), "the books of ancient philosophers and ... the accumulated experience of artisans over hundreds of years," in which their own work was rooted (2005: 102). Dismissing this lineage of ideas for the sake of novelty was not only disingenuous but misguided, Libavius believed, leading to an intellectual climate in which "hardly anyone agreed with anyone else, and each person wanted to seem to have brought forth something new, the knowledge and art of which he laid claim to only for himself" (Moran 2005: 101). For the sake of the future, Libavius argued, such thinking and practice would have to stop.

And so it did, Moran tells us, as the secretive work of court-sponsored alchemy gradually gave way to the relatively more open and accessible work of university-based chemistry. Not that academic chemistry, or "public alchemy" (2005: 111), as Moran suggests Libavius envisioned it, was without its costs. Writing in the early years of the Cold War, Taylor could not help but comment on the dubious success of Libavius' vision. The "transmutation of metals, has now been realized by science," he wrote, "and the alchemical vessel is the uranium pile. Its success has had precisely the result that the alchemists feared and guarded against, the placing of gigantic power in the hands of those who have not been fitted by spiritual training to receive it" (Taylor 1952: 179).

What is an anthropologist in the twenty-first century to make of all this? Am I suggesting that the questions facing the early modern European protagonists discussed here are similar to the questions facing anthropologists who want to reach wider and different audiences with more strategic sorts of writing? Or am I perhaps suggesting that we should all do as Libavius did and work toward the achievement of a common, single vision of what anthropology could and should be about—a vision that all of us can agree on and believe in? If there *are* specific lessons to be learned from the debates that occupied people such as Libavius, I am in no position to teach them; I am as uncertain as anyone about the future of the discipline that occupies and employs me.

That noted, one general lesson might indeed be taken from the account just given. If the work of today's anthropologists is to have a future, and if the writing we do is to play a role in building this future, then variety is a good thing. Moran argued that what made the written work of alchemists so influential over the long term was just that—its variety. "Through the messy mixture of conflict and diversity," he noted, "alchemical writers extended the repertoire of imaginable opinion. Theirs was a clamorous 'voice,' a commotion at the interface between reason and passion, theory and practice, belief and experience" (2005: 187). It stands to reason that in our own efforts to extend the repertoire of imaginable opinion, we might be better served by searching out more clamor than by pursuing consensus.

Clamor need not only feature in our collective work, however. Clamor is also something for which individual anthropologists have an affinity, thanks to the processes that are essential to our work—the part of what we do that requires us take diverse perspectives and opinions seriously. For those of us who want to do it, making the most of this latter sort of clamor requires extending our existing collaborative tendencies, discussed in the previous section, into the parts of what we do that can be most isolating. "Collaborative ethnography" projects (Lassiter 2005a) are certainly one way of proceeding, but there are other possibilities as well. As some of the case studies collected in this volume suggest, projects conceived out of the mingling of anthropological processes with existing social and political processes in particular contexts stand to offer a great deal to all involved.

Not that such collaborations will or need always be deemed successful or worthy of imitation, nor need they necessarily involve writing. All that is important is that such efforts be acknowledged, both within the discipline and in the institutions that house and support it, as valid ways of doing anthropology. Without such acknowledgment, there will be even less incentive than already exists for breaking disciplinary habits. Given the current state of the productivity regimes in which many of us work, the greatest deterrent to the development of new ways of doing anthropology is the possibility that some efforts simply will not count or, perhaps more insidiously, that some will not count as much as others. Without new ways of doing anthropology, how will those who follow us ever know how to do anthropology in any ways but those in which it is done today?

Anthropology from the Future

In this chapter I have tried to make something out of mixing an unlikely comparison with insights drawn from some unlikely conversations I have had in northern Madagascar over the past couple of years. Whether or not the end result has proven insightful, I hope it is acknowledged as a product of the very processes I have argued are essential to the sort of anthropological work I do. Regardless of how this work is taken by others, I draw some comfort from knowing that at least *I* have learned something from working through the material presented here, and thus, even if I have failed to make the work relevant to others, I have failed productively, in a way that will affect my own future doings, conversations, and collaborations.

This last comment should not be taken as a sign of the tired cynicism that can creep into one's work in the weeks leading up to a deadline. Rather, it is a sign of my renewed confidence in the proposition with which I began the chapter—that what is most valuable about anthropological work is the processes it involves. Not that anthropological products, including this volume, are not important; without products, the potential value of our processes could be neither realized nor communicated. Still, my sense is that if twenty-first-century anthropology is to have a legacy, it will be a legacy owing more to our processes than to any particular products that came from them. To illustrate what I mean by this, let me end with a series of questions that should put anthropological work in the sort of perspective I have in mind.

How will anthropological work look from the future? Not *in* the future, but *from* the future, or, more precisely, from future hindsight. And not five or ten years from now, either, or even thirty years from now, when I will likely be asked to leave whatever job I might have. How will the anthropological work of today look four hundred years from now, when those who consider our efforts are as distant from us in time as we are from the early modern European alchemists to whom I have been referring? Will the boundaries that so many have fought to uphold be acknowledged, or will we be grouped with others whose work ours will be said to have resembled? If the latter, which others might those be? With regard to the broader historical and intellectual narratives in which we will be contextualized, will our work be celebrated as essential or derided as out of touch? Will we be praised for being ahead of the curve or faulted for failing to see it coming, whatever "it" might be? Or will we be accused of having seen it coming but having done too little to stop, stem, or steer it? Worst of all, perhaps, might our descendants not remember us much at all?

Of all the lessons that might be garnered from the history and legacy of alchemy, perhaps the best to end with is the following: The potential and value of a field of study cannot be determined solely by what or whether it is seen to deliver. Despite the failures for which they are so well known, early modern European alchemists contributed significantly to the development of ways of thinking and doing that literally changed the world. And in retrospect, they did so not so much by virtue of their faith or productivity but by simply doing what they did and, in the process, teaching others as much through their failures as through their successes. A similar legacy for anthropology might well be something worth working toward.

Reflections on the Symposium

Douglas E. Foley

Most anthropologists acknowledge that in the wake of postcolonial, feminist, critical race, cultural Marxist, and postmodern critiques, anthropology has "reinvented" itself (Hymes 1972). In the introduction to this volume, Field and Fox's excellent synopsis of the 2005 Wenner-Gren symposium on which the book is based demonstrates how the field is evolving. The conference participants made it clear that they no longer try to produce holistic portraits of culture that exist outside world history. Long gone is the lofty goal of salvage ethnology, that of discovering cultural and linguistic universals before modernity destroys human diversity.

As the focus and purpose of anthropological research have changed, so have the field methods used to study new topics. Like Luke Lassiter (2005b), Field and Fox emphasize the rise of collaborative field methods. The conference participants had practiced varying degrees of collaboration with their subjects. Doretti and Brunell assisted victims of Argentina's dirty war in identifying the remains of loved ones. Frank, Basch, and Toussaint became resources for tribal elders, woman's groups, and Aboriginal communities, respectively, in addressing their various needs. Rappaport and Hale worked as political allies with activist groups, co-theorizing and co-writing their ethnographies. Walsh and Woodson each worked closely with informants to validate views and indicators of modernization and poverty. Block and Frank had assimilated into the culture of occupational therapy to better serve their respective clients. Sundar and Craig Howe, whose paper does not appear in this collection, wrote, respectively, cultural critiques of Indian anthropology and of the new United States National Museum of the American Indian.

> All the participants still subscribed to the classic methodological practices of extended fieldwork, field notes, direct observation, interviews,

and personal experience as the basis of knowing. But as Fox and Field point out, the conference participants were much less worried about "going native" and "over-identifying" with their subjects than earlier anthropologists were. They had dropped the positivist pretense that an ethnographer can be a neutral, detached, objective observer. In varying degrees, all the participants embraced the notion that ethnographies are the products of complex encounters and thus are more intersubjective and interpretive than objective. Consequently, all of them were trying to get closer to their subjects through various types of collaboration. Their motives were many, but most were doing so for ethical and political reasons. Their aim was to make anthropology a more useful, publicly engaged science that addressed pressing social and political problems. Many traditional anthropologists will find these new collaborative practices problematic. They represent for them a breakdown of a time-honored distinction between basic and applied research and the rise of a politicized, subjective, unscientific anthropology.

During the discussions, the participants tried on many professional identity labels—applied, public policy, citizen, action, activist—but no consensus emerged on how to conceptualize and label these new practices. Hale settled on the label "activist anthropology," which has some affinities with Sol Tax's earlier notion of "action anthropology" (Foley 1999). Hale argued for a high degree of political and methodological collaboration that leads to co-theorized and co-written ethnographies. The chapters by Rappaport, Doretti and Brunell, Frank, Basch, and Toussaint represent, to varying degrees, excellent examples of Hale's activist anthropology. According to both Tax and Hale, wrestling with the contradictions of political collaboration leads to more complex, accurate, ethical, and useful ethnographies.

To flourish in academe, collaborative or activist anthropology—which-ever label you prefer—must be founded on more than high-minded ethics. This is so because traditional anthropologists can easily trivialize alliances with and heartfelt accounts of the downtrodden as "going native" and thus lacking scientific objectivity. One counter to such "objectivist baiting" is standpoint epistemology, which restates Hegel's old master-slave argument that the slave has greater insight into his oppressed condition than does the master. Because all interpretation and knowledge production is situated in history and politics, why not interpret the world from the perspective least corrupted by power and dominance? Most standpoint theories, whether or not they acknowledge their debt to Hegelianism, have those philosophical roots. Traditional anthropologists who imagine themselves objective scientists may find this new commitment to "partial" and "situated" knowledge claims troubling, but collaborative or activist anthropologists generally prefer this more limited, less grandiose notion of science. Although few of the contributors to this book make their epistemological assumptions explicit, feminist standpoint theorists provide collaborative-activist ethnographers with a defensible epistemological foundation for their field practices (Foley 2002).

The chapters by Block, Frank, and Basch contain interesting reflections on developing an interdisciplinary professional identity in the face of the status politics of academe. But few of the conference papers presented what the authors had learned from the post-1960s anthropological debates. I have chronicled my understanding of these debates elsewhere (Foley 1999; Foley and Valenzuela 2005), and doing so helped me understand my own ethnographic practice. So in the remainder of this essay, I contrast collaborative-activist ethnographic approaches with other major postpositivist ethnographic approaches. Contrasting ethnographic genres highlights what is distinctive about collaborative-activist ethnographic practices.

After reviewing many ethnographies of United States American culture, Kirby Moss and I (Foley and Moss 2000) concluded that "anthropology as cultural critique" (Marcus and Fisher 1986) had become the most popular genre in contemporary American anthropology. The anthropology of cultural critique is a capacious umbrella that incorporates postcolonial, feminist, critical race, cultural Marxist, poststructuralist, and postmodern critiques. Perhaps its most seminal characteristic is that it views the cultural world through a multiple dominance/power (class, race, gender, sexual preference) perspective. This broad theoretical lens generates critiques of institutions, popular cultural practices, and public policies and uses interdisciplinary research techniques from anthropology, media studies, history, and literary studies.

The influence of theoretical debates in Britain, France, and Germany and in Continental philosophy has been especially important in the emergence of anthropology as cultural critique. The theoretical works of the big three—Bourdieu, Foucault, and Gramsci—and of numerous feminist writers dominate this genre of American ethnography (Foley and Moss 2000; Foley and Valenzuela 2005). Cultural critics work from these grand theoretical traditions in a way that challeges naturalized, taken-for-granted cultural and institutional practices. Well-known practitioners of this genre are, among many others, Nancy Scheper-Hughes, Michael Taussig, Emily Martin, Phillipe Bourgois, Louise Lamphere, and George Marcus.

Many anthropologists who have adopted a cultural critique notion of ethnography imagine themselves doing the political work of raising ordinary people's consciousness and transforming the conventional wisdoms and dated theoretical paradigms of the academy. Methodologically, most cultural critics are more collaborative than earlier scientific ethnographers were, but the modernist ideals of the rational, intellectual, and autonomous author interpreting everyday reality in a deeper, more theoretical manner does not lend itself to co-theorized and coauthored ethnographies. Most cultural critics maintain a greater degree of intellectual and political autonomy and distance than is advocated in collaborative-activist ethnography.

Some anthropologists associate the anthropology of cultural critique with postmodernism, a broad, complex philosophical critique of the social sciences that has filtered into anthropology in fragmented ways. Put far too simply, postmodernism, with its deconstructionist methodology, is radically skeptical and critical of the eighteenth-century modernist, Enlightenment dream of progress through rational social and physical science. There are actually few practicing postmodern ethnographers in American anthropology, but because of their relentless critique of positivism and ethnographic realism, several have had considerable influence. In varying degrees, ethnographers such as Stephen Tyler, Michael Taussig, Kathleen Stewart, Guillermo Gomez-Pena, and Patti Lather distance themselves from modernist grand theory, authoritative knowledge claims, linear theories of historical progress, modernist reflexive practices, and realist representations of their subjects. They generally strive to deconstruct earlier ethnographic misrepresentations of their subjects and represent them without deploying grand theories.

Methodologically, postmodern ethnographers are not particularly collaborative in the sense of co-theorizing and co-writing their ethnographies, and they consider the various types of reflexivity that cultural critics valorize a modernist, rationalist conceit that will not produce greater objectivity and better representations. In theory, postmodern ethnographers strive to represent their subjects through "evocative" texts—that is, texts that are more ambiguous and poetic than modernist "realist" ethnographies with grand theory and strong knowledge claims (Foley 2002). At this writing, postmodern ethnography has come and gone. A sure sign of its demise is the number of anthropologists now bashing postmodernism without acknowledging its role in transforming anthropological practice.

Anthropologists who practice some form of cultural critique have learned a few things from the postmodern critique. They are more skeptical about being scientists in the grand, positivist sense, and they worry more about their authorial power and their representational and narrative practices. But most cultural critics in anthropology still subscribe to a modernist principle of academic knowledge production that postmodern thinkers renounced: the production of grand theory and generalizable knowledge. Such knowledge purports to explain how social and cultural institutions such as patriarchy, racial and class formations, the mass media, and even the professions work. Like earlier modernist, Enlightenment thinkers, cultural critics generally advocate a science rooted in egalitarian, democratic ideals. Although not framed in the allegedly value-neutral, positivist language of "X causes Y" explanations, cultural critiques do purport to produce knowledge that explains our lived reality and helps to improve our social and cultural institutions and practices.

The collaborative-activist anthropologists at the Wenner-Gren conference expressed many of these same modernist notions of science and knowledge production. Politically engaged "collaborative anthropologists" produce in-depth, theorized ethnographies much like those of cultural critics, but with one significant difference. The local political allies of collaborative-activist anthropologists usually demand that the anthropologists produce another form of knowledge that cultural critiques rarely produce. Activist anthropologists must also produce, for lack of a better construct, a great deal of "local knowledge"—that is, ungeneralizable knowledge that might help people get their appropriated land back or recover the remains of a loved one. The knowledge needed to address particular local political inequities may not readily translate into the "generalizable knowledge" stories that academics admire and reward.

In addition, political activists may be more interested in glowing portraits of their cause than in complex, critical portraits. Several of the contributors to this volume note their struggles to bridge the enormous gap between what academe and local political groups demand and to resist political-correctness pressures to censor their data. These were problems my colleagues and I found especially difficult to overcome during our study of the Chicano civil rights movement (Foley 2000).

The egalitarian ideal of co-theorized and co-written ethnographies takes anthropology in some exciting new directions, but several of us wondered whether privileged university professors could really answer Maori scholar Linda Tuhiwai Smith's (1999) call to decolonize research. Can academics really let working-class and tribal leaders decide who researches what? Moreover, will the political legislatures that govern universities and the professional associations that govern academic disciplines really accept such a democratic, politicized, and collaborative model of inquiry? It seems that collaborative-activist anthropology must overcome some powerful institutional barriers if it is to enter the mainstream of anthropological practice.

I believe would-be collaborative anthropologists must think of their labor the way homemakers do. For the time being, they will have to be content with doing unpaid labor that is grossly undervalued in academe. When they publish useful op-ed pieces in newspapers, or policy briefs, or videos that help local people redress injustices, they probably will not get credit for it as academic production. In addition, they must learn how to produce much more accessible and varied accounts of their collaborative research. Videos, policy briefs, popular ethnographies, and investigative newspaper articles are not academic journal articles, and few anthropologists have much training, if any, in these genres. Finally, activist anthropologists must become a strong enough force in professional associations and in their universities to broaden the definition of what counts as knowledge production.

Many politically progressive academic anthropologists doing cultural critiques will not embrace the burden of double labor, undervalued production, lower salaries, and political-correctness pressures. In the end, they will channel their activist aspirations the way I did, into the safer, acceptable model of academic production called the anthropology of cultural critique. And if they were political activists, they will feel guilty about the compromises made to survive in academe (Foley and Valenzuela 2005).

Field and Fox may be correct in saying that collaborative-activist ethnographic practices are already widespread. What this optimistic view does not provide, however, is an account of where collaborative, activist anthropology is actually taking place. From what I have seen, the most politically active anthropologists are nomadic, untenured academics in less prestigious colleges or in interdisciplinary professional schools, or they have been pushed outside the academy entirely. And as Hale notes, there are a few clusters of activist anthropologists in big-name, publish-or-perish universities who work harder than their colleagues, tolerate political-correctness pressures, and publish both universal and local knowledge. The hopeful sign is that the number of "citizen anthropologists" who are more collaborative and serve the public interest is growing.

Nevertheless, I must reiterate Lassiter's view that "collaborative ethnography" is not the only way to produce socially and politically relevant studies. Following the sociologist Jack Douglas (1976), the less collaborative, more detached, covert approach of investigative reporting may, in some circumstances, be needed. The genre of insider, whistle-blower accounts has produced revealing ethnographies of the tobacco industry and the CIA. There is nothing collaborative about these critiques, but they do fulfill Laura Nader's call to "study up," and they definitely serve the public interest.

In addition, there are many politically involved "applied" or "policy-oriented" investigators who "work within the system," like Basch, Woodson, and Doretti and associates. My colleague Angela Valenzuela is not collaborative methodologically, but she is highly collaborative politically. She is a trusted ally of Chicano legislators who want to reform neoconservative school policies. They are not interested in co-theorizing or coauthoring her research. They expect her to be an expert witness and writer of authoritative studies and policy briefs (Foley and Valenzuela 2005).

Finally, I second Fox and Field's cautionary note that this volume may misrepresent collaborative-activist anthropology as an emerging world anthropological practice. During the discussion of Sundar's and Toussaint's papers at the symposium, the group was very clear about the need for many histories of the field of anthropology. Concern was expressed that this volume might produce a colonizing discourse that represented the United States experience as universal. The chapters situated in Latin America suggest that colleagues to the south may actually be more activist and collaborative than US anthropologists. Europe and Australia also have their fair share of experimentation with collaborative methods and politics. Sundar's account of Indian anthropology, however, highlights the enduring hegemony of more traditional anthropological practices. Perhaps the Wenner-Gren Foundation needs to host an international conference on this topic. In the absence of more conferences, I hope this volume provokes more reflection on why and how anthropology is changing yet in some ways staying the same.

References

Abbott, Andrew. 1988. *The System of Professions: An Essay on the Division of Expert Labor.* Chicago: University of Chicago Press.

Adamson, Walter L. 1980. *Hegemony and Revolution: A Study of Antonio Gramsci's Political and Cultural Theory.* Berkeley: University of California Press.

Addams, Jane. 1999 [1910]. *Twenty Years at Hull-House.* New York: Signet.

Agrawal, Arun. 1995. "Dismantling the Divide between Indigenous and Western Knowledge." *Development and Change* 26 (3): 413–39.

Ahmad, Abdul Ghaffar M. 2003. *Anthropology in the Sudan: Reflections by a Sudanese Anthropologist.* Amsterdam: International Books and OSSREA.

Allport, Carolyn. 2005. "Fighting for Our Rights." *Frontline: National Tertiary Education Union Women's Journal* 12: 2.

Alvarez, María D., and Gerald F. Murray. 1981. "Socialization for Scarcity: Child Feeding Beliefs and Practices in a Haitian Village." Report submitted to USAID/Haiti. August. Port-au-Prince: USAID/Haiti.

Anderson, Ian. 2003. "Aboriginal Australians, Governments, and Participation in Health Systems." In *Health, Social Policy and Communities,* eds. P. Liamputtong Rice and H. Gardner, 224–40. Oxford: Oxford University Press.

Anderson, Mark, and Sarah England. 1998. "Authentic African Culture in Honduras? Afro–Central Americans Challenge Honduran Indo-Hispanic Mestizaje." Paper presented at the 21st Latin American Studies Association International Congress, Chicago.

Anglade, Georges. 1982. *Atlas critique d'Haïti.* Groupe d'Études de Recherches Critiques d'Espace (ERCE), Département de Géographie, Université de Québec à Montréal et Centre de Recherches Caraïbes de l'Université de Montréal.

Anonymous. 2000. "Sxabwes/El ombligo": El juego didáctico de las matemáticas." *C'ayu'ce* 4: 42–43. Popayán.

AOTA (American Occupational Therapy Association). 2004. "Consumer Information: What Is Occupational Therapy?" http://www.aota.org/featured/area6/index.asp, accessed July 28, 2004.

Appadurai, Arjun. 2002. "Deep Democracy: Urban Governmentality and the Horizon of Politics." *Public Culture* 14 (1): 21–48.

Argyrou, Vassos. 1999. "Sameness and the Ethnological Will to Meaning." *Current Anthropology* 40: S29–S40.

Australian Bureau of Statistics and Australian Indigenous Health and Welfare. 2001. *The Health and Welfare of Australia"s Aboriginal and Torres Strait Islander Peoples.* Canberra: Australian Bureau of Statistics.

Australian Law Reform Commission. 1986. *Final Report.* Canberra: Australian Government Printers.

Avirama, Jesús, and Rayda Márquez. 1995. "The Indigenous Movement in Colombia." In *Indigenous Peoples and Democracy in Latin America,* ed. D. L. Van Cott, 83–105. New York: St. Martin's.

Balcazar, Fabricio E., and Christopher B. Keys. 1998. "Developing the Capacity of Minority Communities to Promote the Americans with Disabilities Act." Grant proposal to the National Institute on Disability and Rehabilitation Research.

———, Christopher B. Keys, and Yolanda Suarez-Balcazar. 2001. "Empowering Latinos with Disabilities to Address Issues of Independent Living and Disability Rights: A Capacity-Building Approach." *Journal of Prevention and Intervention in the Community* 21: 53–70.

BARA. 1996a. *A Baseline Study of Livelihood Security in Northwest Haiti.* Prepared by M. Baro, C. Bart, and K. Coelho, with the assistance of M. Langworthy and D. G. Woodson. April. Tucson: BARA, University of Arizona, and Port-au-Prince: CARE/Haiti and iFSIS.

———. 1996b. *A Baseline Study of Livelihood Security in the Southern Peninsula of Haiti.* Prepared by D. G. Woodson and M. Baro, with the assistance of T. J. Finan et al. April. Tucson: BARA, University of Arizona, and Port-au-Prince: CRS/Haiti and iFSIS.

———. 1997. *A Baseline Study of Livelihood Security in the Departments of the Artibonite, Center, North, Northeast, and West, Republic of Haiti.* Prepared by D. G. Woodson and M. Baro, with the assistance of T. J. Finan et al. May. Tucson: BARA, University of Arizona, and Port-au-Prince: ADRA/Haiti and iFSIS.

Barad, Karen. 2003. "Posthumanist Performativity: Toward an Understanding of How Matter Comes to Matter." *Signs: Journal of Women in Culture and Society* 28 (3): 801–31.

Barthélemy, Gérard. 1989. *Le pays en dehors: Essai sur l'univers rural Haïtien.* Montréal: Centre International de Documentation et d'Information Haïtienne, and Port-au-Prince: Henri Deschamps.

Basch, Linda. 2004. "Human Security, Globalization, and Feminist Visions." *Peace Review,* special issue, 16 (1): 5–12.

———, Lucie Wood Saunders, Jagna Wojcicka Sharff, and James Peacock, eds. 1999. *Transforming Academia: Challenges and Opportunities for an Engaged Anthropology.* Arlington, VA: American Anthropological Association.

———, Nina Glick Schiller, and Christina Blanc Szanton. 1994. *Nations Unbound.* New York: Gordon Breach.

Basso, Keith. 1996. *Wisdom Sits in Places: Landscape and Language among the Western Apache.* Albuquerque: University of New Mexico Press.

Bates, Robert H., V. Y. Mudimbe, and Jean O'Barr. 1993. *Africa and the Disciplines.* Chicago: University of Chicago Press.

Benedict, Ruth. 1946. *The Chrysanthemum and the Sword: Patterns of Japanese Culture.* Boston: Houghton Mifflin.

Benmayor, R. 1991. "Testimony, Action Research, and Empowerment: Puerto Rican Women and Popular Education." In *Women's Words,* eds. D. Patai and S. B. Gluck, 159–74. New York: Routledge.

Bennett, John W. 1996. "Applied and Action Anthropology: Ideological and Conceptual Aspects." *Current Anthropology* 36, Supplement: S23–S53.

———. 2005. "Malinowski Award Lecture 2004: Applied Anthropology in Transition." *Human Organization* 64 (1): 1–3.

Berggren, Gretchen, Sarah Castle, Lincoln Chen, Winifred Fitzgerald, Catherine Michaud, and Marko Simunovic. 1993. "Sanctions in Haiti: Crisis in Humanitarian Action." Preliminary report, November. Cambridge, MA: Harvard Center for Population and Development Studies.

Bergquist, Charles. 1990. "In the Name of History: A Disciplinary Critique of Orlando Fals Borda's *Historia doble de la costa.*" *Latin American Research Review* 25 (3): 156–76.

Beteille, Andre. 1993. "Sociology and Anthropology: Their Relationship in One Person's Career." *Contributions to Indian Sociology,* n.s. 27 (2): 291–304.

———, 2000. "Teaching and Research." In *Situating Sociology: A Symposium on Knowledge, Institutions and Practices. Seminar,* special issue, 495: 20–23.

Biolsi, Thomas, and Larry J. Zimmerman, eds. 1997. *Indians and Anthropologists: Vine Deloria, Jr. and the Critique of Anthropology.* Tucson: University of Arizona Press.

Block, Pamela. 2000. "Sexuality, Fertility, and Danger: Twentieth-Century Images of Women with Cognitive Disabilities." *Sexuality and Disability* 18 (4): 239–54.

———. 2004. "Disability Studies in the Belly of the Beast." *Disability Studies Quarterly* 24 (4): n.p. (online journal). Special issue, "Disability Studies in the Education of Public Health and Health Professionals: Can It Work for All Involved?"

———, Fabricio E. Balcazar, and Christopher B. Keys. 2001. "From Pathology to Power: Rethinking Race, Poverty, and Disability." *Journal of Disability Policy Studies* 12 (1):18–27.

———, Beth Bock, Bruce Becker, and Sarah Everhart. 2001. "Alcohol and Substance Use by Adolescents and Young Adults with Recent Spinal Cord and Traumatic Brain Injuries." *Disability Studies Quarterly* 21 (2): n.p. (online journal).

———, and James H. Rimmer. 2000. "Shake It Up for Alcohol and Substance Use Reduction: Health Promotion and Capacity Building for Persons with Traumatic Spinal Cord Injuries." Grant proposal to the National Institute on Disability and Rehabilitation Research. CFDA Program 84.133, award no. H133G010094.

———, Sarah Everhart Skeels, and Christopher B. Keys. 2006. "Participatory Intervention Research with a Disability Community: A Practical Guide to Practice." *International Journal of Disability, Community, and Rehabilitation* 5 (1): n.p. (online journal).

———, Sarah Everhart Skeels, Christopher B. Keys, and James H. Rimmer. 2005. "Shake-It-Up: Health Promotion and Capacity Building for People with Spinal Cord Injuries and Related Neurological Disabilities." *Disability and Rehabilitation* 27 (4): 185–90.

Blundell, Valda, and Donny Wooloogoodja. 2004. *Keeping the Wandjinas Fresh.* Fremantle, Australia: Fremantle Arts Center Press.

Boas, Franz. 1912. "Changes in the Bodily Form of Descendants of Immigrants." *American Anthropologist* 14 (3): 530–62.

———, 1916. "New Evidence in Regard to the Instability of Human Types." *Proceedings of the National Academy of Sciences* 2: 713–71.

———, 1945. *Race and Democratic Society.* New York: J. J. Augustin.

———, 1960 [1888]. "The Central Eskimo: Domestic Occupations and Amusements." In *The Golden Age of American Anthropology*, eds. M. Mead and R. L. Bunzel, 246–50. New York: George Braziller.

———, 1962. *Anthropology and Modern Life.* New York: Norton.

Bolaños, Graciela, Abelardo Ramos, Joanne Rappaport, and Carlos Miñana. 2004. *¿Qué pasaría si la escuela…? Treinta años de construcción educativa.* Popayán: Programa de Educación Bilingüe e Intercultural, Consejo Regional Indígena del Cauca.

Bonilla, Víctor Daniel. 1977. *Historia política de los paeces.* Bogotá: Carta al CRIC, 4.

——, 1982. "Algunas experiencias del proyecto 'Mapas Parlantes.'" In *Alfabetización y educación de adultos en la región andina,* ed. J. E. García Huidobro, 145–61. Pátzcuaro, Mexico: UNESCO.

——, Gonzalo Castillo, Orlando Fals Borda, and Augusto Libreros. 1972. *Causa popular, ciencia popular: Una metodología del conocimiento científico a través de la acción.* Bogotá: Publicaciones de La Rosca.

Bose, Pradip K. n.d. "The Anthropologist as 'Scientist'?: Nirmal Kumar Bose." In *Anthropology in the East: The Indian Foundations of a Global Discipline,* eds. P. Uberoi, N. Sundar, and S. Deshpande. New Delhi: Permanent Black. In press.

Bourdieu, Pierre. 1996. *The State Nobility.* Stanford, CA: Stanford University Press.

Breines, Estelle B. 1986. *Origins and Adaptations: A Philosophy of Practice.* New York: Geri-Rehab, Inc.

Brinkerhoff, Derick W., and Jean-Claude Garcia-Zamor, eds. 1986. *Politics, Projects, and People: Institutional Development in Haiti.* New York: Praeger.

Buckley, Thomas. 2002. *Standing Ground: Yurok Indian Spirituality, 1850–1990.* Berkeley: University of California Press.

Cardoso de Oliveira, Roberto. 2000. "Peripheral Anthropologies 'versus' Central Anthropologies." *Journal of Latin American Anthropology* 4 (2)–5 (1): 10–30.

Carrara, Sergio. 1996. *Tributo a Vênus: A luta contra a sífilis no Brasil da passagem do século aos anos 1940.* Rio de Janiero: Editora Fiocruz.

Carrithers, Michael. 1992. *Why Humans Have Cultures: Explaining Anthropology and Social Diversity.* Oxford: Oxford University Press.

Castillo-Cárdenas, Gonzalo. 1987. *Liberation Theology from Below: The Life and Thought of Manuel Quintín Lame.* Maryknoll, NY: Orbis.

Chakrabarty, Dipesh. 2003. "Globalisation, Democratisation and the Evacuation of History?" In *At Home in Diaspora,* eds. J. Assayag and V. Beneit, 127–47. Delhi: Permanent Black.

Chambers, Erve. 1987. "Applied Anthropology in the Post-Vietnam Era: Anticipations and Ironies." *Annual Review of Anthropology* 16: 309–37.

Chambers, Robert. 1997. *Whose Reality Counts? Putting the Last First.* London: Intermediate Technology Publications.

Champagne, Duane. 1998. "American Indian Studies Is for Everyone." In *Natives and Academics: Researching and Writing about American Indians*, ed. D. A. Mihesuah, 181–89. Lincoln: University of Nebraska Press.

———, and Carole Goldberg. 2005. "Changing the Subject: Individual versus Collective Interests in Indian Country." *Wicazo Sa Review* 20 (1): 49–69. University of Minnesota Press.

Chapple, Eliot D. 1943. "Anthropological Engineering: Its Use to Administrators." *Applied Anthropology* 2: 23–32.

———, 1946. "The Natural Group in Industry." *Journal of Educational Sociology* 19: 534–39.

Charkiewicz, Ewa. 2004. "Global Bio-Politics and Corporations as the New Subject of History." Unpublished manuscript.

Cheah, Peng. 1997. "Posit(ion)ing Human Rights in the Current Global Conjecture." *Public Culture* 9: 233–66.

Chow, Rey. 1995. *Primitive Passions: Visuality, Sexuality, Ethnography, and Contemporary Chinese Cinema*. New York: Columbia University Press.

Clark, F. A., D. Parham, M. E. Carlson, G. Frank, J. Jackson, D. Pierce, R. J. Wolfe, and R. Zemke. 1991. "Occupational Science: Academic Innovation in the Service of Occupational Therapy's Future." *American Journal of Occupational Therapy* 45: 300–310.

Clifford, James. 1988. "Identity in Mashpee." In *The Predicament of Culture*, J. Clifford, 277–346. Cambridge, MA: Harvard University Press.

———, 1997. *Routes: Travel and Translation in the Late Twentieth Century*. Cambridge, MA: Harvard University Press.

Coffey, Wallace, and Rebecca Tsosie. 2001. "Rethinking the Tribal Sovereignty Doctrine: Cultural Sovereignty and the Collective Future of Indian Nations." *Stanford Law and Policy Review* (Spring): 191–210.

Cohn, Bernard. 1990. "Notes on the History of the Study of Indian Society and Culture." In *An Anthropologist among the Historians*, B. Cohn, 136–71. Delhi: Oxford University Press.

Collins, Patricia Hill. 1991. *Black Feminist Thought: Knowledge, Consciousness, and the Politics of Empowerment*. New York: Routledge.

Committee of Concerned Citizens. 2002. *Third Report: A Detailed Account of the Efforts of the Committee during the Five Years to Intervene in the Climate of Social Turmoil and Violence in Rural Andhra Pradesh, Specially in Telengana, in the Interests of the Common People of the State*. Hyderabad: Committee of Concerned Citizens.

Connerton, Paul. 1989. *How Societies Remember*. Cambridge: Cambridge University Press.

Cook, Sherburne F. 1976. *The Conflict between the California Indian and White Civilization*. Berkeley: University of California Press.

Cooke, Bill, and Uma Kothari, eds. 2001. *Participation: The New Tyranny?* London: Zed.

Cowan, Jane K. 2006. "Culture and Rights after *Culture and Rights*." *American Anthropologist* 108 (1): 9–24.

CRIC (Consejo Regional Indígena del Cauca). 2000. "Informe final: Profesionalización, Consejo Regional Indígena del Cauca." Popayán: PEBI-CRIC. Manuscript.

Crough, Greg, and Christine Christophersen. 1993. *Aboriginal People in the Economy of the Kimberley.* Darwin: North Australian Research Unit, and Canberra: Australian National University.

Current Anthropology. 1968. "Social Responsibility Symposium." Vol. 9, no. 5 (December). Articles by Kathleen Gough, Gerald Berreman, et al.

Dagua Hurtado, Abelino, Misael Aranda, and Luis Guillermo Vasco. 1998. *Guambianos: Hijos del aroiris y del agua.* Bogotá: Los Cuatro Elementos.

Dasgupta, Sangeeta. n.d. "Recasting the Oraons and the 'Tribe': Sarat Chandra Roy's Anthropology." In *Anthropology in the East: The Indian Foundations of a Global Discipline,* eds. P. Uberoi, N. Sundar, and S. Deshpande. New Delhi: Permanent Black. In press.

Declaration of Barbados. 1971. In *The Situation of the Indian in South America,* ed. W. Dostal, 376–81. Geneva: WCIP.

Deloria, Vine Jr. 1969. *Custer Died for Your Sins: An Indian Manifesto.* New York: Macmillan.

Desai, I. P. 1996. "Craft of Sociology in India: An Autobiographical Perspective." In *Theory and Ideology in Indian Sociology: Essays in Honour of Prof. Yogendra Singh,* ed. N. K. Singhi, 167–99. Jaipur: Rawat Publications.

Dewey, John. 1990. *The School and Society* and *The Child and the Curriculum.* Chicago: University of Chicago Press.

Dirks, Nicholas. 2001. *Castes of Mind: Colonialism and the Making of Modern India.* Princeton, NJ: Princeton University Press.

Douglas, Jack. 1976. *Investigative Social Research: Individual and Team Research.* Thousand Oaks, CA: Sage.

DuBois, W. E. B. 1989 [1903]. *The Souls of Black Folk.* New York: Bantam.

Dupuy, Alex. 1991. "Political Intellectuals in the Third World: The Caribbean Case." In *Intellectuals and Politics: Social Theory in a Changing World,* ed. C. C. Lemert, 74–92. London: Sage.

EAAF/Witness. 2002. *Following Antigone: Forensic Anthropology and Human Rights.* Film.

Edgerton, Robert B. 1992. *Sick Societies: Challenging the Myth of Primitive Harmony.* New York: Free Press.

Environmental Concern, Inc. 1972. "Preliminary Report, Tule River Indian Reservation Comprehensive Planning Program."

Ervin, Alexander M. 2000. *Applied Anthropology: Tools and Perspectives for Contemporary Practice*. Boston: Allyn and Bacon.

Escobar, Arturo. 1998. "Whose Knowledge, Whose Nature? Biodiversity, Conservation, and the Political Ecology of Social Movements." *Journal of Political Ecology* 5: 53–82.

Fals Borda, Orlando. 1980–86. *Historia doble de la costa*. 4 vols. Bogotá: Carlos Valencia Editores.

———, and Mohammad Anisur Rahman. 1991. *Action and Knowledge: Breaking the Monopoly with Participatory Action-Research*. New York: Apex Press.

Fass, Simon. 1988. *Political Economy in Haiti: The Drama of Survival*. New Brunswick, NJ: Transaction.

Fatton, Robert Jr. 2002. *Haiti's Predatory Republic: The Unending Transition to Democracy*. Boulder, CO: Lynne Rienner.

Fernandez, James. 1987. "Anthropology as a Vocation: Listening to Voices." Online guest editorial for *Cultural Anthropology: A Perspective on the Human Condition,* by Emily A. Shultz and Robert Lavenda. http://www.us.oup.com/us/pdf/cultant/fernandez.pdf.

Field, Les. 1999. "Complicities and Collaborations: Anthropologists and the 'Unacknowledged Tribes' of California." *Current Anthropology* 40 (2): 193–209.

———, 2003. "Unacknowledged Tribes, Dangerous Knowledge: The Muwekma Ohlone and How Indian Identities Are 'Known.'" *Wicazo Sa Review* (University of Minnesota Press) 18 (2): 79–94.

———, 2005. "Beyond Applied Anthropology." In *A Companion to the Anthropology of North American Indians,* ed. T. Biolsi, 472–89. Oxford: Blackwell.

———, n.d. "Extinction Narratives and Pristine Moments: Evaluating the Decline of Abalone." Manuscript.

Fisher, Melissa. 2004. "Corporate Ethnography in the New Economy." *Anthropology News* 45 (4): 15.

Flacks, Dick. 1991. "Making History and Making Theory: Notes on How Intellectuals Seek Relevance." In *Intellectuals and Politics: Social Theory in a Changing World,* ed. C. C. Lemert, pp. 3–18. London: Sage.

Foley, Douglas. 1999. "The Fox Project: A Reappraisal." *Current Anthropology* 40 (2): 171–91.

———, 2000. "Studying the Politics of Raza Unida Politics: Reflections of a White Anthropologist." *Reflexiones: New Directions in Mexican American Studies* 3 (Spring): 51–81.

———, 2002. "Critical Ethnography: The Reflexive Turn." *International Journal of Qualitative Studies in Education* 15 (4): 469–90.

———, and Kirby Moss. 2000. "Studying US Cultural Diversity: Some Non-Essentializing Theories." In *Teaching Cultural Diversity,* eds. I. Susser and T. Patterson, 343–64. New York: Blackwell.

———, and Angela Valenzuela. 2005. "Critical Ethnography: The Politics of Collaboration." In *The Handbook for Ethnographic Research,* 3rd ed., eds. N. Denzin and Y. Lincoln, 217–34. Thousand Oaks, CA: Sage.

Forgacs, D., ed. 1988. *An Antonio Gramsci Reader: Selected Writings 1916– 1935.* New York: Schocken.

Fox, Gretchen, Dana Powell, and Dorothy Holland. 2004. "Center for Integrating Research and Action: An Experimental Public Anthropology." Department of Anthropology, University of North Carolina. Unpublished manuscript.

Fox, Jonathan. 2005. "Lessons from Action-Research Partnerships." *LASA Forum* 35 (1): 5–8.

Fox, Richard G. 1985. *Lions of the Punjab: Culture in the Making.* Berkeley: University of California Press.

———, and Andre Gingrich. 2002. "Introduction." In *Anthropology, by Comparison,* eds. A. Gingrich and R. G. Fox, 1–24. London: Routledge.

Frank, Gelya. 1980. "Detailed History of the Tribe's Land Tenure." *Restoration of Tule River Indian Reservation Lands.* Hearing before the United States Senate Select Committee on Indian Affairs 96, 1 of S.1998, pp. 74–141, February 5. Washington, DC: US Government Printing Office.

———, 1992. "Opening Feminist Histories of Occupational Therapy." *American Journal of Occupational Therapy* 46 (11): 989–99.

———, 2005. "Final Report of the Tule River Tribal History Project, Phase I, Summer 2004." Presented to the Tule River Tribal Council, Porterville, CA, April 8. 37 pp.

———, and Carole Goldberg. n.d. *Defying the Odds: One California Tribe's Struggle for Sovereignty in Three Centuries.* New Haven, CT: Yale University Press. Forthcoming.

Frankenberger, Timothy R., Claude Bart, Jennifer J. Mamtjeo, and M. Katherine McCaston. 1994. *A Livelihood Systems Approach to Title II Food Aid: A Means to Incorporate Food Security Objectives into Future Programming.* Prepared for USAID/Washington, Bureau for Humanitarian Response, Office of Program, Planning and Evaluation. Tucson: Office of Arid Lands Studies, University of Arizona.

Freeman, Derek. 1983. *Margaret Mead and Samoa: The Making and Un-making of an Anthropological Myth*. Cambridge, MA: Harvard University Press.

———, 1999. *The Fateful Hoaxing of Margaret Mead: A Historical Analysis of Her Samoan Research*. Boulder, CO: Westview Press.

Gagnon, Alain C. 1987. "The Role of Intellectuals in Liberal Democracies: Political Influence and Social Involvement." In *Intellectuals in Liberal Democracies*, ed. A. Gagnon, 3–16. London: Praeger.

Galison, Peter. 2003. *Einstein's Clocks, Poincaré's Maps: Empires of Time*. New York: W. W. Norton.

Gayton, A. H. 1930a. "Yokuts-Mono Chiefs and Shamans." *University of California Publications in American Archaeology and Ethnology* 24 (8): 361–420.

———, 1930b. "The Ghost Dance of 1870 in South-Central California." *University of California Publications in American Archaeology and Ethnology* 28 (3): 57–82.

———, 1946. "Culture-Environment Integration: External References in Yokuts Life." *Southwestern Journal of Anthropology* 2 (3): 252–68.

———, 1948a. *Yokuts and Western Mono Ethnography, I: Tulare Lake, Southern Valley, and Central Foothill Yokuts*. Berkeley: University of California Press.

———, 1948b. *Yokuts and Western Mono Ethnography, II: Northern Foothill Yokuts and Western Mono*. Berkeley: University of California Press.

———, and Stanley S. Newman. 1940. *Yokuts and Western Mono Myths*. Berkeley: University of California Press.

Geertz, Clifford. 1973. *The Interpretation of Cultures: Selected Essays*. New York: Basic Books.

Gill, Carol J. 1998. "Disability Studies: Looking at the FAQs." *Alert* 9 (3): 1–5. Department of Disability and Human Development, University of Illinois, Chicago.

———, 2001. "Divided Understandings: The Social Experience of Disability." In *Handbook of Disabilities Studies*, eds. G. L. Albrecht, K. D. Seelman, and M. Bury, 351–72. Thousand Oaks, CA: Sage.

Glass, Aaron, director. 2004. *In Search of the Hamat'sa: A Tale of Head-hunting*. DVD, 33 minutes. Produced in the Program for Culture and Media, New York University. Distributed by the Royal Anthropological Institute, Great Britain.

Goodale, Mark. 2006. "Introduction to 'Anthropology and Human Rights in a New Key.'" *American Anthropologist* 108 (1): 1–8.

Gordon, Edmund T. 1991. "Anthropology and Liberation." In *Decolonizing Anthropology: Moving Further Toward an Anthropology of Liberation*, ed.

F. Harrison, 149–67. Washington, DC: American Anthropological Association.

———, 1998. *Disparate Diasporas: Identity and Politics in an African-Nicaraguan Community.* Austin: University of Texas Press.

———, and Mark Anderson. n.d. "Conceptualizing the African Diaspora." Proceedings of the City University of New York Kenneth B. Clark Colloquium Series. IRADAC II.

———, Galio C. Gurdian, and Charles R. Hale. 2003. "Rights, Resources, and the Social Memory of Struggle: Reflections on a Study of Indigenous and Black Community Land Rights on Nicaragua's Atlantic Coast." *Human Organization* 62 (4): 369–81.

Graeber, David. 2005. "The Auto-Ethnography That Can Never Be and the Activist's Ethnography That Might Be." In *Auto-Ethnographies: The Anthropology of Academic Practices,* eds. A. Meneley and D. J. Young, 189–202. Peterborough, ON: Broadview Press.

Greenwood, Davydd J., and Morten Levin. 1998. *Introduction to Action Research: Social Research for Social Change.* Thousand Oaks, CA: Sage.

Gritzer, Glenn, and Arnold Arluke. 1989. *The Making of Rehabilitation: A Political Economy of Medical Specialization, 1890–1980.* Berkeley: University of California Press.

Grossberg, Lawrence, Cary Nelson, and Paula Treichler, eds. 1992. *Cultural Studies.* New York: Routledge.

Guha, Ramachandra. 1998. "Between Anthropology and Literature: The Ethnographies of Verrier Elwin." *Journal of the Royal Anthropological Institute* 4 (2): 325–43.

Guldin, Gregory Eliyu. 1994. *The Saga of Anthropology in China: From Malinowski to Moscow to Mao.* Armonk, NY: M. E. Sharpe.

Gwaltney, John L. 1981. "Common Sense and Science: Urban Core Black Observations." In *Anthropologists at Home in North America: Methods and Issues in the Study of One's Own Society,* ed. D. A. Messerschmidt, 46–61. Cambridge: Cambridge University Press.

———, 1993. *Drylongso: A Self-Portrait of Black America.* New York: New Press.

Halbwachs, Maurice. 1980 [1950]. *The Collective Memory.* Trans. F. J. Ditter Jr. and V. Y. Ditter. New York: Harper and Row.

Hale, Charles R. 2001. "What Is Activist Research?" *Items* 2 (1–2): 13–15. Social Science Research Council.

———, 2006a. "Activist Research v. Cultural Critique: Indigenous Land Rights and the Contradictions of Politically Engaged Anthropology." *Cultural Anthropology* 21 (1): 96–120.

————, 2006b. *"Más que un indio": Racial Ambivalence and Neoliberal Multiculturalism in Guatemala.* Santa Fe, NM: School of American Research Press.

Haraway, Donna. 1988. "Situated Knowledges: The Science Question in Feminism and the Privilege of Partial Perspective." *Feminist Studies* 14 (3): 575–99.

————, 1991. *Simians, Cyborgs, and Women: The Reinvention of Nature.* New York: Routledge.

Harrison, Faye. 1999. "New Voices of Diversity, Academic Relations of Production, and the Free Market." In *Transforming Academia: Challenges and Opportunities for an Engaged Anthropology,* eds. L. G. Basch et al., 72–85. Arlington, VA: American Anthropological Association.

Hawke, Steve, and Michael Gallagher. 1989. *Noonkanbah: Whose Land, Whose Law?* Fremantle, Australia: Fremantle Arts Center Press.

Hayner, Priscilla. 2002. *Unspeakable Truths: Confronting State Terror and Atrocity.* New York: Routledge.

Hays, Terence E., ed. 1992. *Ethnographic Presents: Pioneering Anthropologists in the Papua New Guinea Highlands.* Berkeley: University of California Press.

Hinson, Glenn. 2000. *Fire in My Bones: Transcendence and the Holy Spirit in African American Gospel.* Philadelphia: University of Pennsylvania Press.

Hinton, Leanne. 1994. *Flutes of Fire: Essays on California Indian Languages.* Berkeley, CA: Heyday Books.

————, with Matt Vera and Nancy Steele. 2002. *How to Keep Your Language Alive: A Commonsense Approach to One-on-One Learning.* Berkeley, CA: Heyday Books.

Holland, Dorothy. 2003. "Some Notes on Anthropological Knowledge beyond the Discipline." Paper presented at the SAR workshop "Public Interest Anthropology," Chicago.

Horton, Miles, and Paolo Freire. 1990. *We Make the Road by Walking: Conversations on Education and Social Change.* Philadelphia: Temple University Press.

Howe, Craig. 2002. "Keep Your Thoughts above the Trees: Ideas on Developing and Presenting Tribal Histories." In *Clearing a Path: Theorizing the Past in Native American Studies,* ed. N. Shoemaker, 161–79. New York: Routledge.

Huizer, Gerrit, and Karl Mannheim, eds. 1979. *The Politics of Anthropology: From Colonialism and Sexism towards a View from Below.* The Hague: Mouton.

Hurtado, Albert L. 1988. *Indian Survival on the California Frontier.* New Haven, CT: Yale University Press.

Hutchinson, Charles F., and Robert E. Hall. 1993. *Famine Mitigation Activity Report: Baseline Vulnerability Assessment for Haiti*. Prepared for the Office of US Foreign Disaster Assistance. Washington, DC: USAID Bureau for Food and Humanitarian Assistance.

Hymes, Dell, ed. 1972. *Reinventing Anthropology*. New York: Pantheon.

IEG (Institute of Economic Growth Society). 1952. *Memorandum of Association*. Delhi.

Jaffe, JoAnn M. 1990. "Labor, Land, Livestock, and Markets: Persistence and Accumulation in the Peasant Economy of Haiti." Ph.D dissertation, Cornell University.

Jebb, Mary Anne. 2002. *Blood, Sweat and Welfare: A History of White Bosses and Aboriginal Pastoral Workers*. Nedlands: University of Western Australia Press.

Jimeno, Myriam. 1999. "Desde el punto de vista de la periferia: Desarrollo profesional y conciencia social." *Anuário Antropológico* 97: 59–72. Rio de Janeiro.

Johnson, Mary. 2005a. "After Terry Schiavo." *Ragged Edge Online*. April 2. http://www.raggededgemagazine.com/focus/postschiavo0405.html.
———, 2005b. "We Need to Talk!" *Ragged Edge Online*. January 28. http://www.raggededgemagazine.com/mediacircus/weneedtotalk.html.

Jones, Delmos J. 1970. "Towards a Native Anthropology." *Human Organization* 29 (4): 251–59.

Kardiner, Abram. 1945. *Psychological Frontiers of Society*. New York: Columbia University Press.
———, and Ralph Linton. 1939. *The Individual and His Society*. New York: Columbia University Press.

Kasnitz D., and R. Shuttleworth. 2001. "Introduction: Engaging Anthropology in Disability Studies." *Disability Studies Quarterly* 21 (3): n.p. (online journal).

Keen, Ian. 1988. "Twenty-five Years of Aboriginal Kinship Studies." In *Social Anthropology and Australian Aboriginal Studies: A Contemporary Overview*, eds. R. M. Berndt and R. Tonkinson, 79–123. Canberra: Aboriginal Studies Press.
———, 2004. *Aboriginal Economy and Society*. Oxford: Oxford University Press.

Kelley, Robin D. G. 2002. *Freedom Dreams: The Black Radical Imagination*. Boston: Beacon Press.

Keys, Christopher B. 1987. "Synergy, Prevention, and the Chicago School of Sociology." *Prevention in Human Services* 5 (2): 11–34.

Kielhofner, Gary. 2004. "Disability Studies." In *Conceptual Foundations of Occupational Therapy*, 3rd ed., 238–53. Baltimore, MD: Williams and Wilkins.

————, 2005. "Rethinking Disability and What To Do About It: Disability Studies and Its Implications for Occupational Therapy." *American Journal of Occupational Therapy* 59 (5): 487–96.

————, and Janice Burke. 1977. "Occupational Therapy after Sixty Years: An Account of Changing Identity and Knowledge." *American Journal of Occupational Therapy* 31: 657–89.

Kirshenblatt-Gimblett, Barbara. 1998. *Destination Culture: Tourism, Museums, and Heritage.* Berkeley: University of California Press.

Kitching, Heather J., Gelya Frank, Rani Bechar, Amber Bertram, Colleen Harvey, Allison Joe, and Jeanine Blanchard. 2004. "Direct Cultural Intervention: Meeting the Needs of Communities." Paper presented at the 28th annual conference of the Occupational Therapy Association of California, Pasadena, 7 November.

Kloos, Peter, and Henri J. M. Claessen, eds. 1991. *Contemporary Anthropology in the Netherlands: The Use of Anthropological Ideas.* Amsterdam: VU University Press.

Kluckhohn, Clyde 1949. *Mirror for Man: The Relation of Anthropology to Modern Life.* New York: Whittlesey House.

Kroeber, A. L. 1900, 1903. Unpublished field notebooks, Yokuts. Bancroft Library, University of California, Berkeley. Microfilm.

————, 1906. "Yokuts Names." *Journal of American Folklore* 19: 142–43. Reprinted in Robert F. Heizer, *A Collection of Ethnographical Articles on the California Indians,* 54–55. Ramona, CA: Ballena Press, 1976.

————, 1907a. "The Yokuts Language of South Central California." *University of California Publications in American Archeology and Ethnology* 2 (5): 169–377.

————, 1907b. "Indian Myths of Central California." *University of California Publications in American Archeology and Ethnology* 4 (4): 167–250.

————, 1925. *Handbook of the Indians of California.* Bureau of American Ethnology Bulletin no. 78. Washington, D.C.: Smithsonian Institution.

————, 1963. "Yokuts Dialect Survey." *Anthropological Records* 11 (3).

Kronenberg, Frank, Salvador Simó Algado, and Nick Pollard. 2005. *Occupational Therapy without Borders: Learning from the Spirit of Survivors.* London: Elsevier Press.

Kuklick, Henrika. 1991. *The Savage Within: The Social History of British Anthropology, 1885–1945.* Cambridge: Cambridge University Press.

Laitin, David. 1986. *Hegemony and Culture: Politics and Religious Change among the Yoruba.* Chicago: University of Chicago Press.

Lakoff, George, and Mark Johnson. 2003. *Metaphors We Live By.* 2nd ed. Chicago: University of Chicago Press.

Lal, Vinay. 2003. *The History of History.* New Delhi: Oxford University Press.

Lambek, Michael. 2005. "Our Subjects/Ourselves: A View from the Back Seat." In *Auto-Ethnographies: The Anthropology of Academic Practices,* eds. A. Meneley and D. J. Young, 229–40. Peterborough, ON: Broadview Press.

Lame, Manuel Quintín. 1971 [1939]. *En defensa de mi raza.* Ed. Gonzalo Castillo Cárdenas. Bogotá: Comité de Defensa del Indio.

———, 2004 [1939]. *Los pensamientos del indio que se educó dentro de las selvas colombianas.* Ed. Cristóbal Gnecco. Popayán: Editorial Universidad del Cauca, and Cali: Editorial Universidad del Valle.

Lamphere, Louise. 2003. "Perils and Prospects for an Engaged Anthropology: A View for the U.S." *Social Anthropology* 11: 13–28.

———, 2004. "The Convergence of Applied, Practicing, and Public Anthropology in the Twenty-First Century." Unpublished ms.

Landsberger, Henry. 1958. *Hawthorne Revisited.* Ithaca, NY: Cornell University Press.

Lassiter, Luke Eric. 2005a. "Collaborative Ethnography and Public Anthropology." *Current Anthropology* 46 (1): 83–106.

———, 2005b. *The Chicago Guide to Collaborative Ethnography.* Chicago: University of Chicago Press.

Latta, F. F. 1949. *Handbook of Yokuts Indians.* Oildale, CA: Bear State Press.

Lawless, Elaine. 1993. *Holy Women, Wholly Women: Sharing Ministries of Wholeness through Life Stories and Reciprocal Ethnography.* Philadelphia: University of Pennsylvania Press.

Leach, Edmund. 1976. *Culture and Communication: The Logic by which Symbols Are Connected. An Introduction to the Use of Structuralist Analysis in Social Anthropology.* Cambridge: Cambridge University Press.

Lesser, Alexander. 1981. "Franz Boas." In *Totems and Teachers: Perspectives on the History of Anthropology,* ed. S. Silverman, 1–33. New York: Columbia University Press.

Leys, Ruth. 1990. "Adolph Meyer: A Biographical Note." In *Defining American Psychology: The Correspondence between Adolph Meyer and Edward Bradford Tichner,* eds. R. Leys and R. Evans, 39–57. Baltimore, MD: Johns Hopkins University Press.

Lidz, Theodore. 1967. "Adolf Meyer and the Development of American Psychiatry." *American Journal of Psychiatry* 123: 320–32.

Lief, Alfred, ed. 1948. *The Commonsense Psychiatry of Adolf Meyer: Fifty-two Selected Papers, Edited, with Biographical Narrative.* New York: McGraw-Hill.

Lilla, Mark. 2001. *The Reckless Mind: Intellectuals in Politics.* New York: New York Review Books.

Linton, Ralph, ed. 1945. *The Science of Man in the World Crisis.* New York: Columbia University Press.

Linton, Simi. 1998. *Claiming Disability: Knowledge and Identity.* New York: New York University Press.

Lipsitz, George. 1998. *The Possessive Investment in Whiteness.* Philadelphia: Temple University Press.

Liu, Xin, ed. 2002. *New Reflections on Anthropological Studies of (Greater) China.* China Research Monograph, Institute of East Asian Studies, University of California, Berkeley, and Centre for Chinese Studies.

Locher, Uli. 1984. "Migration in Haiti." In *Haiti, Today and Tomorrow: An Interdisciplinary Study,* eds. C. R. Foster and A. Valdman, 325–36. Lanham, MD: University Press of America.

———, 1991a. "L'évolution récente de l'enseignement primaire." In *Haïti et l'après-Duvalier: Continuités et ruptures,* eds. C. Hector and H. Jadotte, 357–76. Montréal: CIDHICA, and Port-au-Prince: Éditions Henri Deschamps.

———, 1991b. "Primary Education in Haiti." In *Forging Identities and Patterns of Development in Latin America and the Caribbean,* eds. H. P. Diaz, J. W. A. Rummens, and P. D. M. Taylor, 85–104. Toronto: Canadian Scholars' Press.

———, Glenn R. Smucker, and Drexel G. Woodson. 1983. *Comparative Evaluation of Three Haitian Rural Development Projects.* Prepared for USAID/Haiti. Washington, DC: Creative Associates, Inc.

Loomis, Barbara. 1992. "The Henry B. Favill School of Occupations and Eleanor Clarke Slagle." *American Journal of Occupational Therapy* 46 (1): 34–37.

López, Luis Enrique. 1996. "No más danzas de ratones grises: Sobre interculturalidad, democracia y educación." In *Educación e interculturalidad en los Andes y la Amazonía,* ed. J. Godenzzi Alegre, 23–80. Cuzco: Centro de Estudios Regionales "Bartolomé de Las Casas."

Lorde, Audre. 1984. "Uses of the Erotic: The Erotic as Power." In *Sister Outsider,* A. Lorde, 53–59. New York: Crossing Press.

Lowe, Pat, and Jimmy Pike. 1991. *Jilji Country.* Broome, Australia: Magabala Books.

Lowenthal, Ira P., and Harland H. D. Attfield. 1979. *Integrated Rural Development in Haiti: Problems, Progress, and a Proposal.* Report submitted to the Agricultural Development Office. Port-au-Prince: USAID/Haiti.

Lundahl, Mats. 1979. *Peasants and Poverty: A Study of Haiti.* London: Croom Helm.

————, 1992. *Politics or Markets?: Essays on Haitian Underdevelopment.* London: Routledge.

MacClancy, Jeremy, ed. 2002. *Exotic No More: Anthropology on the Front Lines.* Chicago: University of Chicago Press.

Maguire, Robert. 1984. "Strategies for Rural Development in Haiti: Formation, Organization, Implementation." In *Haiti, Today and Tomorrow: An Interdisciplinary Study,* eds. C. R. Foster and A. Valdman, 161–72. Lanham, MD: University Press of America.

————, 1997. "From Outsiders to Insiders: Grassroots Leadership and Political Change." In *Haiti Renewed: Political and Economic Prospects,* ed. R. I. Rotberg, 154–69. Washington, DC: Brookings Institution Press.

Marcus, George, and Michael J. Fischer. 1986. *The Anthropology of Cultural Critique: An Experimental Moment in the Human Sciences.* Chicago: University of Chicago Press.

Mattingly, Cheryl. 1998. *Healing Dramas and Clinical Plots.* Cambridge: Cambridge University Press.

————, and Nedra Gillette. 1991. "Anthropology, Occupational Therapy, and Action Research." *American Journal of Occupational Therapy* 45: 972–78.

Maxwell, Simon, and Timothy R. Frankenberger. 1992. *Household Food Security: Concepts, Indicators, Measurements. A Technical Review.* New York: UNICEF, and Rome: IFAD.

Mayo, Elton. 1933. *The Human Problems of an Industrial Civilizaton.* New York: Macmillan.

McNeil, John M. 2001. "Americans with Disabilities: Household Economic Studies. US Bureau of the Census." In *Current Population Reports,* 70–73. Washington, DC: US Government Printing Office.

Mead, Margaret. 1928. *Coming of Age in Samoa.* New York: Blue Ribbon Books.

————, 1979. "Anthropological Contributions to National Policies during and Immediately after World War II." In *The Uses of Anthropology,* ed. W. Goldschmidt, 145–58. Washington, DC: American Anthropological Association.

Merlan, Francesca. 1998. *Caging the Rainbow: Places, Politics, and Aborigines in a North Australian Town.* Honolulu: University of Hawaii Press.

Merry, Sally Engle. 2003. *Human Rights and Gender Violence: Translating International Law into Local Justice.* Chicago: University of Chicago Press.

Métraux, Alfred, with Edouard Berrouet and Dr. and Mrs. Jean Comhaire-Sylvain. 1951. *Making a Living in the Marbial Valley (Haiti).* UNESCO Occasional Papers in Education 10. Paris: UNESCO.

Meyer, Adolf. 1921. "The Philosophy of Occupation Therapy." *Archives of Occupational Therapy* 1 (1): 1–10.

Milton, Kay. 1994. *Environmentalism and Cultural Theory: Exploring the Role of Anthropology in Environmental Discourse.* London: Routledge.

Minnegal, Monica, ed. 2005. *Sustainable Communities, Sustainable Environments: Conference Proceedings.* Melbourne: Melbourne University, School of Social Anthropology, Geography and Environmental Sciences.

Mintz, Sidney W. 1995. *Sweetness and Power: The Place of Sugar in Modern History.* New York: Penguin Books.

———, and Eric R. Wolf. 1989. "Reply to Michael Taussig." *Critique of Anthropology* 9 (1): 28–31.

Mohanty, Satya P. 2000. "The Epistemic Status of Cultural Identity: On *Beloved* and the Postcolonial Condition." In *Reclaiming Identity: Realist Theory and the Predicament of Postmodernism,* eds. P. Moya and M. R. Hames-Garcia, 29–66. Berkeley: University of California Press.

Mondé, Carl. 1980. *Organisation paysanne et développement rural: L'exemple de Papaye.* Petite-Rivière de Bayonnais: Projet Pilote de Groupman.

Moral, Paul. 1978 [1961]. *Le paysan Haïtien (étude sur la vie rurale en Haïti).* Facsimile reproduction of the original edition. Port-au-Prince: Éditions Fardin.

Moran, Bruce T. 2005. *Distilling Knowledge: Alchemy, Chemistry, and the Scientific Revolution.* Cambridge, MA: Harvard University Press.

Morphy, Howard. 1998. *Aboriginal Art.* London: Phaidon.

Moya, Paula, and Michael R. Hames-Garcia. 2000. *Reclaiming Identity: Realist Theory and the Predicament of Postmodernism.* Berkeley: University of California Press.

Muelas Hurtado, Bárbara. 1995. "Relación espacio-tiempo en el pensamiento guambiano." *Proyecciones Lingüísticas* 1 (1): 31–40. Popayán.

Munshi, Indra. n.d. "Patrick Geddes: Sociologist, Environmentalist and Town Planner." In *Anthropology in the East: The Indian Foundations of a Global Discipline,* eds. P. Uberoi, N. Sundar, and S. Deshpande. New Delhi: Permanent Black. In press.

Murray, Gerald F. 1977. "Haitian Peasant Land Tenure: A Case Study in Agrarian Adaptation to Population Growth." Ph.D dissertation, Columbia University.

———, 1980. "Population Pressure, Land Tenure, and Voodoo: The Economics of Haitian Rural Peasant Ritual." In *Beyond the Myths of Culture: Essays in Cultural Materialism,* ed. E. B. Ross, 295–321. New York: Academic Press.

Naples, Nancy A. 2003. *Feminism and Method: Ethnography, Discourse Analysis, and Activist Research*. New York: Routledge.

Nene, Yamilé, and Henry Chocué. 2004. "Las luchas de Quintín Lame." In *Los pensamientos del indio que se educó dentro de las selvas colombianas*, Manuel Quintín Lame, 103–10. Popayán: Editorial Universidad del Cauca and Cali: Editorial Universidad del Valle.

Nespor, Jan. 1989. "Strategies of Discourse and Knowledge Use in the Practice of Bureaucratic Research." *Human Organisation* 48 (4): 325–32.

Nora, Pierre. 1989. Between Memory and History: *Les Lieux de Memoire*. *Representations* 26 (Spring): 7–24.

Oriol, Michèle. 1994. *Les collectivités territoriales entre 1991 et 1993: Essai d'analyse institutionnelle et de prospective*. With the collaboration of P.-A. Guerrier and D. Saint-Lot. Port-au-Prince: Projet Intégré pour le Renforcement de la Démocratie en Haïti (PIRÈD).

PAHO/WHO. 1994. *Food, Health and Care in Haiti: A Nutrition Situation Analysis*. Port-au-Prince: Pan-American Health Organization and World Health Organization.

Peacock, James. 1997. "The Future of Anthropology." *American Anthropologist* 99 (1): 9–29.

———, 1999. "Toward a Proactive Anthropology." In *Transforming Academia: Challenges and Opportunities for an Engaged Anthropology*, eds. L. Basch et al., 21–31. Arlington, VA: American Anthropological Association.

Peirano, Mariza G. S. 1991. "The Anthropology of Anthropology: The Brazilian Case." PhD dissertation, Harvard University.

Pels, Peter. 1999. "Professions of Duplexity: A Prehistory of Ethical Codes in Anthropology." *Current Anthropology* 40: 101–36.

Phillips, George Harwood. 1975. *Chiefs and Challengers: Indian Resistance and Cooperation in Southern California*. Berkeley: University of California Press.

———, 1993. *Indians and Intruders in Central California, 1769–1849*. Norman: University of Oklahoma Press.

———, 1997. *Indians and Indian Agents: The Origins of the Reservation System in California, 1849–1852*. Norman: University of Oklahoma Press.

———, 2004. *"Bringing Them under Subjection": California's Tejón Indian Reservation and Beyond, 1852–1864*. Lincoln: University of Nebraska Press.

Pickering, Andrew. 2001. "Science as Alchemy." In *Schools of Thought: Twenty-Five Years of Interpretive Social Science*, eds. J. W. Scott and D. Keates, 194–206. Princeton, NJ: Princeton University Press.

Plattner, Stuart, and Daniel Gross. 2002. "Anthropology as Social Work: Collaborative Models of Anthropological Research." *Anthropology News* 43 (8).

Polanyi, Karl. 1944. *The Great Transformation.* New York: Farrar and Rinehart.

———, Conrad M. Arensberg, and Harry W. Pearson, eds. 1957. *Trade and Market in the Early Empires.* Glencoe, IL: Free Press.

Pundalik, Vidyadhar. 1970. "Irawati Karve: Chaitanya: Ek Gyot." *Manus,* Diwali special, 34–39. Pune.

Ramos, Abelardo, and Cabildo Indígena de Mosoco. 1993. *Ec ne'hwe's': Constitución política de Colombia en nasa yuwe.* Bogotá: CCELA-UniAndes.

Rappaport, Joanne. 1990. "Anthropology and Violence in Colombia: An Interview with Hernán Henao." *Latin American Anthropology Review* 2 (2): 56–60.

———, 1994. *Cumbe Reborn: An Andean Ethnography of History.* Chicago: University of Chicago Press.

———, 1998. *The Politics of Memory: Native Historical Interpretation in the Colombian Andes.* Durham, NC: Duke University Press.

———, 2005. *Intercultural Utopias: Public Intellectuals, Cultural Experimentation, and Ethnic Dialogue in Colombia.* Durham, NC: Duke University Press.

———, and Abelardo Ramos Pacho. 2005. "Una historia colaborativa: Retos para el diálogo indígena-académico." *Historia Crítica* 29: 39–62. Bogotá.

Rawls, James J. 1984. *Indians of California: The Changing Image.* Norman: University of Oklahoma Press.

Redfield, Robert. 1947. "The Folk Society." *American Journal of Sociology* 52: 293–308.

Riaño-Alcalá, Pilar. 2006. *Dwellers of Memory: Youth and Violence in Medellín, Colombia.* New Brunswick, NJ: Transaction.

Ribeiro, Gustavo Lins. 2004. "World Anthropologies: Cosmopolitics, Power and Theory in Anthropology." Unpublished manuscript.

———, and Arturo Escobar. 2006. *World Anthropologies: Disciplinary Transformations within Systems of Power.* Oxford: Berg.

Richman, Karen E. 1992. "'They Will Remember Me in the House': The *Pwen* of Haitian Transnational Migration." PhD dissertation, University of Virginia. (Revised as *Migration and Vodou in Haiti,* Gainesville: University Press of Florida, 2005.)

Ridington, Robin, and Dennis Hastings. 1997. *Blessing for a Long Time: The Sacred Pole of the Omaha Tribe.* Lincoln: University of Nebraska Press.

Ritter, David, and Frances Flanagan. 2004. "Lawyers and Rats: Critical Legal Theory and Native Title." In *Crossing Boundaries: Cultural, Legal, Historical and Practice Issues in Native Title,* ed. S. Toussaint, 128–41. Carlton, Australia: Melbourne University Press.

Robbins, Bruce. 1990. "Introduction: The Grounding of Intellectuals." In *Intellectuals: Aesthetics, Politics, Academics,* ed. B. Robbins, ix–xxvii. Minneapolis: University of Minnesota Press.

Roberts, Gareth. 1994. *The Mirror of Alchemy: Alchemical Ideas and Images in Manuscripts and Books.* London: British Library.

Rose, Deborah Bird. 1992. *Dingo Makes Us Human.* Cambridge: Cambridge University Press.

Rose, Nikolas. 1999. *Powers of Freedom: Reframing Political Thought.* Cambridge: Cambridge University Press.

Royal Commission into Aboriginal Deaths in Custody. 1991. *Final Report.* Canberra: Australian Government Printers.

Roy-Burman, B. K. 2000. "Frozen Ice and a Silent Spring." In *Situating Sociology: A Symposium on Knowledge, Institutions and Practices,* special issue of *Seminar* 495: 50–54.

SACAD and FAMV. 1993–94. *Paysans, systèmes et crise: Travaux sur l'agraire Haïtien.* 3 vols. D. Pillot, A. Bellande, and J.-L. Paul, eds. Pointe-à-Pitre, Guadeloupe: Groupe de Recherche/Formation SACAD (Systèmes Agraires Caribéens et Alternatives de Développement), Université des Antilles et de la Guyane, and Port-au-Prince: FAMV (Faculté d'Agronomie et de Médecine Vétérinaire), Université d'État d'Haïti.

Sahlins, Marshall. 1976. *Culture and Practical Reason.* Chicago: University of Chicago Press.

Sahmat. 2003. *Against Communalisation of Archaeology: A Critique of the ASI Report.* New Delhi: Sahmat.

Sanday, Peggy Reeves. 2003. "Public Interest Anthropology: A Model for Engaged Social Science." Paper presented at the SAR workshop "Public Interest Anthropology," Chicago.

Savain, Roger E. 1993. *Haitian-Kreol in Ten Steps/Dis pa nan Kreyòl Ayisyen-an.* 4th ed. Rochester, VT: Schenkman.

Scheper-Hughes, Nancy. 1995. "The Primacy of the Ethical: Propositions for a Militant Anthropology." *Current Anthropology* 36: 409–40.

Schwartz, Kathleen Barker. 1992. "Occupational Therapy and Education: A Shared Vision." *American Journal of Occupational Therapy* 46 (1): 12–18.

Schwartzman, Helen B. 1992. *Ethnography in Organizations.* New York: Sage.

Seigfried, Charlene Haddock. 2002. "Introduction." In *Democracy and Social Ethics,* Jane Addams, ix–xxxviii. Urbana: University of Illinois Press.

Shaffer, Simon. 1994. *From Physics to Anthropology and Back Again.* Cambridge: Prickly Pear Press.

Shah, A. M. 2000. "Sociology in a Regional Context." In *Situating Sociology: A Symposium on Knowledge, Institutions and Practices,* special issue of *Seminar* 495: 45–49.

Shore, Chris, and Susan Wright, eds. 1997. *Anthropology of Policy: Critical Perspectives on Governance and Power.* London: Routledge.

Sluka, Jeffrey A. 2000. "Introduction: State Terror and Anthropology." In *Death Squad: The Anthropology of State Terror,* ed. J. Sluka, 1–45. Philadelphia: University of Pennsylvania Press.

Smith, Linda Tuhiwai. 1999. *Decolonizing Methodologies: Research and Indigenous Peoples.* New York: St. Martins.

Smucker, Glenn R., and Dathis Noriac. 1996. *Peasant Organizations in Haiti: Trends and Implications.* Port-au-Prince: Comité Haïtien de Développement et L'Institut de Consultation, d'Évaluation et de Formation, and Rosslyn, VA: Inter-American Foundation.

———, and Nina P. Schlossman, eds. 2001. *Evaluation Report of the Enhanced Food Security II Program, USAID Mission.* 2 vols. Prepared for USAID Haiti Mission, Food for Peace Office. Arlington, VA: John Snow, Inc.

Society for Disability Studies. 2004. "General Information: Mission Statement." http://www.uic.edu/orgs/sds/generalinfo.html, accessed July 28, 2004.

Spencer, Jean Cole, Laura Krefting, and Cheryl Mattingly. 1993. "Incorporation of Ethnographic Methods in Occupational Therapy Assessment." *American Journal of Occupational Therapy* 47: 303–9.

Srivastava, Vinay. 2000. "Teaching Anthropology. In *Situating Sociology: A Symposium on Knowledge, Institutions and Practices,* special issue of *Seminar* 495: 33–39.

Staples, Annalisa R., and Ruth L. McConnell. 1993. *Soapstone and Seed Beads: Arts and Crafts at the Charles Camsell Hospital, a Tuberculosis Sanatorium.* Alberta: Provincial Museum of Alberta.

Starn, Orin. 1986. "Engineering Internment: Anthropologists and the War Relocation Authority." *American Ethnologist* 13: 700–720.

———, 1994. "Rethinking the Politics of Anthropology." *Current Anthropology* 35 (1): 13–38.

———, 2004. *Ishi's Brain: In Search of America's Last Wild Indian.* New York: W. W. Norton.

Starr, Paul. 1984. *The Social Transformation of American Medicine.* New York: Basic Books.

Stepick, Alex. 1984. The Roots of Haitian Migration. In *Haiti, Today and Tomorrow: An Interdisciplinary Study,* eds. C. R. Foster and A. Valdman, 337–49. Lanham, MD: University Press of America.

———, 1998. *Pride against Prejudice: Haitians in the United States.* Boston: Allyn and Bacon.

Steward, Julian H. 1950. *Area Research, Theory, and Practice.* Bulletin 63. New York: Social Science Research Council.

———, 1956. *The People of Puerto Rico: A Study in Social Anthropology.* Urbana: University of Illinois Press.

Stewart, George W. 1884. "The Indian War on Tule River." *Overland Monthly* (January). Reprinted in *Early History of Tulare County, California,* ed. K. E. Small, 84–102, Exeter, CA: Bear State Books, 2001 [1926].

Stocking, George W. 1992. *The Ethnographer's Magic and Other Essays in the History of Anthropology.* Madison: University of Wisconsin Press.

———, ed. 1986. *History of Anthropology,* vol. 4, *Malinowski, Rivers, Benedict, and Others: Essays on Culture and Personality.* Madison: University of Wisconsin Press.

———, ed. 1991. *History of Anthropology,* vol. 7, *Colonial Situations: Essays on the Contextualization of Ethnographic Knowledge.* Madison: University of Wisconsin Press.

———, 2000. "'Do Good, Young Man': Sol Tax and the World Mission of Liberal Democratic Anthropology." In *Excluded Ancestors, Inventible Traditions: Essays Toward a More Inclusive History of Anthropology,* ed. R. Handler, 171–264. Madison: University of Wisconsin Press.

Stony Brook University. 2006. http://www.research.sunysb.edu/research/.

Strand, Kerry, Sam Marullo, Nick Cutforth, Randy Stoecker, and Patrick Donohue. 2003. *Community-Based Research and Higher Education: Principles and Practices.* San Francisco: Jossey-Bass.

Strathern, Andrew, and Pamela Stewart. 2001. "Anthropology and Consultancy: Ethnographic Dilemmas and Opportunities." *Social Analysis* 45 (2): 3–21.

Strathern, Marilyn, ed. 2000. *Audit Cultures: Anthropological Studies in Accountability, Ethics, and the Academy.* New York: Routledge.

Sundar, Nandini. 2000. "Comment: Activism and Academic Angst." *Seminar* 488: 68–73.

———, 2002. "Indigenise, Nationalise and Spiritualise: An Agenda for Education?" *International Social Science Journal* 173: 373–83.

———, 2004. "Toward an Anthropology of Culpability." *American Ethnologist* 31 (2): 145–63.

———, n.d. "In the Cause of Anthropology: The Life and Work of Irawati Karve." In *Anthropology in the East: The Indian Foundations of a Global*

Discipline, eds. P. Uberoi, N. Sundar, and S. Deshpande. New Delhi: Permanent Black. In press.

———, Satish Deshpande, and Patricia Uberoi. 2000. "Indian Anthropology and Sociology: Towards a History (Report of a Seminar)." *Economic and Political Weekly* 35 (24): 1998–2002.

———, Roger Jeffery, and Neil Thin. 2001. *Branching Out: JFM in India.* New Delhi: Oxford University Press.

Sutton, Peter. 2003. *Native Title in Australia: An Ethnographic Perspective.* Cambridge: Cambridge University Press.

Taussig, Michael T. 1980. *The Devil and Commodity Fetishism in South America.* Chapel Hill: University of North Carolina Press.

———, 1987. *Shamanism, Colonialism, and the Wild Man: A Study in Terror and Healing.* Chicago: University of Chicago Press.

———, 1989. "History as Commodity in Some Recent American (Anthropological) Literature." *Critique of Anthropology* 9 (1): 7–27.

Taylor, F. Sherwood. 1952. *The Alchemists.* St. Albans: Paladin.

Thomas, David Hurst. 2000. *Skull Wars: Kennewick Man, Archaeology, and the Battle for Native American Identity.* New York: Basic Books.

Thompson, E. P. 1993. "Time, Work Discipline, and Industrial Capitalism." In *Customs in Common,* ed. E. P. Thompson, 352–403. New York: New Press.

Tickner, J. Ann. 2004. "Feminist Responses to International Security Studies." *Peace Review,* special issue, 16 (1): 43–48.

Tonkinson, Robert. 1991. *The Mardu Aborigines: Living the Dream in the Australian Desert.* 2nd ed. Fort Worth, TX: Holt, Rinehart and Winston.

Toussaint, Sandy. 1999a. *Phyllis Kaberry and Me: Anthropology, History and Aboriginal Australia.* Carlton, Australia: Melbourne University Press.

———, 1999b. "Kimberley Aboriginal Peoples." In *Foraging Peoples: An Encyclopedia of Contemporary Hunters and Gatherers,* eds. R. Lee and R. Daly, 339–42. Cambridge: Cambridge University Press.

———, 2001. "Don't Forget to Ask: Working with Women and with Men in Aboriginal Australia." *Practicing Anthropology,* special edition, 23 (1): 29–32.

———, 2003. "'Our Shame: Blacks Live Poor, Die Young': Indigenous Health Practice and Ethical Possibilities for Reform." In *Health, Social Policy and Communities,* eds. P. Liamputtong Rice and H. Gardner, 241–56. Oxford: Oxford University Press.

———, ed. 2004. *Crossing Boundaries: Cultural, Legal, Historical and Practice Issues in Native Title.* Carlton, Australia: Melbourne University Press.

————, 2006a. "A Time and Place beyond and of the Center: Australian Anthropologies in the Process of Becoming." In *World Anthropologies: Disciplinary Transformations within Systems of Power*, eds. G. L. Ribeiro and A. Escobar, 225–38. Oxford: Berg.

————, 2006b. "Australian Anthropology: The 'Best' and 'Worst' of Globalized Times." *Anthropology News*, January 2006, 15, 19.

Townsend, E., and A. Wilcock. 2004. "Occupational Justice and Client-Centred Practice: A Dialogue in Progress." *Canadian Journal of Occupational Therapy* 71 (2): 75–87.

Trigger, David. 1992. *Whitefella Comin': Aboriginal Responses to Colonialism in Northern Australia*. Cambridge: Cambridge University Press.

————, 2004. "Anthropology in Native Title Court Cases: Mere Pleading, Expert Opinion, or Hearsay?" In *Crossing Boundaries: Cultural, Legal, Historical and Practice Issues in Native Title*, ed. S. Toussaint, 24–33. Carlton, Australia: Melbourne University Press.

Tróchez Tunubalá, Cruz, Miguel Flor Camayo, and Martha Urdaneta Franco. 1992. *Mananasrik wan wetøtraik køn*. Bogotá: Cabildo del Pueblo Guambiano.

Trouillot, Michel-Rolph. 1990. *Haiti, State against Nation: The Origins and Legacy of Duvalierism*. New York: Monthly Review Press. (Originally published as *Les racines historiques de l'état Duvaliérien*, Port-au-Prince: Henri Deschamps, 1986.)

————, 1997. "A Social Contract for Whom? Haitian History and Haiti's Future." In *Haiti Renewed: Political and Economic Prospects*, ed. R. I. Rotberg, 47–59. Washington, DC: Brookings Institution Press.

Tsosie, Rebecca. 2002a. "Introduction: Symposium on Cultural Sovereignty." *Arizona State Law Journal* (Spring): 1–14.

————, 2002b. "Reclaiming Native Stories: An Essay on Cultural Appropriation and Cultural Rights." *Arizona State Law Journal* (Spring): 299–358.

Tule River Tribal Council. 2002. "Survival, Renewal, Vision: The Tule River Tribal Council Commemorates 150 Years of Tulare County History." Ed. Gelya Frank. Special insert in *Visalia Times Delta, Tulare Advance Register*, and *Porterville Recorder*, September 7. 20 pp.

Turner, Terence. 1993. "Anthropology and Multiculturalism: What Is Anthropology that Multiculturalists Should Be Mindful of It?" *Cultural Anthropology* 8: 411–29.

————, 1997. "Human Rights, Human Difference: Anthropology's Contribution to an Emancipatory Cultural Politics." *Journal of Anthropological Research* 53 (3): 273–91.

Turner, Victor W. 1975. "Symbolic Studies." *Annual Review of Anthropology* 4: 145–61.

Uberoi, J. P. S. 1968. "Science and Swaraj." *Contributions to Indian Sociology,* n.s. 2: 119–23.

Uberoi, Patricia. 2000. "Déjà vu?" In *Situating Sociology: A Symposium on Knowledge, Institutions and Practices,* special issue of *Seminar* 495: 14–19.

———, Nandini Sundar, and Satish Deshpande, eds. n.d. *Anthropology in the East: The Indian Foundations of a Global Discipline.* New Delhi: Permanent Black. In press.

Urdaneta Franco, Martha. 1988. "Investigación arqueológica en el resguardo indígena de Guambía." *Boletín del Museo del Oro* 22: 54–81. Bogotá.

Valdman, Albert. 1988. *Ann Aprann Kreyòl: An Introductory Course in Haitian Creole.* Bloomington: Creole Institute, Indiana University.

Van Bremen, Jan, and Akitoshi Shimizu. 1999. *Anthropology and Colonialism in Asia and Oceania.* Richmond, Surrey: Curzon.

Varadarajan, Siddharth, ed. 2002. *Gujarat: The Making of a Tragedy.* New Delhi: Penguin Books.

Vasco Uribe, Luis Guillermo. 2002. *Entre selva y páramo: Viviendo y pensando la lucha indígena.* Bogotá: Instituto Colombiano de Antropología e Historia.

———, Abelino Dagua Hurtado, and Misael Aranda. 1993. "En el segundo día, la Gente Grande (Numisak) sembró la autoridad y las plantas y, con su jugo, bebió el sentido." In *Encrucijadas de Colombia amerindia,* ed. F. Correa, 9–48. Bogotá: Instituto Colombiano de Antropología.

Vincent, Joan. 1990. *Anthropology and Politics: Visions, Traditions and Trends.* Tucson: University of Arizona Press.

Wacquant, Loic J. D. 1996. "Foreword." In *The State Nobility,* Pierre Bourdieu, ix–xxii. Stanford, CA: Stanford University Press.

Walsh, Andrew. 2004. "In the Wake of Things: Speculating in and about Sapphires in Northern Madagascar." *American Anthropologist* 106 (2): 225–37.

———, 2005. "The Obvious Aspects of Ecological Underprivilege in Ankarana, Northern Madagascar." *American Anthropologist* 107 (4): 654–65.

Warner, W. Lloyd, and J. O. Low. 1947. *Sociology of the Modern Factory: The Social System.* New Haven, CT: Yale University Press.

Watson, Ruth, and Leslie Swartz, eds. 2004. *Transformation through Occupation.* Hoboken, NJ: Whurr Publishers.

Weber, M. 1949. "Objectivity in Social Science and Social Policy." In *The Methodology of the Social Sciences,* eds. E. Shils and H. Finch, 50–112. New York: Free Press.

Wolf, Eric R. 1980. "They Divide and Subdivide, and Call It Anthropology." *New York Times,* 30 November, 1980, E-9.

———, 1997. *Europe and the People without History.* Berkeley: University of California Press.

———, 1999. "Anthropology and the Academy: Historical Reflections." In *Transforming Academia: Challenges and Opportunities for an Engaged Anthropology,* eds. L. Basch et al., 32–39. Arlington, VA: American Anthropological Association.

———, 2001 [1984]. "Culture: Panacea or Problem?" In *Pathways of Power: Building an Anthropology of the Modern World,* E. R. Wolf, 307–19. Berkeley: University of California Press.

Woodson, Drexel G. 1990. "Tout mounn sé mounn, men tout mounn pa menm: Microlevel Sociocultural Aspects of Land Tenure in a Northern Haitian Locality." Ph.D dissertation, University of Chicago.

———, 1997. *"Lamanjay,* Food Security, *Sécurité Alimentaire:* A Lesson in Communication from BARA's Mixed Methods Approach to Baseline Research in Haiti, 1994–1996." *Culture and Agriculture* 19 (3): 108–22.

———, 2001. "Food-for-Work." In *Evaluation Report of the Enhanced Food Security II Program, USAID Mission,* eds. G. R. Smucker and N. P. Schlossman, vol. 1 (IV), 1–35. Prepared for USAID Haiti Mission, Food for Peace Office. Arlington, VA: John Snow, Inc.

World Anthropologies Network. 2003. "A Conversation about World Anthropologies." *Social Anthropology* 11 (2): 265–69.

Yerxa, Elizabeth J., Florence Clark, Gelya Frank, Jeanne Jackson, Diane Parham, Doris Pierce, Carol Stein, and Ruth Zemke. 1990. "An Introduction to Occupational Science: A Foundation for Occupational Therapy in the Twenty-First Century." *Occupational Therapy in Health Care* 6 (4): 1–18.

Young, Donna J., and Anne Meneley. 2005. "Auto-Ethnographies of Academic Practices." In *Auto-Ethnographies: The Anthropology of Academic Practices,* eds. A. Meneley and D. J. Young, 1–21. Peterborough, ON: Broadview Press.

Young, Robert J. C. 2001. *Postcolonialism: An Historical Introduction.* Malden, MA: Blackwell.

Yuval-Davis, Nira. 2004. "Transversal Politics and the Situated Imagination." Unpublished ms.

Zemke, Ruth, and Florence Clark, eds. 1996. *Occupational Science: The Evolving Discipline.* Philadelphia: F. A. Davis.

Index

June 5
sunday. seatfille postted Olsen.